DOWNING STREET
THE WAR YEARS

DOWNING STREET
THE WAR YEARS

SIR JOHN MARTIN

Former Principal Private Secretary to Winston Churchill

BLOOMSBURY

First published in Great Britain 1991
Bloomsbury Publishing Limited, 2 Soho Square, London W1V 5DE

Copyright © 1991 by Sir John Martin

The moral right of the author has been asserted

PICTURE SOURCES

W. M. Codrington: page 11 *top*
Harvard University Archives: page 7 *top*
The Trustees of the Imperial War Museum: pages 1, 2, 6,
8, 10 *bottom*, 11 *bottom*, 15, 16, 17, 18, 19,
20, 21, 22, 24, 25, 26 *top*, 27, 28, 29, 32
Izvestiya Sovetov Deputatov Trudyashchikh USSR: page 9
New York Times: page 7 *bottom*
Oxford and County Newspapers: pages 12, 13, 14
Syndication International: page 26 *bottom*
US Army Airforce: page 10 *top*

Map on pages 30–1 by Neil Hyslop, based
on an original by George Philip & Son, Limited
Other illustrations from the author's collection

A CIP catalogue record for this book
is available from the British Library

ISBN 0-7475-0838-0

Typeset by Hewer Text Composition Services, Edinburgh
Printed by Butler and Tanner Limited, Frome and London

ACKNOWLEDGEMENTS

Although originally transcribed or written some fourteen years ago, this book owes its publication now to a call from Correlli Barnett of Churchill College, Cambridge, early last year for materials for the Churchill Archives Centre, of which he is Director. Correlli later visited us in Watlington. This visit moved me to show the typescript to our neighbours, Errol and June Bedford. They were most encouraging and with the advice of Eric Buckley, Emeritus Fellow of Linacre College, Oxford, we selected Bloomsbury as our first choice of publisher. They speedily accepted the project.

A substantial amount of correction and augmentation of the text and the re-identification of various personalities was then required, much of it performed by my wife Rosalind. Our son David helped edit the text and also collated the photographs, largely from the collection of official and press photographs supplied to me during the war by Captain Horton of the Ministry of Information. Other photographs have been kindly provided by Lady Rowan, widow of Leslie Rowan, and by the Imperial War Museum, which has proved invaluable for obtaining precise details of many of the illustrations.

Churchill's own *The Second World War* and Martin Gilbert's massive and authoritative works on Churchill and on the war have been the main sources for checking facts. Gilbert's biography cites in appropriate context many recollections provided by me and furnishes a far better memoir than any I could have written.

Thanks are due to Bloomsbury Publishing for their enthusiasm and help in the book's production. Thanks are due too to Errol Bedford and Arthur Spencer for reading proofs and making many helpful corrections.

This book is presented as an original source rather than as a scholarly work, but so far as possible all annotations have been checked for accuracy.

ROUTE KEY TO MAP IN PICTURE SECTION

1 Atlantic Charter Meeting: Newfoundland, Iceland, August 1941.
2 1st Washington Conference: Washington, Ottawa, Pompano, December 1941.
3 1st Washington Conference: Washington, Ottawa, Bermuda, December 1941–January 1942.
4 2nd Washington Conference, June 1942.
5 1st Moscow Conference: Cairo, Teheran, The El Alamein Front, Moscow, August 1942.
6 Casablanca Conference: Cairo, Adana, Cyprus, Tripoli, Algiers, January–February 1943.
7 3rd Washington Conference: New York, Washington, May 1943.
8 3rd Washington Conference: Algiers, Tunisia, June 1943.
9 1st Quebec Conference: Halifax, Washington, August–September 1943.
10 Cairo Conference – Teheran Conference: Algiers, Malta, Alexandria, November 1943.
11 Cairo Conference – Teheran Conference: Cairo, Teheran, Tunis, Marrakesh, November 1943–January 1944.
12 Normandy visit, June 1944.
13 Normandy visit, July 1944.
14 Italy, the Italian Fronts and the South of France invasion coast, August 1944.
15 2nd Quebec Conference: Halifax, Quebec, New York, September 1944.
16 2nd Moscow Conference: Naples, Cairo, Moscow, October 1944.
17 Paris and the French Fronts, November 1944.
18 Greece, December 1944.
19 Paris and Belgium, January 1945.
20 Malta Conference – Yalta Conference: Malta, Saki, Yalta, Sebastopol, Athens, Alexandria, Cairo, January–February 1945.
21 Belgium and Holland, March 1945.
22 Potsdam Conference: Bordeaux, Berlin, July 1945.

CONTENTS

CONTENTS

INTRODUCTION

My wartime diary begins in May 1940 when I was selected to work as a Private Secretary in the office of the Prime Minister. It was an unwritten rule in those days that detailed diaries should not be kept in government departments. To observe this rule and yet have some record of the period as seen from 10 Downing Street, I kept a short diary for five years, confined largely to a brief note of where each day was spent and of the people met.

For my own interest and that of my family I used extracts from this diary in the following memoir. A more general account of life is taken from my periodical letters to my mother (who lived in Edinburgh) and other members of my family. Since the diary was so brief and the letters deliberately avoided disclosure of confidential matter, they throw little or no light on the course of events, but I hope they may give some impression of what life was like for those who spent their finest and indeed many other hours in the Prime Minister's office.

For the first few months the extracts are worked into a short consecutive narrative, month by month, but after February 1941 this form is abandoned and only a short list of the month's principal events precedes the diary. The latter does not pretend to provide anything but the barest summary within which the letters can be placed. To save space the diary extracts do not reproduce entries where the only content was, as often, 'At No. 10', and it can be assumed every day was spent there unless otherwise indicated.

With the passage of fifty years since these events and the assurance of experts that even these small details are of value for the student in the history of the period, it now seems appropriate to make them available to a wider public, though I feel I owe some apology for adding to the already considerable number of memoirs of that time.

John Martin
August 1990

1940

MAY and JUNE

After the preliminary overture in Norway, the 'phoney' war ended with a crash on 10 May 1940. I had no reason to suppose that within a few days my own life would be so completely changed. Since January I had been a Principal in the Far Eastern Department of the Colonial Office, congenial work and not too heavy. After the first alarms of September 1939 routine had been little changed and I enjoyed weekend expeditions into the country in a late spring of exceptional beauty. In April, on a short holiday in Perthshire, I had climbed Ben Lawers in hot sunshine.

On Sunday 5 May I walked in the park. It was a peaceful day, bright and warm: the grass was fresh, the chestnut trees were hung with shining candles of blossom, the paths thronged with strollers whom shortage of petrol had kept in town. Five days later we were startled from enjoyment of the sunshine by news that the invasion of Holland had begun. That very morning, as if to underline the sudden change, I received a letter from a Dutch friend with the postal stamp 'Vacantie in Vredigen Vaderland'. Eleven days later I was summoned by the Permanent Under-Secretary of State, who told me that I was to be one of the Prime Minister's Private Secretaries. I was astonished and aghast; but he gave me no time to plead my inadequacy, pointing out that in war one must go where one is posted.

My selection by the Treasury (who were then responsible for staff matters in the Civil Service) had to be confirmed by the Prime Minister; but I was told that Mr Churchill was too busy to see me immediately and on the next day he flew to Paris. While waiting I was given a kind and reassuring welcome by the Principal Private Secretary, Eric Seal, and 'Mags' Stenhouse, the head of the permanent staff of assistants in the Prime Minister's office (to whose expert knowledge, wisdom and splendid leadership of 'the Girls' so much was due in the coming years), and spent my first day at No. 10 being introduced to my new colleagues and my duties. 'A most frightening day' I described it to my mother: 'I have never felt so empty inside'; but I no longer felt out of the war. I was to work with two others in a room next to the Cabinet Room, with a battery of telephones (though these were far outnumbered by the array I was to see in the anteroom to Stalin's study in the Kremlin).

On 23 May I was at last introduced to Winston in his room at the House of Commons. 'Stand over in the window,' he said. There were no questions, no conversation – just a searching gaze, while he looked me up and down. Then – 'I understand that you are going to be one of my Secretaries.' The interview was over. He believed he could sum up a man in such a swift scrutiny. It is only fair to add that it has been said that he was not a good judge of men and that he was hard to convince that his geese were not swans. Anyhow I became one of the geese, even if I cannot flatter myself that I was one of 'the geese that saved the Capitol'.

Two days later I was able to write home: 'I am enjoying life enormously and have got over the funk with which I began.' The day in the office had begun at 9.45 a.m. and ended at 3.15 a.m. the following morning, but the stimulus of excitement made up for the loss of sleep and as one long day followed another I learnt the truth of one of Churchill's favourite sayings, 'Eels get used to skinning.'

One of the first regulars I met at No. 10 was the famous black cat, a dignified animal that had appeared beside Chamberlain at the front door in the days of Munich and was often mentioned in the newspapers at the time. On my first night, when I slept on a bed rigged up in the next room, quite expecting to see the ghosts that must haunt the place, he was my only visitor, introducing himself with a miaow, rolling on his back and 'writing letters' on the carpet with his paws. He had a fan mail of his own. Besides fish handed in at the front door, people used to send him postal orders, which the office-keeper expended on condition powders. But the stigma of appeasement remained and he was sometimes known as the Munich Mouser, regarded as on the Treasury establishment, unlike Nelson, the Churchill cat, who was a pampered member of the household. The Munich Mouser continued to live in the

Treasury next door, occasionally coming along the corridor to No. 10 and taking his exercise in the garden. He was to have a sad end later, being found dead in mysterious circumstances in a room in the Foreign Office across the street. Winston had a special fondness for cats and would talk to Nelson, sat demurely on a chair at the dining-room table. He enjoyed repeating the story about two cats lying by the fireside and one of them saying to the other, 'These humans are very intelligent: I believe they understand quite a lot of what we say.' While on the subject of cats, I remember Margaret Bondfield reproving Nye Bevan in the House for his 'feline' attacks on the Prime Minister and telling Churchill afterwards that when she went home that night she apologised to her cat.

I became Private Secretary at a grim moment of the war, when the German armour swinging round the north of the Maginot line had plunged deep into France. The collapse of the French army was only a few days away and the fate of the British Expeditionary Force hung in the balance. Sir Arthur Bryant wrote later (*The Turn of the Tide*, 112) that, with the possible exception of two days in the winter of 1941–42, 20 May 1940 was for the democracies the most disastrous day of the war. On 22 May, the day of my introduction to No. 10, the Prime Minister was away on a visit to Paris for consultations with the French Premier M. Reynaud and Marshal Weygand, Commander of the French forces. Three days later Lord Gort, C in C of the British Expeditionary Force, took the decision to march to the sea, as the only alternative to destruction or surrender, and on 26 May the evacuation from Dunkirk began. Through all those terrible days the Prime Minister remained utterly steadfast; but it was easy to feel the intensity of the responsibility that weighed upon him; and the imagination and emotion with which he watched the agony of France, eager to bring any support and comfort he could, yet steeling himself in face of desperate entreaties and his own generous instincts to hold back that bare minimum of aircraft strength on which our hope of continuing the struggle in Britain depended. His anxiety for the British Army was relieved at last as we brought him hour by hour the mounting tally of the troops brought safely home from the Dunkirk beaches.

Through all those hectic days the Prime Minister worked tirelessly early and late. I have written elsewhere (in *Action This Day*) of the nights at Admiralty House, where he was still living –

'the Midnight Follies' we called them. Here I recall one typical evening, when I was left alone with him as duty Private Secretary. He had dictated an important message to Lord Gort. The draft was sent over to the War Office for clearance by the Secretary of State and the Chief of the Imperial General Staff; but their reply was delayed. Again and again Churchill rang for me and asked with increasing impatience if it had been received. I was continually on the telephone to the War Office but without effect. At last he went off grumbling to bed, instructing me to report to him in his bedroom as soon as I had an answer. Half an hour passed and the War Office remained silent. I thought I must go upstairs and report lack of progress. I found him dressed only in a vest, pacing up and down. I gave my report. He turned angrily away from me; no word was spoken, there was only an angry grunt. Such moments were unnerving for a raw Private Secretary. But there were more heart-warming experiences, as when on another strenuous evening he put his hand on my shoulder and said, 'You know, I may seem to be very fierce, but I am fierce only with one man – Hitler.'

It is not surprising that when memory peers back to those now distant years with Churchill it recalls most readily the impressions of the first year and especially of that first summer. It may have been 'the finest hour'; but when we were living through it, it was a time of agony piled on agony. 'The month of June' he wrote afterwards 'was particularly trying for all of us.' He enjoined on his colleagues the duty of the stiff upper lip and told Parliament that 'if we get through the next three months we shall get through the next three years'; but at the time no solid grounds for confidence were visible. Yet, when he said at a meeting of Ministers 'quite casually' that 'whatever happens at Dunkirk, we shall fight on' there was the remarkable demonstration of support (described in *The Second World War*, II, 88), to which he often afterwards referred in disclaiming for himself all credit for the will to resist. Perhaps nothing brings back the strange elation which carried men away in those days and lifted them above logical calculations so clearly as the proposal for an Act of Union offered to the French Government on 16 June, two days after the German entry into Paris. There was at the time some mystery about the origin of this proposal and indeed not less about its implications. It was a day of great emotional stress – a day of Prayer for France, when the tricolor floated over Westminster Abbey. But by evening Reynaud had resigned and for a time the alliance was at an end. Next morning I wrote, 'The French news has come as no surprise, though its final shape is still uncertain. I cannot feel consternation or alarm, only grief for France and particularly for Paris, which I knew before I knew London and for which I have always had a special affection. Our turn will come now.'

Meanwhile on 10 June Mussolini, the 'jackal', had joined Hitler. After long uncertainty it was a relief to know where we stood. In contrast to the bellicose speech of Duff Cooper, the Minister of Information, promising new ruins in Italy, to many the idea of fighting Italy seemed repugnant – a sort of matricide – though they comforted themselves with the thought that it was the Italians' own fault if their country chose the side of the enemies of Christian civilisation.

The horror of the collapse of France and our withdrawal from the Continent was in strange contrast to the continuing brilliance of the summer. 'What a summer to waste on war,' I wrote and once, when I took a day off and walked on the Downs above Goring, 'the country looked incredibly lovely and peaceful and even the Downs themselves, which so often seem bleak and are attractive for their bleakness, were this time coloured with an astonishing profusion of flowers.'

Although the full power of the Luftwaffe was not unleashed against London till September, in earlier months we had occasional alerts. A letter home described one of these. 'The sirens went at 1 a.m., when the Cabinet was just breaking up after a late session. Sir John Anderson [Home Secretary and later Lord President of the Council] dutifully went down to the air-raid shelter with two other ministers, Mrs Churchill, Mary [the Churchills' youngest daughter, aged 17] and the domestic staff. There were long wooden benches and it looked exactly like a meeting in a village hall. Upstairs the PM and the others walked about, sometimes in the garden. The searchlights were rather beautiful. Nothing happened and about three o'clock, with Duff Cooper and others, I walked home through the empty streets and went to bed, so sleepy that the All Clear failed to awaken me.' Outside No. 10, on the Horseguards' Parade, was an RAF squad looking after a barrage balloon. We knew it as 'Tinskip' because of its resemblance to the rotund Dominions Secretary, Lord Caldecote [the recently ennobled Sir Thomas Inskip]. One day, in the process of filling, it gave out a strange noise.

7

'That's Tinskip,' explained a Private Secretary. At that moment Lord Caldecote himself came into the room. 'It sounds like the braying of an ass,' he said, to suppressed giggles.

At night, of course, we were under the curtain of the blackout. Once coming away weary and late I walked into the invisible barbed-wire fence at the end of Downing Street and had to be disentangled by a policeman. With the surrounding offices we were a beleaguered city, protected by wire, pill-boxes and other barricades. 'The system of passes,' I wrote, 'has got to absurd lengths, so that those who are regular visitors to a number of Departments and are entitled to their various passes collect quite a pocketful. The other day Sir Edward Bridges [secretary to the War Cabinet] knelt down and dealt out all his passes on the floor, like Patience cards. On this scene entered Neville Chamberlain [now Lord President of the Council], looking solemn, and observed that he only required a joker.' Sentries controlling entry through the barrier had a difficult task. I remember one self-important junior minister making a fuss because he was not recognised and was asked to produce his pass. It was said that a competition was organised in the Foreign Office to see who could get past with the least adequate credentials; that at times a railway season ticket and the card of membership of a golf club were accepted; and that finally the prize went to a man who walked confidently through the entrance holding out a slice of cake. Months later at Chequers, where there was a strong security guard all round the house, I had a lesson in the vulnerability of any such system. Working in the Private Secretaries' room just inside the front door, I noticed an unfamiliar major in the lobby and asked who he was. It turned out that he had tested our security by walking unidentified past a saluting sentry, entered the house unchallenged, went upstairs and asked a housemaid to direct him to the Prime Minister's bedroom. Only on return to the front door was his imposture discovered.

Among the memories of those early days is that of receiving Lady X who called to offer her valuable pearl necklace to the nation, symbolical of the mood when (as Churchill recalled) 'Romans in Rome's quarrel/Spared neither land nor gold.' Another day I went on my first outside expedition with the Prime Minister – to visit some of the coast defences, spending the night in his special train. For the first time I saw the tremendous enthusiasm with which he was invariably welcomed in all his public appearances. A big crowd gathered outside the hotel where we stopped for lunch and gave him a rousing cheer. Already the first of the stirring broadcasts had brought his inspiration into almost every home. Perhaps the reader in later years may find himself less moved than were the hearers at the time and may sometimes be critical of a style of rhetoric less familiar now. To appreciate their impact one must recreate in one's mind the atmosphere of that summer of 1940, reflecting the overwhelming suddenness and horror of the French collapse, the anxiety for the British forces involved (for many, a close, personal fear) and the immediacy of the threat that hung over our island. The very frankness of the references to the military situation, accompanied by rock-like defiance, bred confidence.

DIARY

May

21 Told that I was to be one of PM's Private Secretaries. Taken to No. 10. Dinner with E. A. Seal [Principal Private Secretary] at R.A.C.

22 Began at No. 10. Other Private Secretaries are Seal, Bevir, Miss Watson, Colville, Peck. PM in Paris.

23 Introduced to Churchill in room at House of Commons.

24 Evening at Admiralty House – crazy gang of 'Prof' Lindemann [later Lord Cherwell, PM's scientific adviser and personal assistant], Brendan Bracken [MP, Minister of Information] and [Major Desmond] Morton [PM's personal assistant].

25 At Admiralty House till 3 a.m. next day.

26 Day of Prayer. Reynaud flew over. Hinsley [Cardinal Archbishop] shouted down at Westminster Cathedral (? really an epileptic).

28 Reynaud's broadcast on Leopold of Belgium's surrender. Roger Keyes [Admiral of the Fleet] back.

29 News from Dunkirk.

June

1 In afternoon went with Edward Muir [Oxford friend, then at Ministry of Works] to Haslemere.

2 Haslemere. Bright and very hot. Walk on Blackdown. Signposts painted out.

3   Returned to town. Late duty at Admiralty House. PM preparing speech and considering support to be given to France.
4   News of Paris bombed yesterday. A perfect summer day. Such contrast. PM's speech on withdrawal from Dunkirk.
9   Late at Admiralty House. (To CIGS with telegram.) It has been a very hot week.
10 To Andover in afternoon. [I spent many weekends off with my sister and her family, Alan and Detta Gulland, who lived near Andover.] Italy entered war against Britain and France.
11 At Andover. Returned to town in evening.
14 Germans entered Paris.
16 'Act of Union' communicated to French Government. Special train (in which PM was to have left on another visit to France) cancelled. Reynaud resigned. Pétain to form Government.
18 Day off. Walked on Downs above Goring.
22 French accept German armistice terms.
24 French accept Italian armistice terms.
25 As last night's Cabinet was breaking up (c.1 a.m.) Red Warning (first since September).
26 With PM visited coastal defences Southwold to Harwich.
29 News of raid on (demilitarized) Channel Islands.
30 At St Columba's for Communion. Afterwards at No. 10 till 11 p.m. Broadcast by Chamberlain (break in voice).

LETTERS

22 *May*   Thanks so much for the kind things you say in your letter. It came as a great encouragement at the beginning of a most frightening day.
24 *May*   ... My appointment at No. 10 is now definite. It is going to be a hard and exciting job; but I need no longer feel left out of the war. I have never felt so empty inside as on Wednesday and Thursday, when expecting to be presented to the PM, and jitters on that account were combined with the black news from France.
25 *May*   I have been living in such a whirl that it is almost impossible to settle down for a peaceful moment to write a letter of my own. From now on it seems clear that I will only live for this job, with the exception of an occasional hour in the evening and

(if the war allows) an occasional 'weekend' not necessarily on Saturday and Sunday. Yesterday, for example, began at quarter to ten in the morning and ended at the Admiralty, where I was lucky to find a taxi, at 3.15 a.m. on the following morning. It is all tremendously exciting and the stimulus of the excitement seems to make up for lack of sleep . . . I enjoy it all enormously and have got over the complete funk with which I began. There are three of us working in the room next the Cabinet Room – Seal, Bevir and myself, while there are two younger Secretaries in another room [John Peck and Jock Colville] and also Miss Watson, so we are quite a crowd; but with the stream of phone calls and alarms and excursions everyone is needed, particularly while the PM alternates between Admiralty House (where he still lives) and No. 10.

30 May   The PM's confidence and energy are amazing. 'Nobody left his presence without feeling a braver man' was said of Pitt; but it is no less true of him.

2 June   We have worked out an elaborate arrangement of shifts which ought to make it possible for each PS to have a 'weekend' once, if not twice, a fortnight. It is really necessary for any but supermen like the PM himself (though even he goes to sleep most days for about an hour after lunch). He has a boxful of papers left outside his room each night and works through this in bed in the morning, dictating to a shorthand-writer, and generally does not get up and dress till quite late. About eleven he comes over to No. 10 for the daily Cabinet meeting, which lasts till about two. There is such coming and going of Ministers and Chiefs of Staff etc. for this. (Yesterday we had Lord Gort on his return from France.) Then the PM returns to Admiralty House for lunch and rest, usually working in Downing Street (or having another meeting of Ministers there or in the House of Commons) from about 4.30 until dinner time. He dines at Admiralty House and there sees a succession of Ministers or Chiefs of Staff and others until bedtime not much before midnight and sometimes a good deal later.

The chief difficulty as a novice is understanding what he says and great skill is required in interpreting inarticulate grunts or single words thrown out without explanation. I think he is consciously odd in these ways. Anyhow he is certainly a 'character' and I shan't soon forget an interview with him in his bedroom walking about clad only in a vest.

11

It has been an anxious week, waiting hour by hour for the latest news of the British Expeditionary Force. Their successful evacuation is an incredible achievement, which could not have been hoped for a week ago.

There is going to be little time for amusements or for private reading. Bevir and I take day about helping the younger PS who remains in attendance until the PM actually goes to bed, i.e. we stay over at Admiralty House till 11.30 or later. On the alternate day we get away 'early' but that is not before about 8.15.

We have a very pleasant garden at Downing Street. Our windows look out on it and I have a key by which I can let myself out at the back.

6 June The Simons [Viscount Simon, former Chancellor of the Exchequer, and his wife] are now out of the house next door, so we hope the Chamberlains will soon move from the upper part of No. 10.

13 June Have ordered a new flannel suit and some shirts – rather scandalous no doubt, but, even as a public example, I can hardly go about in rags at No. 10 and fortunately my tailor hasn't put up his prices while the old stocks last.

The Churchills are now moving into No. 10 and I took the opportunity yesterday to look through the house. It is much bigger than it looks from the front, having an inner court, but much of the space is taken up by large rooms for receptions, including a fine hall for state dinners. It will simplify our arrangements a good deal when we no longer have alternative headquarters at Admiralty House (where, for example, I spent yesterday evening up to nearly midnight).

17 June The PM gave me such a kind and human goodnight when he went up to bed at one o'clock this morning – put his hand on my arm and said he was sorry there had been no time in all the rush of these days to get to know me.

21 June Back in the evening on Tuesday in time for the PM's broadcast. His halting delivery at the start seems to have struck people and we had for example a telegram from someone saying that he evidently had something wrong with his heart and ought to work in a recumbent position. The fact was, I gather, that he spoke with a cigar in his mouth.

24 June You needn't fear that I don't get my food properly. It is less often at Graham Terrace now, that being too far from the scene of operations; but my Club in Pall Mall is handy. Have slept twice at No. 10 in the last few days, where we have installed a bed in one of the office rooms, and a good, though short, night's sleep is possible. Both nights we had 'yellow' warnings.

Saturday night was particularly hectic. The PM had rashly gone down to Chequers but returned for a hastily summoned Cabinet, which went on till a late hour. Bevir and I were the only Private Secretaries there and we had a very hectic time, with a great many people coming and going and all the telephones (there were eight instruments) perpetually ringing.

A tiresome complaining letter from X. I wish he could see some of the pathetically brave and loyal letters we get from humble people in the PM's mail.

30 June   I don't suppose you imagined that I was sitting a few yards away outside the door of the room in which Chamberlain made his speech this evening, having fortunately thought of putting beside him the water which became necessary towards the end. I wonder if you heard the birds in the garden, which sounded almost too loud – and heedless of their relative brought in to die on our floor by the black cat.

My letters ought to be full of interest these days; but when it comes to writing them down all the incidents seem too official for record or else too trivial. E.g. there was a letter saying the Prime Minister was a tonic for the nation, which our office accidently referred to the Ministry of Health. When I told Winston that six people had died of heart failure during the air-raid warning, he said that *he* was more likely to die of over-eating, but he didn't want to die yet when so many interesting things were happening. I saw him this evening after his bath wrapped only in a huge towel, looking like one of the later Roman Emperors.

JULY

The threat of invasion hung over us and seemed each day closer. Intensive preparations continued, to meet the expected landings. Precious supplies of arms arrived from the United States and the PM made great efforts to ensure their safe arrival and speedy distribution. For none was the suspense greater. Yet lunching with him, along with Mrs Churchill, Mary, Pamela [Churchill, wife of

PM's son Randolph] and Mr Attlee, I thought him, I wrote afterwards,

> in very good form (after his successful broadcast) and it was a most enjoyable meal. He likes his food and was amusing about food faddists and the rationing ideas of those who would feed people on oatmeal, potatoes and milk, 'washed down on gala occasions with a glass of lemonade'. He is in a very confident frame of mind, more so now than ever . . . He seems very playful in his family and fond of animals, playing with a little dog and making absurd remarks to it. And to me he couldn't have been nicer.

There was a steadfast mood in the country. We still received masses of letters declaring determination and support, some most moving and others ludicrous with a constant stream of bright ideas for winning the war and strange Heath-Robinson inventions.

It was still a perfect summer. 'Tuesday was a brilliantly hot day and I went for a mild walk along the river at Windsor, sunbathing on a grassy bank. It was amusing to see how every reference to the Thames, e.g. at a lock, had been painted out, though Germans could hardly have mistaken it for any other river.' Stuck up in the Private Secretaries' room was a notice, received as an advertisement, 'Please understand that there is no depression in this House and we are not interested in the possibilities of defeat. THEY DO NOT EXIST. Queen Victoria.'

At the beginning of the month came the tragedy of the action against the French fleet, following 'a hateful decision, the most unnatural with which I have been concerned', as the PM wrote afterwards. He was referring to the decision to have the Royal Navy sink the French fleet at Oran to prevent its falling into German hands. Sir Alexander Cadogan, Permanent Under-Secretary at the Foreign Office, commented in his *Diaries*, 'it was necessary, but it was not pleasant, like having a tooth out'. I was in the official box when the Prime Minister made his report to Parliament. There was a remarkable scene at the end of his statement, when the entire crowded House (except, I think, three Independent Labour Party members) rose to their feet and cheered. There had been nothing like it, people said, since Munich. Churchill himself was quite overcome and his eyes filled with tears.

14

Ten days later emotions were again stirred by the celebration of Quatorze Juillet. The tricolor once more floated from the tower at Westminster Abbey. 'It is strange,' I wrote, 'how many French sailors (and also some soldiers) are about. There are also crowds of Anzacs, looking rather bored. Great crowds in the streets. I had no idea there was such a large French colony in London.' Incidentally the Ministry of Works had chosen, with a certain lack of tact, an office in Trafalgar House, Waterloo Place, for the Free French. I received a letter from a friend working there which ended 'Malgré cette adresse je reste votre ami'.

One day the Prime Minister's hairdresser came up from the country and hung about for two days, waiting for a chance to cut his hair. He had cut all the family's hair since they were children and, when it was time for Winston's to be done, cancelled all engagements and came up to town for the purpose.

An appeal went out for aluminium pots and pans to be collected to be 'recycled' (as we say now) as material for building aircraft. Some people even bought new ones to add to the scrap-heap.

DIARY

July
2 Day off. Walk on towing path at Windsor.
3 Another day off. Walk in Richmond Park.
15 Lunch with PM, Mrs Churchill, Mary, Mrs Randolph Churchill and Mr Attlee. Afternoon off – cinema.
16 Day off. Walk on towing path at Richmond.
23 Day off. Walk on Downs from Goring. Kingsley Wood's Budget – Income Tax 8/6.
28 Two hours off in morning. Walked up to park.
29 Neville Chamberlain's operation. To Andover in afternoon.
30 Returned to London in evening.

LETTERS

4 July In the evening a cinema party, the first such recreation for about two months and fortunately we went to a shriekingly funny French film (*Neuf Célibataires*) which made me laugh loud and helplessly.

7 July Sometimes when master is away we take the sun in the garden, a surprisingly pleasant place – a lawn with a tree and a long border along a wall, gay with great profusion of colours. The Chamberlains had taken great interest in it and their efforts have certainly been rewarded. Our room looks out on to it, as does the Cabinet room, where the summer scents and songs of birds might make you imagine you were in the library of a country house.

Last night, when I was alone, the office-keeper, who looks after No. 10 and has been there for forty years, came and talked at great length about his various Prime Ministers. Stories particularly of Balfour, whose reading at family prayers at Whittinghame seems to have impressed him a great deal, and of Chamberlain at the time of Munich.

14 July How did you like the speech ['The War of the Unknown Warriors']? It read very well at its first draft; but I had seen it so often by the time I listened that it had lost some of its freshness. I had a great hunt for a quotation he wanted to use and which after all he decided to leave out – just as well, as I thought it rather unsuitable. I was all packed up for Chequers on Friday and was looking forward to an aeroplane flight which was part of the programme (and for which the PM dressed rather self-consciously in Air Force uniform); but in the end it was decided that one of the juniors couldn't be left in charge here, so as an ancient I had to stay to hold the fort. If only there wasn't such a rush this work in a *house*, instead of an ordinary office, would be very pleasant. I'm afraid it will be very spoiling for anything else.

18 July 'Gestapo' ought to have the accent on the 'a'; but Winston takes a delight in pronouncing foreign words in an English way: e.g. Graf Spee pronounced as spelt, and Quimper pronounced to rhyme with whimper.

My niece demanded a letter on Downing Street paper. I sent this and hear that its arrival produced a summons to the headmistress, who no doubt thought that she had been corresponding with the Prime Minister (because of the address on the back of the envelope).

I didn't get to bed till quarter past two last night and the PM summoned me to his bedroom, where he was working on a bed table, before nine this morning. Some day I propose to sleep for a week without stopping.

25 July Did you hear Lord Halifax's [Foreign Secretary] fine broadcast? It was a brave speech and I believe entirely sincere. Another minister who stands up for the Church is Lord Lloyd [Secretary of State for the Colonies], a pillar of St Mary's, Graham Terrace.

28 July There was some idea of all of us PSs enrolling in the Home Guard; but nothing has come of it. All the offices have Guards, who patrol at night and drill and do musketry at lunchtime. I feel very rusty on all that, but after all not surprising as OTC days were no less than seventeen years ago.

AUGUST

As reports came in of increasing concentration of German barges across the Channel and as the Luftwaffe increased the tempo of their attacks, the prospect of invasion seemed daily nearer. Air attacks, first on the Kentish promontory and the Channel coast, and then on the radar stations and airfields of south-east England, were now continuous. On the 15th came a massive onslaught on the Tyne and the Yorkshire coast, and on the 24th the first bombs by day on Central London. We were cheered by the high figure of German losses, but did not know what each day would bring. In a balanced statement of our situation to the House of Commons on 20 August the Prime Minister paid his tribute to the fighter pilots – 'never in the field of human conflict was so much owed by so many to so few'. Later the words were cheapened by many parodies; but when first spoken they were an inspiring reflection of the national mood. 'This was a time when it was equally good to live or die.'

I spent the first of many weekends on duty at Chequers. Normally the Prime Minister would go down there on Friday evening and return to London on Monday morning. One Private Secretary, with shorthand writers, accompanied him, while another provided a rear link in Downing Street, keeping in touch by 'scrambler' telephone and relays of despatch riders.

First impressions were recorded in a letter:

Brilliant August weather and the place could not be seen in more lovely conditions. The house stands high, so we are not worried with heat, and all the surroundings are rural and peaceful. It is a big red-brick house of various periods – 15th and 16th centuries and later. Inside, a large central hall, originally an open courtyard, is surrounded by various rooms, with a gallery on one side on the first floor. The whole place is like a museum, stuffed with old furniture and pictures of varying interest, and treasures including relics of Cromwell. On one side is a large terrace and rose garden and on the other a lawn, while, beyond, the park and woods stretch to the horizon . . . I have breakfast in bed and do my first business with the PM (who himself spends most of the morning working in bed) in my dressing-gown; then spend most of the day in a small office overlooking the rose garden. Tea in the Great Hall with Mrs Churchill and other meals all together *en famille* in the dining-room.

We have a military guard outside, with sentries who challenge at every turn and have a nightly password. I was rather dreading my first weekend here in sole charge; but after all enjoyed it hugely, though it was no picnic and it was tantalising not to be able to explore the surrounding country, and shortage of sleep may begin to tell by Monday.

German planes were heard more than once at night, with their distinctive engine hum, and bombs were dropped a few miles away.

These weekends at Chequers were much used for the entertainment of official guests. It is amusing to notice that, in recording the names of guests on my first weekend, after mentioning General Freyberg, GOC New Zealand forces, Lord Gort and Air Marshal Dowding, C in C Fighter Command, I added among 'various lesser fry' General de Gaulle. One of the clear pictures in my memory from one of the Chequers visits is of taking a message to Lord Halifax in his bedroom, where I found him reading his Bible, his lanky form sprawled in an armchair before the fire, towards which his long legs were stretched out, the flames illumining his blue velvet bedroom slippers.

In this month the Prime Minister was increasingly concerned with the Middle East. A guest at Chequers was General Wavell, who had been brought home to discuss the problems of his Command. Cadogan noted in his diary at the time that 'Wavell was not very impressive'. That was how he struck the Prime Minister. He seemed strangely unforthcoming and negative. He seemed to make no attempt to 'get across', though it was important for him to have the Prime Minister's confidence at a time when his Command was making such large demands on scarce resources of men and materials and receiving such generous support from the Prime Minister and the Chiefs of Staff. Their decision to divert these resources in this 'blood transfusion' was an agonising one to take. ('Awful and right,' Churchill afterwards described it – *The Second World War*, II, 379.)

A fortnight later we were again at Chequers. I was crippled by a twisted ankle, 'the result of dashing off impetuously to stop the guard's wireless'. (Churchill was extremely sensitive to noise. At Downing Street there were continual calls to 'stop that hammering', often a long way off. One afternoon I was sent out from the Cabinet room to stop the hammering by a detachment of Guardsmen piling sandbags on a balcony of the Admiralty across the Horse Guards. I felt like an inverted Mussolini as I shouted up at them from the ground, an insignificant civilian.)

At Chequers 'it was not a very good day. The PM was irritable, worrying about Mrs Churchill, left behind in London, where air raids were threatened, and for other reasons. In the end he decided to return to London after dinner and we drove back in the dark.' Those drives were rather fun as we had police gongs in the cars and drove at a great pace, ignoring traffic lights and gonging other cars out of the way.

In London there were frequent air-raid warnings, with magnificent searchlight displays and occasionally the sound of distant gunfire. One night the Prime Minister went to sleep in a makeshift bed in our underground shelter. When the All Clear went he was snoring peacefully: no one dared to waken him, so he spent the night there and said in the morning that he had not had such a good night's sleep for a long time.

One day I lunched with Dr Weizmann, Chairman of the Jewish Agency, and a distinguished chemist, whom I had come to know before the war when concerned with Palestine affairs in the Colonial Office – a magnetic personality, for whom I always felt much admiration not untinged with a warmer feeling. He was of course aware of Churchill's sympathy with Zionism, but must also have been conscious of the Prime Minister's wish to keep aloof at a time when he could not give practical effect to that sympathy (apart from opposition to the policy of withholding arms from the Jews in Palestine) or enter into any commitments regarding arrangements to be made in any post-war settlement.

Much the most important event of the month was the agreement with President Roosevelt (finally announced early in September) for the transference of fifty United States destroyers, linked with the leasing to the United States of bases in British territories in the Western hemisphere, 'an event which brought the United States definitely nearer to us and to the war'. In a statement in Parliament on 20 August the Prime Minister underlined the significance of these transactions: 'Undoubtedly this process means that these two great organisations of the English-speaking democracies, the British Empire and the United States, will have to be somewhat mixed up together in some of their affairs for mutual and general advantage.'

DIARY

August
  2 To Chequers in the evening.
  3 Chequers. German plane over *c.*1 a.m. Bombs about 4 miles away at Great Missenden. Lord Gort to stay. Sir H. Dowding to dinner.
  4 Chequers. Gen. de Gaulle, Gen. Spears [PM's personal representative with French Premier and head of British Mission to de Gaulle] and Major Morton to lunch. Visit to Fighter Command HQ at Stanmore. Air Marshal Portal [C in C Bomber Command] to dinner.
  5 Returned to London. Signature of Anglo-Polish Agreement at No. 10 (Gen. Sikorski, [Polish Premier and C in C Poles in exile], M. Zalewski, [Polish Foreign Secretary], PM and Lord Halifax).
  9 Great RAF fights in Channel. 60 Germans down.
 11 60 Germans down again.
 12 Day off. In Battersea Park and to St Albans, visiting Cathedral and Roman Theatre.
 15 Air-raid warning in the evening, but no planes over Whitehall.
 16 Another uneventful warning in morning. Lunch at No. 10 – other guests Duke and Duchess of Marlborough and Sir James Hawkey [Chairman of Epping Conservative Association, Churchill's last constituency]. To Chequers. Lord Lloyd, Sir

Alan Brooke [Viscount Alanbrooke, C in C Anti-Aircraft Defences and Home Forces, and CIGS] and Sir Hugh Dowding to dinner.

17 At Chequers. Another hot, bright weekend. Ismay [Gen. Sir Hastings Ismay, 'Pug', PM's Chief of Staff] and Lindemann also here. Also at dinner Duncan and Diana Sandys [the Churchills' MP son-in-law and eldest daughter], Lord Beaverbrook, Air Marshal Portal and Brendan Bracken. German plane overhead after midnight.

18 Chequers. Last week was one of great air battles and heavy losses for German raiders. Lord and Lady Halifax, de Gaulle, Spears and Morton to lunch. Major Jefferis showed his new gun. Returned to London after dinner.

21 Afternoon off.

22 Day off. Owing to ankle sprained last Saturday, did not go for long walk, only along towing path Richmond to Kew. Tired and rather depressed. Air raid at night. Bombs in City and bombs at West India Dock.

23 Air-raid warnings in afternoon and at night.

24 Air warnings at night.

25 Day off. Visited friends at Northwood.

31 Frequent air-raid warnings continue daily.

LETTERS

1 August Instructions have been given for everyone to have about a week's holiday before the autumn; but it hardly seems possible to go off while there is every day the chance of invasion.

Have you heard of the Camden fruit preserving solution? I gather you can buy the tablets from Boots for 6d a bottle and with them you can bottle fruit without sugar. This I know from having made enquires for Mrs Churchill.

Isn't old Chamberlain tough? He has made an incredible recovery and Horder says he should actually be at his desk in a fortnight.

You ask about sleeping in the office. It means hauling along a suitcase each time. I shave in the morning and when relieved (about 9.15 to 9.30) come along to Graham Terrace for a bath and breakfast. It makes a long stretch. E.g. yesterday I was on duty till after 1.30 this morning: got up at quarter to 8, relieved at 9.15 and back at the office again about 11 a.m., remaining till 8.30 this evening.

7 *August*   At Chequers on Sunday. Mrs Churchill returned to town and there were only the PM, Air Marshal Portal, Prof. Lindemann and myself. Winston was in very good form. I only wish I hadn't such a sieve-like memory and could remember all the talk afterwards. He always talks very freely on these occasions and is extremely good company. I believe Chequers was very different in MacDonald's time. Someone who visited then told me that they ate their meals in complete silence – very embarrassing for the guest.

11 *August*   I have had a succession of late nights since last weekend and have only once been to bed before one a.m. and often later; but I propose to take tomorrow off.

15 *August*   The news of the RAF's successes is almost incredibly good. We are perpetually being told to ring up headquarters to get the latest reports. Perhaps I can now mention that there were bombs a few miles from Chequers one of the nights we were there. The German plane or planes overhead had quite a distinctive sound, unlike any other planes I ever heard. Here we have still had nothing more than warnings. The sirens made me late for dinner last night.

25 *August*   Written on guard at the office – a much idler way of spending Sunday than at Chequers. I could hear the enemy plane or planes overhead last night (about midnight) and the search-lights looking for them made a fine spectacle. The morning alarm delayed the arrival of my relief and so of my breakfast but led to nothing more exciting.

28 *August*   No need for you to worry about 'raids' here, which seem only designed to keep us awake, though on Saturday night some damage was done by bombs on the docks. Last night and the night before the alarm came at almost the same time, just after the news. The hum of a single plane could be heard and from time to time there was a magnificent searchlight display and occasion-ally the sound of distant gunfire. The wail of the siren is our worst trouble so far.

9.57 p.m. There go the sirens again.

Thursday. A plane kept circling about, eluding the searchlights, but there was nothing more so I went to bed and slept as usual, waking for the All Clear about 4 a.m.

SEPTEMBER

'September, like June, was a month of extreme opposing stresses for those who bore the responsibility for British war direction' (Churchill, *The Second World War*, II, 403). The evidence of impending invasion, in the massive accumulation of ships and barges at the German-occupied ports across the Channel, increased daily. Tension and excitement mounted accordingly. Vigilance was redoubled as the period of most favourable conditions of moon and tide for the enemy approached (between the 15th and the 30th). On the 7th the code signal 'Cromwell', meaning 'invasion imminent', was issued by Home Forces Command and at some places the ringing of church bells called out the Home Guard.

In Parliament on the 5th the Prime Minister had warned that, while August had been 'a real fighting month' in the air, this month 'we must be prepared for heavier fighting' and in what was perhaps the most stirring of his broadcast speeches, on the 11th, he declared that 'we must regard the next week or so as a very important period in our history. It ranks with the days when the Spanish Armada was approaching the Channel or when Nelson stood between us and Napoleon's Grand Army at Boulogne.' It was an invocation of the national spirit – of Londoners, 'who have been bred to value freedom far above their lives', of 'our famous island race . . . a people who will not flinch or weary of the struggle – hard and protracted though it will be'. For, on the 7th, following a declaration by Hitler of his intention to wipe out London, the Luftwaffe had switched from daylight raids on RAF installations in the south of England to night raids on London, and the long agony of the metropolis had begun. For fifty-seven nights the bombing was unceasing. Already on 1 September I wrote:

We are becoming accustomed to ceaseless air warnings, losing count of their number. By day they lead to nothing except an occasional very distant sound of explosives; but by night the lonely prowlers are more of a nuisance, zooming round overhead apparently aimlessly, with sometimes (very rarely) a dull boomp as a bomb falls and the sound of gunfire. The only trouble is the interruption of sleep. Apart from that, no one seems to mind very much and by day people are tending to disregard the sirens.

The Prime Minister soon called for a reduction of the 'banshee howlings' of the sirens and for their use as an alert and not as a local alarm, the latter being given by trained look-out men or 'Jim Crows' when immediate danger was expected at any point. This system ended the double danger of waste of time through unnecessary descents to the air-raid shelters or disregard of the signals.

On the 3rd I took a day off and walked along the ridge from Merstham to Caterham and beyond, hoping to see something of the air battle. There was a siren warning and activity by our own fighters; but I saw no Germans.

Puzzle. In what circumstances did the Prime Minister write 'there must be a drain and a sump'? Answer: In minute of 3 September about draining Anderson shelters (*The Second World War*, II, 313).

On the afternoon of Saturday 7 September came a raid on the London docks. It was a sunny day and we could watch the silvery German planes wheeling overhead in a brilliantly blue sky, surrounded by the white puffs of anti-aircraft shell-bursts. A great fire was started in the docks and I stood with crowds on the Embankment at Charing Cross watching the clouds of smoke billowing upwards in the east. At night the sky glowed red and the raiders returned to their easy mark, like bees round honey.

I was just returning to No. 10 from early dinner when the alarm went and I heard the whizz and dull boomp of a bomb not far away. The cat was waiting at the garden gate to take refuge with me. Things became too lively to remain upstairs, so we all went down to our underground shelter and I spent the night there in my clothes on a bunk. We had occasional explosions and at one moment the light went off for a while. In the morning it was surprising to find London still there, though a stretch of Victoria Street was roped off. On succeeding mornings more and more of the gloomy office buildings in that street lay slumped in ruins.

On the 9th, 10th and 11th there were more raids and again sleep was interrupted. On the 10th I received a telegram from my mother asking 'How are you?', to which I replied, 'Many thanks. Well but sleepy. Don't worry. London is a big place.' I think it was on the night of the 11th (though in *The Second World War* it was said to have been the 10th) that

> there was an intense and continuous barrage from the A A guns, which had hitherto seemed oddly inactive, and this had an immense effect on people's morale. Tails are up and, after the fifth sleepless night, everyone looks quite different this morning – cheerful and confident. It was a curious bit of mass psychology – the relief of hitting back. I have bought a Jaeger sleeping-bag for nights spent on the floor at No. 10.

On the morning of the 12th 'I drove with the PM into the City and to Holborn Viaduct Station. Although there was plenty of damage to be seen, it was surprising how localised it was. There was great enthusiasm from the crowds.' 'We must take September 15 as the culminating date,' Churchill wrote afterwards. That Sunday morning, on the way to Chequers, I accompanied him on a visit to No. 11 Fighter Group headquarters at Uxbridge. As it happened we there witnessed the control of 'one of the decisive battles of the war'. Churchill himself has given a vivid picture of the scene in his history of the war. Air Marshal Park, who was in general control, hovered in the background, issuing instructions from time to time, while detailed conduct of the operation was commanded by the quiet orders of a surprisingly young-looking officer, afterwards identified as Lord Willoughby de Broke. It was not until later in the day, at Chequers, that we realised the magnitude of the British victory. The Prime Minister recorded how, when he awoke from his afternoon sleep, I came in with the evening budget of news:

> It was repellent. This had gone wrong here; that had been delayed there; an unsatisfactory answer had been received from so-and-so; there had been bad sinkings in the Atlantic. 'However,' said Martin as he finished this account, 'all is redeemed by the air. We have shot down one hundred and eighty-three for a loss of under forty.'

(It did not matter that these figures were found afterwards to be exaggerated.) I was surprised when I read the Prime Minister's narrative after the war to find that he had remembered my phrase 'all is redeemed by the air'. I myself had remembered it as a conscious imitation of his own style. Two days later, as we now know, Hitler ordered the indefinite suspension of the invasion plans.

After return from Chequers I took a few days' leave in Scotland. Back at my desk on the 27th I could report that

> London seems little more damaged than a fortnight ago, though the wounds are not far to seek. There are several traces in Whitehall, including one large hole from an explosion which had shaken my master's slumber on Thursday night. A piece of shrapnel is embodied in a panel of my room as a reminder to treat seriously our Jim Crow's alarm bell.
>
> Have you read of the bombed shop which stuck up 'Open as usual', while its neighbour, with shattered windows, replied with 'Opener than usual'?

Among buildings hit in September's raids was Buckingham Palace, which served to 'unite the King and Queen to their people by new and sacred bonds of common danger' (Churchill in the House of Commons, 17 September).

Not all the anxieties this month were at home. In North Africa the Italians began their advance across the Egyptian frontier, while the British armoured reinforcements were still on their long voyage round the Cape. There was the unhappy, unsuccessful Dakar enterprise. Germany, Italy and Japan signed a Tripartite Pact. But the beginning of the month had brought the Prime Minister immense relief in the final announcement of the agreement about the Western hemisphere bases and the fifty American destroyers, with its implications and with the heartening experience, in its negotiation, of the resolute and understanding support of the President of the United States.

By the end of the month arrangements had been made to transfer the Prime Minister's headquarters to the 'Annexe' beside the Central War Room at Storey's Gate. Here there were underground offices, conference rooms and bedrooms (sometimes called 'cabins' by the Royal Marine orderlies), while on the ground floor a flat was provided for the Prime Minister and Mrs Churchill, with steel shutters which could be closed over the windows during raids.

From now on I slept regularly at No. 10 or the Annexe, returning to my lodgings in Graham Terrace for bath and breakfast.

DIARY

September

2 Afternoon off.

3 Day off. Walk from Merstham to Caterham.

7 Air attack in afternoon and at night.

8 Slept in air-raid shelter on mattress on floor.

9 More raids at night.

10 Best man at Colin Hardie's wedding in Westminster Cathedral. Slept (interrupted by air raids) at Graham Terrace.

11 More raids.

12 More raids.

13 With PM to Chequers in afternoon, calling at Dollis Hill (where emergency headquarters had been prepared) and Uxbridge (11th Fighter Group) on the way.

14 Returned to town in afternoon. Spent night at Central War Room. More raids.

15 Back to Chequers, calling at Uxbridge and watching control of battle in 11th Fighter Group operations room.

16 Returned to London. Left for Scotland by night train from Euston. No lights after an hour or so because of 'red' warning.

17–24 At Connel Ferry (on leave).

25, 26 In Edinburgh, leaving night of 26th.

27 Arrived Euston 4½ hours late. Back to work.

LETTERS

6 *September* More banshee wailings nightly and daily, with fireworks at night. It will be a relief to get a few quiet nights' sleep.

29 *September* I do not now sleep much if at all at Graham Terrace. I shall ordinarily be at No. 10, going to Chequers every third weekend and in the three-week period having off (a) two consecutive nights and (b) three consecutive nights, which should allow occasional visits to the country. Each morning I hope to get along to Graham Terrace for bath and breakfast; but otherwise will spend the twenty-four hours at the office, at my club (for meals) or in the cellar. A cheerful existence!

The PM was in very good form and actually realised that I had been away.

OCTOBER

After a relatively quiet start to the month there was a renewal of heavy raids on London. On the 14th a bomb fell on the Treasury courtyard, smashing windows in No. 10, and much damage was done by incendiaries, particularly in Pall Mall and Piccadilly. On the 17th another bomb fell in the yard at Downing Street. Much of the Treasury was destroyed and four people were killed in the basement. (In his history – *The Second World War*, II, 306 – the Prime Minister seems to combine the memories of this raid with those of the raid on the 14th.) To meet the danger from incendiaries the system of fire-watchers was developed. For some time from the beginning of the month the Prime Minister slept in the Railway Executive's deep shelter in the former Down Street station; but thereafter his home at night was in the Annexe at Storey's Gate, though No. 10 continued to be used at times during the day. By the end of the month the invasion threat had slackened. It was not known that Hitler had in fact on 12 October postponed Operation 'Sea Lion' until the following summer. As late as 17 October Sir Alan Brooke noted in his diary that 'evidence is amassing . . . of an impending invasion of some kind or other'.

On the resignation of Sir Neville Chamberlain, Sir John Anderson became Lord President, with general oversight of Home affairs, being succeeded as Home Secretary and Minister of Home Security by Herbert Morrison. Anderson had little in common with Churchill and they were not intimate friends; but, while intervening himself on the Home Front from time to time, the Prime Minister was content to leave its general supervision for the rest of the war to a colleague of such strength of character, wisdom and experience. At this time Churchill also became Leader of the Conservative Party.

Strong reinforcements had now reached General Wavell. The next main objective was to strengthen further the forces in the Middle East and especially in the desert. The Prime Minister was dissatisfied with the distribution of the forces already in the area and with the disparity between ration and fighting strength, and arranged for Anthony Eden, Dominions Secretary, to undertake a special inspection.

On 28 October the Italians invaded Greece. I was awakened early in the morning at Chequers with news of Mussolini's ultimatum. Thinking that Churchill would wish to be informed at once of this new extension of the war, I went up to his bedroom, woke him up and told him. He looked at me, grunted, and rolled over and immediately went to sleep again. Later in the morning, after he was awake, when I went to him with the usual round-up of overnight news, he looked sternly at me and said, 'Never do that again. Why did you do it?' It took me a moment to realise what I had done wrong. Then I said I thought he might wish to summon the Cabinet. 'What could they do? Just gape round the table.' Then he told me never again to awaken him when Hitler invaded a new country. Two days later, on the invitation of the Greek Government, a British force occupied Suda Bay in Crete. 'One salient fact leaped upon us – CRETE! The Italians must not have it.' (*The Second World War*, II, 472.)

DIARY

October

4   In evening to Andover.

5   At Andover. Out on push bike for first time for several years.

6   At Andover. Visit to Oxford.

7   Returned to London.

14   Bomb in Treasury courtyard in evening.

15   Little time to enjoy birthday letters; but came back to Graham Terrace for lunch. With PM visited ruins of Carlton Club, wrecked last night.

17   Another bomb in the yard at Downing Street. A large part of the Treasury demolished and four people killed in basement.

18   In evening to Andoversford, to visit Abells.

19, 20   At Andoversford (Foxcote Manor).

21   Returned early to London. We are in process of moving to 'Annexe' in old Board of Trade.

25   To Chequers in afternoon.

26   At Chequers. Lord Halifax and Lord Lothian, [Ambassador to US], arrived. Virginia Cowles at lunch. Introduced to young Winston [infant son of Randolph and Pamela Churchill]. Reports of German–Vichy agreement.

27   At Chequers. News of de Gaulle's broadcast from Leopoldville

and setting up of Council of Defence. Sir Archibald [Secretary of State for Air] and Lady Sinclair to lunch.

28 Wakened early by news of Italian ultimatum to Greece, regarded by Greece as declaration of war. Returned to London.

29 From now No. 10 includes 'No. 10 Downing Street Annexe'. PM usually goes in the evenings to 'The Barn' (the Railway Executive's deep shelter).

30 At Andover.

LETTERS

2 *October* That holiday had the unwelcome result of making it less easy to overcome the obstacles to sleep in our underground shelter; but I am getting accustomed to these again. The nights seem to be quieter, though anyhow in our shelter we hardly notice the explosions and the damage to property is, on the whole, remarkably small. Generally people are settling down wonderfully cheerfully to their new way of life.

We have had a great day of interviews in connection with the reconstruction of the Cabinet . . . It must be wearing for the PM; but he is still in particularly good form.

6 *October* In spite of continual air-raid warnings the raids seem much lighter and there has been no startling damage in the last few days. In our shelter at night we hear nothing of the barrage that is apt to keep people awake above ground.

16 *October* I shall remember this birthday (15th) by the evening before it when we had, as it seemed, the worst night of air raids since that first weekend in September. A high explosive bomb fell a few yards from No. 10. I was upstairs and dashed down to the shelter as I heard it fall, to the accompaniment of the most terrific explosion. It is difficult to remember exactly what happened; but I seemed to fly down with a rush of 'blast', the air full of dust and the crash and clatter of glass breaking behind. There was a rush of several of us into the shelter and we tumbled on top of one another in a good deal of confusion. Afterwards it was several minutes before the air cleared and, with the clouds of dust and the acrid, sooty smell, we thought that the house or the Treasury next door was on fire. Fortunately that was not so and by the light of

torches we were able to survey the damage. The mess in the house was indescribable – windows smashed in all directions, every-thing covered with grime, doors off hinges and curtains and furniture tossed about in a confused mass. Fortunately the PM has been using the basement and was dining there at the time at the opposite side of the house, with steel shutters closed, so was none the worse.

Meanwhile incendiaries and high explosives were being drop-ped wholesale in the West End and there was a line of fire in the direction of Pall Mall and Piccadilly. The Carlton Club was wrecked and burnt. The Reform Club had been on fire; but was not (as far as I could see today) too badly damaged, though we can't use it. (During the night I telephoned the hall porter at the Reform and asked how things were. A calm voice replied, 'The Club is burning, Sir.') St James's Club in Piccadilly was burnt out. A big house in St James's Square was reduced to a heap of rubble – and so on. The hut of the soldiers who guard Downing Street was completely demolished: fortunately they had taken refuge elsewhere.

Last night was bad in parts of London, but not so bad here, though there was no water in the morning (now restored). At Graham Terrace there is no gas and when you try to turn it on water runs into the meter.

So my birthday treat was to visit the ruins of the Carlton Club with the PM, who stumped in and wandered about amongst the wreckage, regardless of the impending roof. The dining room was like a bit of Pompeii, with unfinished meals and decanters of wine on the tables. At a bedroom door we found the Chief Whip David Margesson's bedroom slippers awaiting him. At the entrance steps the Prime Minister pointed to a piece of marble statuary half buried in rubble. Lifted up it was seen to be the head of Pitt.

27 October   Chequers. We have had fewer visitors than usual; but a particularly interesting couple over the weekend – Lord Halifax and Lord Lothian. Lothian is very ready to talk and gave us a long account of the reactions in America to our battle. He was Private Secretary to the Prime Minister in Lloyd George's days and was here when Chequers was handed over to the nation. Archie Sinclair and his wife have also been here today. She is a very natural, downright sort of person, whom I liked very much. I was introduced this morning to young Winston, Randolph's son. He is absurdly like his grandfather; but, as one of the daughters said, 'so are all babies'. (Someone else said that every baby resembles either Churchill or Max Beaverbrook.)

The talk at dinner here is quite the best entertainment I know. I feel peeved that I haven't the sort of memory that could treasure up the PM's *obiter dicta* to chuckle over afterwards.

All week we seem to have lived in a madhouse at the office, with the din of builders and carpenters added to the confusion of translation from No. 10 to the Annexe . . . For the moment we continue to sleep at No. 10 and with a waning moon the night raids have been less intense. It is extraordinary how little attention is paid to the occasional daytime raids: people mostly go about in the streets as if nothing was happening.

Nelson (the PM's cat) has been evacuated to Chequers under the evacuation scheme; but Treasury Bill (alias the Munich Mouser) still prowls about the ruins of his home.

31 October Two nights off at Andover. I wasn't wakened in the morning and slept for eleven to twelve hours without a break.

No – there is no thought of evacuating London. We have only moved to a safer building than No. 10, though for the moment I sleep there. At present the PM has most of his meals in one place, and spends his evening and sleeps in a second, while we have our main office in a third. The difficulties of life are considerable.

NOVEMBER

On 5 November Roosevelt was re-elected President, to Churchill's 'indescribable relief' (*The Second World War*, II, 489). From the beginning of the month German air attacks were extended to industrial centres throughout the country (starting with the massive blitz on Coventry on the 14th) and to the ports; but London was not entirely spared and suffered a heavy raid on the 15th. A bomb on Sloane Square Station struck an Underground train and there were heavy casualties. This month the Prime Minister paid the first of the weekend visits to Ditchley Park near Blenheim, as the RAF insisted on his doing so, especially at the time of the full moon, when Chequers was a dangerously attractive target. Here the PM and his party were entertained with lavish and thoughtful hospitality by

Ronald Tree and his gifted wife, Nancy. By a miracle of organisation they maintained in their beautiful home the standards and atmosphere of a pre-war house-party. In retrospect the Ditchley weekends stand out as a happy oasis in the gloomiest years of the war.

In the late afternoon of the 14th we set out from No. 10 for Ditchley. Just before starting from the garden gate I handed the Prime Minister a box with a top secret message. A few minutes later he opened this and read the contents – which I subsequently understood were a report that the German 'beam' seemed to indicate a raid on London. The cars had now reached Kensington Gardens; but he immediately called to the driver to return to Downing Street. He was not going to sleep quietly in the country while London was under what was expected to be a heavy attack. (I was informed in 1970 by Miss Stenhouse and Miss Davies that they were sent to spend the night at the Dollis Hill headquarters, and the rest of the female staff sent home, by Brendan Bracken and Anthony Bevir, on the ground that the 'beam' pointed at Whitehall.) As it turned out, the raid was not on London after all but was the blitz which shattered the heart of Coventry. Next day the Prime Minister's party again set out for Ditchley and we were there when London's turn for a heavy raid came that evening.

Eden continued his enquiry in the Middle East. In exchanges of messages he was at cross purposes with the Prime Minister, who, in ignorance of the plans for operations in North Africa, kept pressing for more vigorous support for Greece, while Eden urged that we could not send sufficient forces to have influence on the fighting there without imperilling our whole position in the Middle East. On return to England, however, he was able to unfold the North African plans to Churchill, who received them with gusto and 'purred like six cats' (The Second World War, II, 480).

In successful naval operations in the Mediterranean, half the Italian battle fleet was disabled at Taranto.

DIARY

November

8 To Oxford in afternoon, staying in Magdalen with Colin Hardie.

9 Oxford. *Iolanthe* at the Dragon.

10 Oxford. At St Aldate's Church (packed). Talk with Reginald Coupland [Beit Professor of Colonial History, Oxford; member of 1936 Royal Commission on Palestine of which author was secretary].

11 Returned to London.

14 False start for Ditchley. 'The moonlight sonata': the raid was on Coventry.

15 To Ditchley Park, Enstone (Mr and Mrs Ronald Tree). Also Leonora Cobbett, Brendan and Captain [later Admiral Tom] Phillips, Vice-Chief of Naval Staff.

16 At Ditchley. Sir Alan Brooke for the night.

17 Ditchley. Sir R. Glyn [Conservative MP for Abingdon].

18 Returned to town. Then off to Andover.

19 Andover.

20 Returned to London.

27 Lunch with Mrs Churchill, also Lord Moyne [Minister Resident in Cairo], Sarah and Pamela.

LETTERS

3 November This is written in the catacombs. I no longer 'sleep' at No. 10 (quotation marks because of several interruptions last night), but underneath our office in a neighbouring, more modern building. The completion of our part of it moves slowly and we still have not started the proposed mess; but there is a canteen here run by Marines, which provides a good evening meal – hot tinned soup, sausages etc. Much quieter nights now, but we have not had a night without raids. Today may be the first exception: torrential rain prevented more than one or two planes reaching us and this evening (now 8.25) the sirens have not yet started.

This has been rather a wearing week, what with the difficulty and confusion arising from the three separate places between which (at different times) our office is divided and the din of men altering the new building and fixing brick walls and steel shutters outside the windows. The idea of a peaceful evening by the fireside at home seems something too wonderful to imagine and a concert, theatre or cinema is of course unknown. I am at my desk till bedtime and apart from weekends and a few minutes sometimes snatched at breakfast-time haven't a moment for reading outside my work. Sometimes there is a change of company at lunchtime. I usually lunch in a Scottish atmosphere at the Caledonian Club, where we are boarded out, my own club being *hors de combat*. Such dishes as haggis with bashed neaps and beef scollops appear on the menu. [The proliferation of references to food in this memoir should be understood against the background of five years of wartime diet – dried milk and powdered egg!]

11 November The evenings are almost entirely spent under cover, so that one doesn't notice the raids so much; but we had several loud boomps last night and one time when I was upstairs there was a rattle of incendiaries on the roof making a noise like people playing billiards. Twice I have been a guest for supper in the canteen run in the basement of the Colonial Office, which I can reach by devious routes without going out of doors. It felt like going home and everybody was very kind and welcoming. People of all grades in the Office ought to know one another much better after being thrown together like this every evening.

I wonder if you will see Lord Lloyd, who is going up to Edinburgh to speak in connection with the Livingstone celebrations. I had a particularly nice note from him the other day about a private letter I had sent to Christopher about Palestine.

DECEMBER

On the 8th the Prime Minister sent a long letter to President Roosevelt (on which he had been working since discussions with Lord Lothian at Ditchley in the middle of November), 'one of the most important I ever wrote', on our needs in shipping, aircraft and munitions, and on the financial problem – the approaching moment 'when we shall no longer be able to pay cash for shipping and other supplies'. The President's response was the announcement of Lend-Lease, later described by Churchill as 'the most unsordid act in the history of any nation'.

On the 9th General Wilson launched his eagerly awaited attack in the Western Desert. Sidi Barrani was captured and the best part of five enemy divisions destroyed.

Air raids continued. In a heavy attack on 8 December the House of Commons was hit. The climax came on the 29th, when the

London night sky was lit by great fires that destroyed a large part of the City, consuming or damaging several Wren churches.

Following the untimely death of Lord Lothian, a reluctant Lord Halifax was appointed Ambassador in Washington, Anthony Eden succeeding him as Foreign Secretary, while David Margesson became Secretary of State for War and James Stuart Chief Whip.

I spent Christmas with the Churchills at Chequers. The Principal Private Secretary, Eric Seal, had sent the Prime Minister a minute in which he stated that he was anxious to arrange for everyone to have a week's leave during the Christmas recess and asked if he might have authority for this, adding that, if the Prime Minister could indicate in broad outline what his own plans were, it would be a great help. On the request for authority Churchill wrote 'no', subsequently dictating the following reply:

> Your minute about Christmas holidays surprises me. No holidays can be given at Christmas, but every endeavour should be made to allow members of the staff to attend Divine Service on Christmas Day, either in the morning or afternoon.
>
> My own plans will be to work either here (Chequers) or in London continuously, and I hope that the recess may be used not only for overtaking arrears, but for tackling new problems in greater detail.
>
> On the other hand, I should approve of one week's holiday being worked in and well spread between now and March 31, and you may prepare a roster for me to see on these lines.

Perhaps his tongue was in his cheek. When he set off for Chequers on Christmas Eve he wished the Private Secretaries left behind at No. 10 'a busy Christmas and a frantic New Year'. From Chequers I wrote on Boxing Day:

> The Prime Minister has made a great point of working as usual over the holiday and yesterday morning was like almost any other here, with the usual letters and telephone calls and of course many Christmas greeting messages thrown in. His present to me was an inscribed copy of *Great Contemporaries*. From lunchtime on less work was done and we had a festive family Christmas, with the three daughters, two sons-in-law and one daughter-in-

law and no official visitors. For lunch we had the largest turkey I
have ever seen, a present from Lord Rothermere's farm, sent in
accordance with one of his last wishes before he died. Afterwards
we listened to the King's speech and Vic Oliver, Sarah Churchill's
actor husband, played the piano and Sarah sang. It was the same
after dinner. For once the shorthand writer was dismissed and we
had a sort of sing-song until after midnight. The P M sang lustily,
if not always in tune, and when Vic played Viennese waltzes he
danced a remarkably frisky measure of his own in the middle of
the room. He then sat up and talked till 2 a.m.; but I found him as
brisk as ever this morning, cheerfully munching one of Lloyd
George's apples from Churt.

This Christmas truce (*Heilige Nacht* in truth *stille Nacht*) is a
relief and rather touching. They would be glad to have it in
Graham Terrace, for they had rather a shaking a few nights ago,
when a particularly large bomb or mine exploded at Ebury Bridge
and blew in the area door at No. 6 besides smashing a window in
St Mary's and filling the church with soot.

We had great difficulty in finding a present from the Private
Secretaries for Mrs Churchill. The flower shops seemed to have
nothing at all suitable, being almost empty. Apparently those
bowls of hyacinths that used to appear at Christmas were Dutch.
Most of the big shops were completely cleared out of chocolates
and confectionery; but in the end we found one that could
produce a large box.

On the 31st the Prime Minister sent a message to Pétain, offering
the help of a British expeditionary force if the French Government
decided to cross to North Africa and resume the war against
Germany. There was no reply.

So ended 'this tremendous year' – 'the most splendid, as it was the
most deadly, year in our long English and British story' (*The Second
World War*, II, 555). In his diary Cadogan probably spoke for most
of us when he said, 'I don't frankly see how we are going to win, but
I am convinced that we shall not lose.' I saw the old year out and the
new year in at the Central War Room, with a glass of champagne
provided by Jock Colville.

DECEMBER 1940

DIARY

December

20 To Oxford, to spend the weekend at Corpus with Sir Richard Livingstone [President of Corpus Christi College].

21 Oxford. In afternoon drove to Witney to see College property damaged in an air raid.

22 Oxford. Visited Coupland on Boar's Hill.

23 Returned to London.

24 Opened my Christmas parcels. Far fewer cards this year. To Chequers in evening.

25 Christmas at Chequers. A Churchill family party.

26 Chequers. Lord Woolton [Minister of Food] to lunch. Sir Wilfred Freeman [Deputy Chief of Air Staff] to dinner.

27 Returned to London.

29 At St Columba's in morning, for the first time for many weeks. Great fires in City.

1941

JANUARY

Operations in the Western Desert continued, with the capture of Bardia and Tobruk. In six weeks the Army had advanced 200 miles and taken 113,000 prisoners. There was growing evidence of German preparations for a Balkan campaign and the Chiefs of Staff decided that after the fall of Tobruk all other operations in the Middle East must have second place to affording the greatest possible aid to Greece. On Greek hesitation, however, to accept our aid, unless British troops were sent in sufficient numbers to act offensively, it was decided to push on to Benghazi, while building up a strategic reserve in the desert. In a letter to President Inönü, Churchill offered to send ten squadrons of fighters and bombers to be stationed on Turkish airfields. The Luftwaffe began to operate in the Mediterranean, attacking the British from Sicily. There were heavy air attacks on Malta, where HMS *Illustrious* lay under repair. British troops entered Eritrea.

The Lord President, Sir John Anderson, and his Committee assumed responsibility for the whole field of economic policy. But the most important event on the Home Front was the visit by Harry Hopkins, Roosevelt's special adviser and assistant. The significance of this visitor did not seem to be immediately realised by the Foreign Office, but it was by Brendan Bracken, who alerted the Prime Minister and welcomed Hopkins with red-carpet treatment at Bournemouth. Next day Hopkins lunched at Downing Street and at the weekend joined the Prime Minister's party at Chequers. In the next few weeks – including a stay at Chequers, where he suffered severely from the cold, later vowing that his victory present would be to instal adequate central heating – he had many talks with Churchill and a warm personal friendship grew up between them.

39

In the coming years this contributed much to foster closer understanding and practical liaison between the Prime Minister and the President, and to resolve any difficulties that arose in the relations between Downing Street and the White House. A frail, gentle-looking man, he was lit from within by a blazing flame of devotion to the cause of freedom. (Once later I was amazed by the vigour and intensity of his passion for peace when he rounded on me for something I said which suggested the possibility of a future third world war.)

He was taken by the Prime Minister on his visit to Scapa to see off Lord and Lady Halifax on their departure for Washington in the newly commissioned *King George V*. It seemed a miracle that he survived the rigours and adventures of the journey. On the way back we stopped at Glasgow and, at a small dinner party with Tom Johnston, the Regional Commissioner for Scotland, and the Lord Provost, he made a short speech in which, all the more impressively for its quiet and gentle delivery, he gave his hearers a moving sense of the firm support which would be coming from across the Atlantic, ending with the words from the Book of Books ('in the truth of which Mr Johnston's mother and my mother were brought up'): 'whither thou goest, I will go; and where thou lodgest, I will lodge ... even to the end' [Ruth I, 60]. On the eve of his departure for the United States he listened to the Prime Minister's broadcast of 9 February, ending with the appeal 'Give us the tools, and we will finish the job', and he took with him to Washington a comprehensive list of British requirements.

A startling incident at Scapa had been when there was a trial of rocket projectiles on HMS *Nelson*. One of the projectiles got entangled in the rigging. There was a loud explosion and a jam-jar-like object flew towards the bridge, where we were standing. Everyone ducked and there was a great bang, but no serious damage was done.

Another visitor from the United States was Wendel Willkie, Roosevelt's opponent in the Presidential election, bringing a letter from the President quoting Longfellow's verse:

Sail on, O ship of State!
Sail on, O Union, strong and great!
Humanity with all its fears,

With all the hopes of future years,
Is hanging breathless on thy fate!

DIARY

January
1   In afternoon to Charlie Chaplin film *The Great Dictator*.
3   By night train to Edinburgh. A mild raid and All Clear just before the train started.
4–6   In Edinburgh.
7   Returned to London.
10   Harry Hopkins (who arrived last night) called on PM. Supper in new Cabinet Office canteen.
14   Left by special from King's Cross with PM, Mrs C, Lord and Lady Halifax, Harry Hopkins, Pug Ismay, Tommy [Commander Thompson, PM's ADC], Sir Charles Wilson [PM's personal physician, later Lord Moran] and the Service mission to US.
15   Arrived Thurso. Blizzards. Crossed Pentland Firth in HMS *Napier*. Lunch in *King George V*. Afternoon on island. Dinner in HMS *Nelson*, in which we spent the night.
16   Morning in HMS *Nelson*. Returned through stormy seas to Thurso and left for the south.
17   Arrived Inverkeithing and visited *Petravie* and *QE* and *Hood* in Rosyth Dockyards. Picked up Tom Johnston, Regional Commissioner, in Edinburgh. Visited Civil Defence Services in Glasgow.
18   Returned to Wendover and thence drove in snow-storm to London. To Andover in afternoon.
19   Andover.
20   Returned to London.
31   News of Lord Lloyd's serious illness. Evening off.
     Dinner at Graham Terrace for first time since early September.

LETTERS

19 January   We set off from King's Cross in a 'Special' on Tuesday and woke up next day in Caithness in the middle of a deserted heath, the ground white with snow and a blizzard howling at the windows. There had been a derailment in front of us and it was some time before this was cleared away and we could get on to Thurso. There was much discussion as to what we should do, for the sea was stormy and my master had a bad cold. In the end it was decided to proceed. We put out in a drifter and were transferred from this on a heaving sea to a destroyer, which took us up to Scapa. I spent most of the time on the bridge and it was a beautiful scene – the mainland and low islands covered with snow, the sea extraordinarily blue and bright sunshine turn-about with lashing blizzards. I had better veil our doings at Scapa, save that we spent the night in a battleship and returned by destroyer the following day, through even more tempestuous seas, which swept the deck in cascades. By a miracle I was not sick. Then down through the night to Inverkeithing, for a visit to the dockyards, where the PM was received with immense enthusiasm. Thence to Edinburgh, where we picked up the Regional Commissioner, Tom Johnston, and his principal officer, Norman Duke, and gave them lunch in our train on the way to Glasgow. The visit was supposed to be a secret; but a mob of hundreds if not thousands was waiting at Queen Street Station and we had to fight our way to our cars and then into the City Chambers. The PM had been asked to meet the Councillors and Bailies and say a few words to them; but to our horror we found a crowd of about 200, a platform and press reporters. The PM rose to the occasion, however, though he had no prepared speech, and made a full-length oration, which went down very well. In the evening we had a small dinner-party with the Lord Provost and Tom Johnston and one or two Councillors, and finally the Lord Provost saw us off in our train about 11.30. It took us direct to Wendover, the station for Chequers, from which I returned direct to London by car in a snow-storm.

26 *January* Graham Terrace. The absence of raids (now for nearly a week) makes a pleasant change and as the debris from previous raids is cleared away this part of London is beginning to look much more normal. It is nice to be able to go out to dinner away from the Office without being blitzed upon . . . Part of the purpose of our journey to the north was to see off Lord and Lady Halifax. We had lunch in the new *King George V*, in which they were to cross the Atlantic, before leaving them. On the deck Lord Halifax wished me good luck in the most friendly way.

FEBRUARY

After the capture of Benghazi the Defence Committee decided against advance upon Tripoli, and concentrated on building up a force to help Greece. Eden, now Foreign Secretary, and the CIGS, Field Marshal Sir John Dill, flew to Cairo to put this decision into effect. In a visit to Athens the offer of British troops was formally accepted by the Greek Government. ('We were prepared to run the risk of failure, thinking it better to suffer with the Greeks than to make no attempt to help them' – Eden's telegram of 26 February from Cairo.) Meanwhile, Rommel had arrived in Africa.

In successful British operations in Italian Somaliland, Kismayu and Mogadishu were taken.

In Eden's absence the PM took charge of the Foreign Office. One of his engagements was an interview with Shigemitsu, the Japanese Ambassador. At such interviews Churchill preferred not to have a secretary present. When asked afterwards to supply a record, he could remember his own remarks, but found it difficult to recall the other side of the conversation.

DIARY

February

1   With Frank Lee [Permanent Under-Secretary, Board of Trade] to his cottage at Much Hadham.
2   At Much Hadham.
3   Returned to town.
9   Bad cold, throat and temperature. Evening broadcast by PM.
10   Cold worse. Went to bed. Temperature 102.6.
11   Still away from office with cold.
12   Ditto.
13   Returned to No. 10; but still not very fit and Seal packed me off to Andover.
14, 15   Andover.
16   Returned to London and No. 10.
20   Lunch with Dr and Mrs Weizmann, before their departure for America.
23   To Chequers. Menzies [PM of Australia] and Cranbornes [Viscount Cranborne, Secretary of State for Colonies] staying.

43

24   Returned to town.

28   Left for Edinburgh by 10.15 p.m. train from King's Cross.

LETTERS

6 February   The death of Lord Lloyd is very sad. He had just established his position in the Colonial Office and seemed likely to provide it with much-needed drive. It is hard to believe that one who was so intensively active only a few days ago has now gone.

This week we have started our private mess, which is a great improvement on the canteen we had used hitherto, with its monotonous sausages and tinned food. We have a Swedish cook, who provides most excellent dinners, with the fresh vegetables and et ceteras that make so much difference. But we seem to have used our week's ration of butter at the first meal.

9 February   I have been busy, among other things, with the preparation for today's broadcast, which looks as if it ought to be a very effective and enheartening speech. We had a rather hectic search for a passenger from the north to whom the PM wanted to speak the other evening. [The passenger was H.J. Scrymgeour-Wedderburn, later Earl of Dundee, who was appointed a Parliamentary Under-Secretary in the Scottish Office.] After a long hunt in Perth station, where his supposed train was then standing, we found a hotel porter who had seen him leave by an earlier train. We managed to get a message to it at Larbert and held it up at Coatbridge, where the man was brought to the station-master's office. It was a race against the express to get the calls through in time.

MARCH

The Lend-Lease Bill was signed by the President, 'an ocean-borne trumpet call that we are no longer alone' (PM in a speech on the 18th).

German troops moved into Bulgaria, which had signed the Axis Tripartite Pact. Eden and Dill again flew to Athens to meet the Greek Prime Minister, who expressed his country's determination to fight on. Although the CIGS concluded that the hazards of the enterprise had considerably increased, Eden, on his return to Cairo, in agreement with the Commanders in Chief and General Smuts

[South African PM, later Field Marshal Smuts], was for going ahead with aid to Greece, and this was approved by the War Cabinet. The first British troops disembarked in Greece on the 9th.

On the 25th Yugoslav envoys signed a pact with the Germans; but two days later a *coup d'état* in Belgrade established a pro-Ally administration. King Peter was proclaimed and the Prince Regent Paul fled. ('Early this morning the Yugoslav nation found its soul,' Churchill said in a speech to the Central Council of Conservative Associations.) Hitler postponed the date for his attack on Russia.

On the last day of the month Rommel launched an attack on Agheila. Meanwhile British Somaliland had been regained, Keren taken and, in an advance into Abyssinia, Diredawa and Harrar captured.

There was a British naval victory off Cape Matapan; but this month there were exceptionally heavy losses at sea, leading to the creation of the Battle of the Atlantic Committee.

There was a renewal of heavy air attacks on Britain – the Luftwaffe's 'tour of the ports'.

DIARY

March

1–9 On leave in Edinburgh.
10 Returned to No. 10. PM at Chequers with bronchial cold.
14 To Chequers.
15 New American Ambassador [J.G. Winant] and Averell Harriman [Roosevelt's special representative on Supply] arrived for weekend. Mrs Eden and Mr and Mrs Tree also staying.
16 Chequers.
17 Returned to London.
21 In afternoon to Oxford, staying with Coupland. Dinner at All Souls. Bombs on aerodrome below Boar's Hill.
22, 23 Oxford. Dinner at All Souls. Conant, President of Harvard, also there.
24 Returned to London.
27 PM announced coup in Belgrade.

APRIL

Germany attacked Yugoslavia and Greece. On the 17th Yugoslavia surrendered, followed on the 24th by Greece. In the subsequent evacuation 50,000 British and Allied forces were brought out.

In the Western Desert Rommel's attack drove forward past Tobruk, which was invested, towards Bardia and Sollum.

British forces captured Asmara and Addis Ababa.

Rashid Ali staged a pro-Axis *coup d'état* in Iraq. The siege of Habbaniya began. British troops disembarked at Basra.

The United States security zone and patrol area in the Atlantic were extended to the meridian of 26 West.

DIARY

April
1   Andover.
2   Returned to London.
6   Germany declared war on Yugoslavia and Greece.
9   News of German capture of Salonika.
11 To Oxford in afternoon, staying with Colin and Christian Hardie.
12, 13   Oxford.
14 Returned to No. 10.
16 Night of heavy air raid. Much damage in Ebury Street and neighbourhood. Windows blown in at Graham Terrace: holes in roof etc.
17 Breakfast in downstairs bedroom at Graham Terrace, upstairs being uninhabitable.
18 Left with PM for Ditchley Park. Other guests there – Gen. Arnold [C in C US Army Air Force], Averell Harriman.
19 At Ditchley. President Beneš [of Czechoslovakia], Monseigneur Sramek, Gen. Nizbosky and Gen. Ingr to lunch, with whom PM visited Czech forces. Sir Charles and Lady Portal arrived.
21 Returned to London. In afternoon to Andover.
22 Andover.
23 Returned to No. 10. Found it had been decided to evacuate Greece.
27 PM's broadcast – 'Westward, look, the land is bright.'

LETTERS

17 April Last night we had one of the worst blitzes we have known in London. Our building rocked with the explosions and there was a good deal of noise even down in the sub-basement where we sleep. It was quite strange, as sometimes last September, to go out in the morning into a brilliantly sunny upper world and find that London had after all not been razed to the ground. There are, however, many new scars and after lunch I visited a street where fires were still burning. The Reform Club is again closed because of an explosion across the street. Poor 6 Graham Terrace was this morning a sorry sight. I was warned what to expect by several completely demolished houses in neighbouring streets and the flames still leaping from a blazing furniture depository round the corner in Ebury Street. At No. 6 almost all the windows had been blown in: several of the frames were smashed and those in the sitting room blown clean off the brickwork and into the room. Everything (bright from spring cleaning at the weekend) was covered with soot, plaster and broken glass. Patches of sky could be seen here and there through the roof. Fortunately little irreparable damage had been done to the furniture or other contents of the house, though everything is covered with dust. Neither Miss Edwards (my landlady) nor her sister was hurt and she is very brave about it – not a tear shed and getting to work to put things straight. I could have no bath, there being only a trickle of water, but she insisted on giving me breakfast on a tray in the downstairs back bedroom, which was almost unaltered.

20 April Ditchley. Back in this lovely house, even more beautiful in the April sunlight. Today I managed to get out for a short walk with Mrs C, but otherwise seldom got very far from my telephone. Yesterday we relaxed with a talkie after dinner. I did have an afternoon off, going with the PM on an inspection of Czech forces with President Beneš and their Prime Minister, Monseigneur Sramek. I thought it rather moving – all those poor exiles, the tiny remnant of an army, and they were so pleased to be visited and eager in their welcome. We had tea in the officers' mess – a band, a singer, their own special cakes and neat whisky handed round in small glasses. As the PM left, a choir of soldiers

47

sang 'Rule Britannia' with great enthusiasm. We also had that sad National Anthem. They showered on the Churchills all sorts of gifts of their own making – drawings, coloured woodwork, embroidery etc.

It is again quite an American party, with three of Roosevelt's envoys. We also have the Chief of the Air Staff [Sir Charles Portal] and Lord Rothermere.

I hope Graham Terrace suffered no more damage in last night's raid – probably not, for most of the bombing was more in the east; but I am more worried about the effect of some heavy rain we have had in the last two days. I asked the Army & Navy Stores to repair the roof as soon as possible; but, the telephone being out of action, don't know if they have done anything about it. By the way, the attitude of the crowd after Wednesday night's raid was interesting. The streets were thronged with people almost in holiday mood, cheerfully surveying the smouldering ruins.

24 April The weekend, though strenuous (never to bed till 2 or 2.30 a.m.), was really refreshing in that lovely house, with cheerful society and lots of spring sunshine. Mrs C took me out for a short walk on Sunday afternoon – so nice and full of talk and interest in things. I thought she showed herself very human in her talk about servants – how they prefer the old-fashioned basement, where they are on their own and can have in their friends quietly, to the modern flat. She visits the kitchen only at a fixed time and thinks it unfair to the servants to invade their part of the house at other times, at least not without giving notice that she is coming.

At Andover I spent a day of warm sunshine. The woods are incredibly gay with primroses, violets, anemones and other flowers and the three children had a most cheerful picnic with me (their mother being at her canteen). They are the picture of health and show no signs of war rations.

Poor Miss Edwards seems hardly quite recovered from her shock. She was rather difficult about repairs to the house. I had arranged for the Army & Navy Stores to send a surveyor to estimate the cost of first-aid and begged them to carry out at once repairs to the roof, through which the sky is visible in many places. The men came with remarkable promptitude, bringing a tarpaulin; but, since it would mean removing some more of the slates, Miss Edwards refused to allow the work to proceed. Thereupon heavy showers of rain fell and she had to muster various pots and pans to collect the drips. The long and the short of it is that we now await repairs by the City of Westminster, with nothing definite about when these are likely to be done.

27 April Still no repairs to the house; but fortunately the cold winds of the last week, though tearing at the pieces of cloth nailed up to cover the gaping windows, have brought not a drop of rain. All first-aid repairs in the area are to be taken over by the Ministry of Works and Buildings. Poor Miss E has been like the king who never smiled again. She must have been much shaken and does not take easily the disturbance of the established order. Actually we are better off than some of our neighbours, many of whom have been compelled to leave their homes. You cannot drive along Ebury Street for the mess of ruins (just round the corner of Eaton Terrace). It was evidently a land mine and the desolation has to be seen to be believed. Piccadilly is still closed to traffic; but gradually the mess is being cleared away and people carry on much as usual. There is certainly no trace of defeatism, and criticism of the Government for what happened in Greece, of which there has been some word in Parliament and Press, seems generally remarkable for its absence. I hope the PM's speech tonight will put heart into any falterers there may be.

MAY

Discussion took place of a memorandum by General Dill, in which he argued that the defence of Britain against invasion was so vital that it would be unjustifiable in the next three months to send to the Middle East more than a maintenance reserve for the tanks already there. The PM opposed this and the flow of reinforcements continued unimpaired. During the month, convoy 'Tiger', conveying tanks and Hurricanes, was brought successfully through the Mediterranean. In the Western Desert British forces took Sollum and Capuzzo, but were driven back by a successful German counterattack.

The Battle of Crete ended in the evacuation of British forces. 'The spear-point of the German lance . . . triumphed and was broken' (*The Second World War*, III, 253). The signal from Admiral Cunningham, C in C Mediterranean, read – 'It takes the Navy three years to build a ship. It will take three hundred years to build a new tradition. The evacuation will continue.'

In the climax of the spring blitz, Liverpool and the Mersey were attacked on seven successive nights. The most destructive attack of the whole blitz was on London on the 10th. The House of Commons chamber (in which the PM had made a long statement on the war situation three days earlier) was destroyed. Its meetings were transferred to Church House.

Rudolf Hess arrived in Scotland.

The siege of Habbaniya ended. British forces advanced on Baghdad and Rashid Ali fled.

On the 27th the *Bismarck* was sunk. The news was brought to me on a slip of paper in the official box at the House of Commons in Church House, where the PM had just been making a statement. I passed it forward to him and he rose again to announce it. Great jubilation.

DIARY

May

3–4 Weekend at Kingham with Sir Cosmo Parkinson [Permanent Under-Secretary, Colonial Office] (staying in Langston Arms).

5 Returned to London.

9 In evening with PM to Ditchley.

10 Ditchley.

11 Ditchley. Arrival of Duke of Hamilton to report on arrival of Rudolf Hess. PM informed me that I am to succeed Seal as Principal Private Secretary.

12 Returned to London. To Andover in afternoon.

13 At Andover. Miss Edwards brought by car to stay, having broken down through blitz.

14 Returned to No. 10. Appointed PPS from today, with rank of Assistant Secretary and allowance of £200.

18 Went to see St Columba's, burnt out in raid a week ago.

22 Celebration of anniversary as PS – ballet followed by supper at Spanish restaurant.

23 To Oxford, staying with Coupland at Boar's Hill.

24 Boar's Hill.

25   Boar's Hill. Dinner at All Souls.
28   President Roosevelt's speech.
29   Decided to take flat at Marsham Court. President's telegram about sending expeditionary force to Iceland.
31   To Chequers. Others there – Harriman and daughter Kathleen, Commanders in Chief Bomber and Fighter Commands.

LETTERS

11 May   Although Ditchley is bright and cheering as ever, it has been rather a worrying weekend for various reasons. For one thing, I don't know what to do about Miss Edwards. She has really broken down and ought to be removed to the country. She was bad enough on Friday when I last saw her. I can't think what she is like now after last night's raid, when Westminster was again plastered. Bevir very kindly went along to see her and arranged for the priest to visit. I had to get in touch with a building and decorating firm for her, as she was quite unable to do it herself and the emergency repairs carried out by the City of Westminster are not sufficient. I have accepted liability for the cost, which I fear will run to more than £20 – ceilings (unsafe) to be replaced and one room to be re-papered. It all seems a gamble, considering that Hitler may huff and puff again any day. Last night was pretty bad. I hear that St Columba's (Pont Street) has been destroyed. There were fires at Westminster Abbey, Westminster Hall and Westminster School. St Thomas's was still burning this morning. A bomb crashed through the Big Ben tower, but Big Ben still strikes the hours.

All this is hearsay, for we have been here since Friday in peace and sunshine though still not in summer warmth. Various guests including Sir Archibald and Lady Sinclair.

Another source of worry has been that Seal, the Principal Private Secretary, is being made a Deputy Secretary of the Admiralty and sent on a mission to the United States and the PM has said that he proposes to appoint me as his successor. He hasn't yet said this to me and the matter is not finally settled. I told you before how I felt about this when the same suggestion was made some months ago. The job is one which ought to be held by someone with much bigger guns than I possess (or in fact at my age could be expected to possess). Ought I in the public interest to fight the proposal? On the other hand it would be a quixotic thing to do and, if the PM is satisfied, who am I to question it? A difficulty would be that it would mean passing over Bevir, who is several years senior. Then I don't want to be too long divorced from the Colonial Office, which is my real home. It is all rather wearing and I wish the point could be settled soon. It is an alarming prospect.

15 May It is all decided that I am to be PPS with effect from yesterday. The PM told me when I put him to bed on Sunday night (or rather Monday morning *c.* 2 a.m.). I was not sure that there might not be a revolt from the Treasury; but everything is now settled. There has been a frightful rush since I got back, trying to find a new PS to replace me.

Miss Edwards is so bad that I asked Detta to take her for a holiday. D nobly agreed and I had her brought down by car on Tuesday, a most pathetic figure. Meanwhile the decorators are at work at Graham Terrace – an almost absurd gamble when one considers the desolation in neighbouring streets (including further ravages from Saturday's raid).

18 May I have had a great many telephone messages and letters and everybody has been extraordinarily nice about my appointment as PPS. I was worried and scared about it while it was still in the air (and there is no doubt that it ought to go – as it has in the past – to someone with bigger guns); but now that everything is settled I feel immense relief and really hope to enjoy myself thoroughly. The PM himself has been most affable and gave me a friendly poke in the ribs when he went off to the country on Friday.

Alas Miss E seems to be getting on D's nerves, but I really can't have her back in London quite yet. She is upset not so much by the blitz itself as by an almost 'mental' concern over the damage to the house and the resulting inconvenience to me. I don't want her to return till the house is shipshape again.

I went today to look at St Columba's. The walls and tower still stand but the inside is completely gutted, the windows gone and the polished granite columns and mosaics badly damaged. Outside, a Scottish royal standard was nailed to the door and a notice stuck up announcing that services today are in the Imperial

Institute and aptly ending 'Nec tamen consumebatur' [the motto of the Church of Scotland].

25 May   Wootton Hill. I am very much touched by all these kind messages of congratulation. It is an alarming job to take on and it has been a real encouragement to have so many friends to see me off and give me a cheer.

It has been an active week and I haven't quite settled down in my new saddle, but hope all will go well now. I managed to get from the Treasury one of their best men as a PS [Leslie Rowan] to fill the vacancy resulting from my promotion and once he has learnt the ropes he ought to be a great help.

The trouble about Miss Edwards could not have come at a more awkward time. The best, and perhaps necessary, course will be to pull up my roots at Graham Terrace and for the rest of the war be content with a room in some block of service flats. As my days and nights are now spent at the office it is only necessary to have a *pied à terre* where I can keep my belongings, go daily for a change of clothes and arrange for laundry etc.

Under a new programme of duties at the office we shall each have alternate weekends off.

JUNE

The British offensive in the Western Desert failed. General Wavell was relieved of his appointment as C in C, Middle East, and replaced by General Auchinleck. Oliver Lyttelton was appointed Minister of State resident in Cairo.

Operations were begun against Vichy forces in Syria. Damascus was captured.

Germany invaded Russia.

Clothes and footwear were rationed.

DIARY

June

1   At Chequers. Gen. Pile [Commander Anti-Aircraft] among guests.
2   Returned to London.
7   To Andover in afternoon.
8   Returned to town in afternoon.

9   Up till 3 a.m. in preparation of PM's speech.

10 PM's speech on Crete in House.

12 Meeting of Allied representatives at St James's Palace. Speech by PM. Government luncheon at Lancaster House. Honours list included barony for Lindemann. Miss Watson and Mrs Hill [PM's personal secretary] MBE. To dinner in mess.

14 Moved belongings from Graham Terrace to Marsham Court.

18 With PM to Weybourne (Norfolk) to see demonstration of UP (rocket) against Queen Bees (unmanned aircraft). (Ismay ruefully compared cost of Queen Bee shot down with a few pounds increase in salary he was struggling to obtain from Treasury for his secretary.)

21 To Haslemere to stay with Edward Muir.

22 Haslemere. Walk round Punchbowl in great heat.

23 Returned to London.

24 Constantia Rumbold to lunch. Late night (till 3.40 a.m.) on PM's shipping speech.

25 Luncheon with PM. Also there Mr and Mrs Reg McKenna, Lady Desborough.

26 Left for Scotland with PM, also Sir Roger Keyes.

27 Landing exercises on Loch Fyne and visit to Combined Training Centre at Inverary.

28 Returned to London. In afternoon went down to Chequers.

29 Chequers. Oliver Lyttelton (about to go to Cairo as Minister of State) with Lady Moira, the Portals and Bridges.

30 Returned to London.

LETTERS

21 June Haslemere. I am thankful to be spending this very hot weekend in the country. Hot it is with a vengeance, all the more so in contrast with the long cold spring that lasted till little more than a week ago. We were nearly boiled alive in the PM's special train in which we visited the Norfolk coast the other day, because no one realised until we got back that the steam heat was turned full on.

Brendan Bracken, the PM's Parliamentary Private Secretary, had me to lunch with Maisky, the Soviet Ambassador. Maisky is a funny little man with a beard, like a stage foreigner. He seemed to know (or at any rate to be willing to disclose) very little about what was going to happen between Germany and Russia, but spent his time in trying to pump Brendan. A surprisingly mild and affable little man to represent the Moscow dictator.

For the third time since the outbreak of war I went to the theatre on Thursday – to *Patience* at the Savoy, very refreshing. Jock Colville came too and produced two young women. We had to dine *after* the theatre (which now starts early) and rashly went to the Savoy Grill, where a helping of sole cost 8s.

29 June I was sorry to send you such a scrappy note in the middle of the week. I wonder if the postmark gave our whereabouts away – though not our destination, which was somewhere on the west coast of Scotland. I can't tell you what we saw, except one picturesque incident when a pipe band led the PM through the streets of the town past the cheering populace.

JULY

The German invasion of Russia continued. A message from the PM to Stalin promised all possible help. A message from Stalin urged the establishment of fronts in North France and Arctic. Missions were exchanged with the USSR and an Anglo-Russian agreement made on mutual help, promising no separate peace.

Syria passed into Allied occupation.

The Japanese completed the occupation of Indo-China. Japanese assets in the US were frozen and similar action was taken by the Dutch and British.

DIARY

July

2   At luncheon in honour of Polish Premier Gen. Sikorski sat next Xavier Zalewski (brother of Foreign Minister) and opposite Czech President Beneš.

4   In afternoon to Oxford to stay with Prof. Coupland.

5, 6   Oxford.

7   Returned to London.

8   Quintin Reynolds [American journalist] to dinner in mess.

9   [Sir Robert] Bruce Lockhart [Director of the Political Warfare Executive] to dinner in mess.

17 Harry Hopkins arrived back and attended meeting of Cabinet.

18 Active afternoon in connection with new ministerial appoint-
ments, including Bracken for Ministry of Information, R.A.
Butler for Board of Education and Duncan Sandys to War
Office.

19 To Andoversford, to stay with Abells at Foxcote Manor.

20 At Foxcote.

21 Returned to London.

22 The new Parliamentary PS, Col. Harvie-Watt, began work.

25 With PM to Tidworth to inspect armoured division and watch
exercise (plus Generals Lee and Chaney of US). Thence to
Chequers. Working late on Production speech. To bed 4.50
a.m.

26 Chequers. Harry Hopkins arrived. To bed after 2 a.m. PM
saying, 'This is a half holiday: we must work tomorrow.'

27 Chequers. Winants, Harrimans, Bonham-Carters, Dorothy
Thompson. Broadcast by Harry Hopkins, who then left for
Moscow.

28 Returned to London. Called on Winant.

AUGUST

The meeting of Churchill with Roosevelt in Newfoundland has been
amply recorded in *The Second World War*, III, in Sir Alexander
Cadogan's *Diaries*, in H.V. Morton's *Atlantic Meeting* and elsewhere.
I set down only a few notes in diary form based on my own short diary,
one surviving letter and other contemporary records.

August

 3 To Chequers in morning. Departure from Wendover in PM's
special train. PM himself in best form and siren-suit. Rueful
disappointment at lunch when Prof, with the aid of the slide-
rule which always accompanied him, calculated the volume of
champagne consumed by the PM throughout his life and
found it was less than that of our railway coach.

 4 Arrived Thurso. Crossed in destroyer *Oribi* to Scapa and went
aboard HMS *Prince of Wales* (Captain Leach). An exhausted
Harry Hopkins, just back from Moscow, was already there.

   One of the London dailies said it was the best kept secret of
the war; but another (the same day) said it was the worst.
Anyhow it was all arranged in just over a week. My master was

Roosevelt, supported by his son, Captain Elliott Roosevelt, meets Churchill.

The Atlantic Charter meeting on HMS Prince of Wales, *August 1941.*

Left to right, front row: Air Chief Marshal Sir Wilfred Freeman, Adm. Sir Dudley Pound (First Sea Lord), Churchill, Gen. Sir John Dill, Sir Alexander Cadogan; back row: Tommy Thompson, Lord Cherwell, me.

Divine Service at sea. (I am visible on the extreme right.)

HMS Prince of Wales, *August 1941.*

Disembarkation in Iceland.

DINNER

ABOARD THE

UNITED STATES FLAGSHIP AUGUSTA
SUNDAY, AUGUST 10, 1941

The dinner menu of US flagship *Augusta*, 10 August
1941, showing signatures of guests.

★ PRESENT ★
⚓ ⚓ ⚓

THE PRESIDENT

THE PRIME MINISTER

LORD CHERWELL

COMMANDER C. R. THOMPSON, R.N.

MR. J. M. MARTIN

REAR ADMIRAL ROSS T. MCINTIRE, (MC), U.S.N.

MAJOR GENERAL EDWIN M. WATSON, U.S.A.

CAPTAIN JOHN R. BEARDALL, U.S.N.

CAPTAIN ELLIOT ROOSEVELT, U.S.A., (A.C.R.)

ENSIGN FRANKLIN D. ROOSEVELT, JR. U.S.N.R.

THE HONORABLE HARRY L. HOPKINS

★ MENU ★

ALMONDS

CREAM OF TOMATO SOUP

CELERY   OLIVES   SALTINES

ROAST TURKEY

BUTTERED BRUSSELS SPROUTS

DRESSING

GIBLET GRAVY

CRANBERRY SAUCE

WHOLE WHEAT BREAD

APPLE PIE

AMERICAN CHEESE

DEMI TASSE

CIGARS   CIGARETTES

CANDIES

AFTER DINNER MINTS

On board U.S.S. AUGUSTA
August 11, 1941

My dear Martin:

If your conscience will permit,
these are to be taken to London. If the
niceties of the war would disturb, I
suggest you give them to some other member
of the party whose will to live well, may
be greater than yours.

Ever so cordially,

Mr. J. M. Martin
H.M.S. PRINCE OF WALES
Ship Harbor, Newfoundland

A letter sent to me
from Harry Hopkins,
enclosing a shipment
list of food parcels.

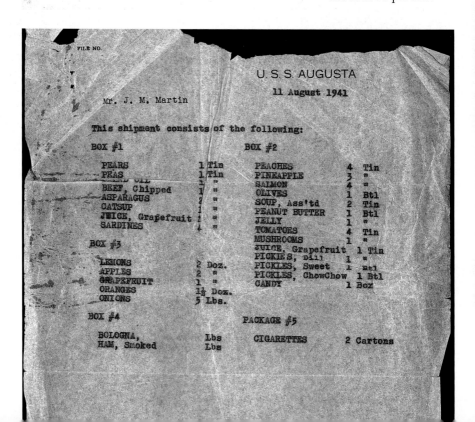

FILE NO.

U. S. S. AUGUSTA

Mr. J. M. Martin

11 August 1941

This shipment consists of the following:

BOX #1

PEARS	1 Tin
PEAS	1 Tin
OIL	1 "
BEEF, Chipped	1 "
ASPARAGUS	2 "
CATSUP	1 "
JUICE, Grapefruit	1 "
SARDINES	1 "

BOX #2

PEACHES	4	Tin
PINEAPPLE	3	"
SALMON	4	"
OLIVES	1	Btl
SOUP, Ass'td	2	Tin
PEANUT BUTTER	1	Btl
JELLY	1	"
TOMATOES	4	Tin
MUSHROOMS	1	"
JUICE, Grapefruit	1	Tin
PICKLES, Dill	1	"
PICKLES, Sweet	1	Btl
PICKLES, ChowChow	1	Btl
CANDY	1	Box

BOX #3

LEMONS	2 Doz.
APPLES	2 "
GRAPEFRUIT	1 "
ORANGES	1½ Doz.
ONIONS	5 Lbs.

BOX #4

| BOLOGNA, | Lbs |
| HAM, Smoked | Lbs |

PACKAGE #5

| CIGARETTES | 2 Cartons |

Official group photograph taken on the steps at 10 Downing Street, 29 September 1941. Left to right: John Colville, Leslie Rowan, Churchill, John Peck, me, Miss Watson, Tommy Thompson, Anthony Bevir, Charles Barker.

On HMS *Duke of York*, December 1941. Left to right: me, Francis Brown, FM Dill, Gen. Hollis, Averell Harriman, Lord Beaverbrook, Maj. Gen. Macready, Churchill, Adm. Pound, Air Marshal Portal.

Churchill with Tommy Thompson (right), Harry Hopkins and his daughter, walking the President's dog, Falla.

Churchill with Professor Conant at Harvard,
December 1941.

White House press conference, December 1941. (I am
sitting at the end of the sofa.)

In clipper on the flight to
Bermuda, 15 January 1942.

With Francis Brown,
working during the flight.

Churchill at the controls.

Soviet photograph of Churchill raising his hat as he greets a smiling Molotov in Moscow.

Churchill and Roosevelt at a press conference at the President's villa near Casablanca, January 1943. (Leslie Rowan is sitting at the back under the vines.)

Churchill and Roosevelt with their Chiefs of Staff at the President's villa, Casablanca, January 1943.

With a Moroccan in Fez,
January 1943.

The Prime Minister, in RAF uniform, with his Chiefs of Staff. Front row: Air Marshal Portal, Adm. Pound, Churchill, FM Dill, Gen. Brooke; back row: Brigadier Dykes, me, Gen. Alexander, Adm. Mountbatten, Gen. Ismay, Lord Leathers, Macmillan, Ian Jacob.

With Rozie on our wedding day, Oxford, 1 May 1943.

My mother (left) with Sir David and Lady Ross after the wedding.

Mrs Churchill greeting Rozie and me at the wedding.

Returning to Oriel College after the wedding. Left to right: my mother, Sir
David Ross, Parry de Winton, Lady Ross, Robin Harrison, me, Rozie,
Christopher Harrison.

On his arrival at the US Capitol, Churchill is greeted by Mr Sol Bloom, Chairman of the House Foreign Affairs Committee, 19 May 1943.

Churchill looks up at the cheering crowds as he disembarks at Halifax, Nova Scotia, 9 August 1943. Beside him are Leslie Rowan, Harry Hopkins and Adm. Adolphus Andrews of the US Navy.

With Churchill and his
daughter Mary, on a visit
to Niagara Falls, August
1943.

A little girl reaches up to take a cigar band from Churchill.
(I am standing behind with Mary Churchill, Tommy
Thompson and Inspector Thompson.)

as excited as a boy, planning all the details of the entertainment of the other fellow – ordering grouse, ordering turtle and ordering a band.

We found ourselves in remarkably spacious and comfortable quarters, with a little mess of our own – for the PM, the three Chiefs of Staff, Cadogan, Hopkins, Cherwell, Tommy and myself – in what was normally the Warrant Officers' Mess – and I never enjoyed a fortnight's meals more. Incidentally, in all the rest of my life I had never eaten so much caviare, for Harry Hopkins had brought ample supplies from Moscow. Every evening there was a film in the Ward-room (including the PM's favourite *Lady Hamilton*).

5   At sea. Fairly rough. Sea-sick and no breakfast ('Tout au contraire' as the PM said). The PM dosed me most tenderly with Mothersill, which he finds an unfailing remedy; but self-respect was restored on the last day of the homeward voyage, when it was again stormy and it was *he* who had to take the Mothersill. The escorting destroyers had been unable to maintain station in the sharply increasing wind and we parted company early in the day. Course was altered to avoid a U-boat reported ahead. (No enemy U-boats, surface craft or aircraft were sighted on the voyage.)

6   A comparatively idle day, PM reading 'Hornblower' and doing no work. Rendezvous with destroyer escort from Iceland. Thick fog.

7   Good progress in fog, which cleared in evening.

8   At sea.

9   Arrived Placentia Bay, Newfoundland, led in through swept channel by USS *McDougal*. When we were about to enter harbour it was discovered that US ships were keeping a zone time 1½ hours ahead of Newfoundland summer time and we were turned around to delay before coming in. We moved slowly into what might have been a Hebridean loch, finally anchoring alongside the President's flagship, USS *Augusta*, about 9 a.m. A Royal Marine band and guard were mounted. The band played the 'Star Spangled Banner' and then across the water came 'God Save the King' in reply. No gun salutes were exchanged as HMS *Prince of Wales* carried no saluting guns.

After the usual naval courtesies the President's Naval ADC called to discuss arrangements for the day (taking Harry Hopkins with him on his return). Then, at eleven o'clock the PM, accompanied by the First Sea Lord, the CIGS, the Vice-Chief of Air Staff, Cadogan, Cherwell and myself) crossed by barge to the *Augusta* to visit the President. Roosevelt met us on the upper deck, supported on the arm of his son, Elliott, accompanied by Gen. Marshall, Admiral Stark, Gen. Arnold, Sumner Welles [Under-Secretary of US State Department] and Franklin Roosevelt Jr. After shaking hands and introducing his party, the PM handed the President a letter from the King, which I had brought with me. The two then went off to a private luncheon while the rest of us were taken below to a cabin for a party with some of the American officers, who (the American Navy being dry) regaled us with large glasses of tomato juice followed by a fork lunch.

In the afternoon a launch from USS *Augusta* brought us over a cargo of presents from the President for the crews of the British ships. Each rating received a box containing fruit, cheese and cigarettes.

10   (Sunday) The President, arriving in USS *McDougal* with his staff and a large number of American sailors, paid his only visit to HMS *Prince of Wales*, to attend Divine Service on the quarterdeck. The PM had given much thought to the preparations for this Service (which he said should be fully choral and fully photographic), choosing the hymns ('O God our Help in Ages Past', 'Onward Christian Soldiers' and 'Eternal Father Strong to Save') and vetting the prayers (which I had to read to him while he dried after his bath). You would have had to be pretty hard-boiled not to be moved by it all – hundreds of men from both fleets all mingled together, one rough British sailor sharing his hymn sheet with one American ditto. It seemed a sort of marriage service between the two navies, already in spirit allies, though the bright peacetime paint and spit and polish of the American ships contrasted with the dull camouflage of the *Prince of Wales*, so recently in action against the *Bismarck*.

The President remained for a time on the quarterdeck, then was taken to the Ward-room Annexe, where the ship's officers were presented, and then, with his staff, was entertained to lunch by the PM, when we ate some of the grouse. After the President's departure, the PM, in very genial mood, asked me if I'd like to go ashore with him. We were a small party, pulled to the beach in a whaler (Cadogan, the Prof, Harriman and Tommy). We went about like the first discoverers, with not a soul to meet, the PM collecting a fistful of flowers. In the evening I accompanied the PM to dinner with the President; only eleven at table (of the Americans – the President; Harry Hopkins; Rear-Admiral Ross McIntyre; the President's doctor; 'Pa' Watson, his aide; Captain Beardall, USN; Elliott Roosevelt and Franklin Jr), with the dog Falla. It was a straightforward American meal of tomato soup, roast turkey with cranberry sauce and apple pie with cheese.

11 A further day of conferences between the PM and the President and the Chiefs of Staff on both sides.

Harry Hopkins sent me large cartons of canned fruit, hams, candies etc. (worth their weight in gold in rationed Britain), accompanied by the following note:

> My dear Martin:
> If your conscience will permit, these are to be taken to London. If the niceties of the war would disturb, I suggest you give them to some other member of the party whose will to live well may be greater than yours.
> Ever so cordially,
> Harry Hopkins

The Governor of Newfoundland, Sir Humphrey Walwyn, lunched with PM.

12 Lord Beaverbrook (Minister of Supply), who had arrived in Newfoundland by air the previous day, came aboard HMS *Prince of Wales*. In the morning the PM went over to the USS *Augusta* for his final conference with the President. Cadogan and Sumner Welles joined in the discussion. Agreement was reached on the text of a Joint Declaration ('The Atlantic Charter') and on a joint message to Stalin. The President handed the PM a letter to the King. The PM remained to lunch with the President, after which he and his staff took leave of

Mr Roosevelt on the deck of the American flagship. At 5 p.m. HMS *Prince of Wales*, with an escort of destroyers, sailed for Iceland, exchanging compliments with USS *Augusta* as she moved away.

13 At sea.

14 Owing to latest U-boat information course altered to further north.

15 At sea, joined by relief destroyer and aircraft escorts from Iceland. *Prince of Wales* carried out anti-aircraft firings at smoke bursts and balloons. In the afternoon we altered course to close a homeward convoy – about seventy-five ships, heavily laden, with many aircraft visible on deck (described by PM as 'a delectable sight'), keeping their stations in very good order. The *Prince of Wales* and escorting destroyers passed through the columns of the convoy and then turned and came through again on the opposite course. Messages were exchanged with the Commodore and we waved to the cheering crews and passengers as we passed near. It was a gallant sight, but the ships of the convoy looked terribly vulnerable in spite of their escort. Then we left them and made course for Iceland.

16 Anchored at Hvalsfiord, where several British and American ships were in harbour. Here we transferred to the Canadian destroyer *Assiniboine* for Reykjavik, where we spent the day. There were crowds in the streets and remarkable enthusiasm, with cheering and clapping, said to be unusual among these stolid, undemonstrative people. It was a lovely sunny day and the place looked most attractive, not unlike somewhere in the West Highlands. We were first driven to the Altingshus, where the PM was received by the Regent and the Icelandic Cabinet. At the Regent's suggestion the PM went out on to the balcony and addressed the crowd in the square, who gave him a tumultuous reception. He then went on to review a big parade of American and British troops, the President's son Franklin standing beside him at the saluting base. After lunch with the British Minister we went for a short drive to see something of the country, visiting a transit camp for RAF trainees and hot springs from which it was hoped to provide the capital with central heating. Tea at Force HQ at Artun and left in destroyer at 5.30, seen off by the Icelandic Prime Minister, Mr Hermann

Jonasson, and again a demonstrative crowd. After visiting HMS *Ramillies* finally weighed anchor in HMS *Prince of Wales* about 8 p.m. with an escort of destroyers, the American ships taking station ahead.

17 At sea. Rather rough.
18 Early morning gun practice before coming in to Scapa. Thence by HMS *Tartar* to Thurso, where Lady Sinclair was waiting to receive us (and promised me grouse for our mess) and we boarded our special train.
19 Arrived back at King's Cross, met by Cabinet and a big crowd. Lunch with Mrs Churchill. To Ministry of Information to see film of PM's meeting with President.
22 I left by night train from Euston for Aviemore.
23–31 On leave at Lynwilg. On 29th climbed Cairn Gorm. In mist, rain and hail at the top I saw three climbers descending, one of whom I learnt afterwards (see Diary, 11 October 1941) was Rosalind Ross.

SEPTEMBER

An Anglo-American Supply Mission was sent to Moscow. The Germans attacked Leningrad and captured Kiev.

DIARY

September
1 Arrived back in London.
4 Luncheon at Mansion House in honour of Canadian PM Mackenzie King.
5 Business over reply to Stalin kept us late, so that PM cancelled departure for Ditchley. Then worked till nearly 3 a.m. He said, 'I feel the world vibrant again.'
6 At Ditchley Park, visiting the establishment at Bletchley on the way. Among guests David Niven and wife, Sir Charles and Lady Portal, Mr and Mrs Dick Law [Parliamentary Under-Secretary at Foreign Office].
7 At Ditchley.
8 Returned to London.
12 In afternoon with Parry de Winton [Oxford friend] to Brecon.
13 At Brecon. Walk on Beacons.

14 Returned to London in evening, the Paddington train being held for me at Newport.

23 Francis Brown began work as Private Secretary. (Letter of 14 September – 'I have had to find a successor to the youngest of the Private Secretaries, Jock Colville, who is being allowed to join the RAF. I have got such a nice boy, whom the PM has accepted, a young captain in the Coldstream Guards'.)

24 PM's appointment as Lord Warden of the Cinque Ports announced. Sherry party at Colonial Office to say goodbye to Sir Alan Burns [on appointment as Governor of the Gold Coast].

25 With PM and Mrs Churchill visited Walmer Castle and PM's Squadron (No. 615) at Manston.

26 In evening to Andover. Very sleepy and in need of fresh air to drive away the remains of a bad cold I have had all week.

27 Andover.

28 Returned to town in evening.

29 Jock Colville's last day. Group photograph with PM on garden steps. I gave a sherry party in our mess, about eighty people.

LETTERS

21 September I seem to have been getting into a habit of not being in bed till after midnight, which (however much the PM may thrive on it) does not conduce to freshness of mind the next day. However, the pressure has not been as great as sometimes and I occasionally get to the flat for a quiet half hour in the afternoon.

I discovered that the desk at which I work used to be the Prime Minister's desk from the time of Gladstone to that of Lloyd George.

The house came to life again on Friday for a luncheon the PM gave to the British and American Missions to Moscow. It was quite a triumph for the Government Hospitality Fund and the Ministry of Works, who only received their orders the evening before. One of the big reception rooms upstairs, at present unfurnished, had to be hastily prepared, floors cleaned, tables and chairs brought in and decorations arranged. We had to do without pictures, but the bare walls (and broken window frames) gave an appropriate note of wartime austerity.

28 September   The PM was greatly taken with the idea of being Lord Warden of the Cinque Ports, an ancient office held by various Prime Ministers in the past. It carries no salary, only the right to certain privileges, such as all whales washed ashore within the limits of his jurisdiction (only that is a liability, because the fish have to be buried, at his expense), and to live in Walmer Castle. We visited that on Thursday – a fine place, but absurdly expensive in these days. Lady Reading told me she used to bring down fourteen servants and there are five gardeners. Mrs Churchill, who said she always wanted to have a cottage by the seaside, seemed to think it much too big. (In a minute of 27 September 1941 printed in *The Second World War*, III, 737, the PM said, 'I very much doubt whether it will ever be possible for me to live at Walmer Castle, or indeed whether anybody will be able to live in such fine houses after the war.')

On announcement of Churchill's appointment as Lord Warden of the Cinque Ports, the following telegram was sent by General Catroux, French plenipotentiary in Beirut: 'Recevez je vous prie mes chaleureuses félicitations pour votre élévation à la Pairie qui réjouit tous mes camarades Français Libres', to which the Prime Minister replied on 28 September: 'Mille remercie-ments mais ce n'est pas si grave que ça (stop) Vive la France Libre. Mister (Repeat Mister) Churchill'.

OCTOBER

Mr Curtin (Labour) became Prime Minister of Australia and maintained the previous Australian Government's insistence on the relief of the Australians in Tobruk.

A protocol was signed in Moscow on the scale of supplies of arms etc. by the UK and USA.

Russian forces withdrew to a line 40 miles west of Moscow.

Mrs Churchill launched her Aid to Russia Appeal. I supported her in refusing to agree that this should be part of the general appeal on behalf of the Red Cross. This certainly contributed to the great success of her Appeal, which, especially in the factories, touched the feeling of popular sympathy for the Russians and their gallant resistance.

OCTOBER 1941

Admiral Keyes was succeeded by Lord Mountbatten as Director of Combined Operations (a title later changed to Chief of Combined Operations). Naval staff had been in despair over their failure to remove Keyes. I told them that their constant attacks on him only aroused the PM's loyalty in support of his old friend: his unsuitability should be left to prove itself.

DIARY

October
3 To Chequers in afternoon. Three Chiefs of Staff and Sir Alan Brooke there. Discussion of 'Ajax' [plan to attack Trondheim – subsequently turned down].
4 Chequers. PM's letter to Sir Roger Keyes, ending his appointment as Director of Combined Operations.
5 Chequers. Two escaped airmen (Sqn Ldr Gibbs and PO Rennie) to lunch. Gen. Paget [C in C Home Forces] for the night.
6 Returned to London.
10 In afternoon to Oxford to stay with Colin and Christian Hardie.
11 Oxford. Rosalind Ross to supper. (Found she was one of the party I had seen on Cairn Gorm.)
12 Oxford. Dinner at Magdalen (talking among others to Vice-President, C.S. Lewis).
13 Returned to London.
15 Only celebration of my birthday was an hour off in flat, unpacking presents etc.
23 Miss Watson and Rosalind Ross to lunch.
24 In evening with Frank Lee to Much Hadham.
25 Much Hadham. [Played] 'word-making' with De la Mares after supper.
26 Returned to London early.
28 King and Queen lunched at No. 10.

LETTERS

2 October My sherry party to say goodbye to Jock Colville was a great success. Almost no one refused the invitation, which rather upset my calculations and there must have been almost eighty people, but they were spread over an hour and a half and the room was never overcrowded. Our Swedish cook produced a wonderful selection of things to eat, including a big cake of the kind I shudder to remember – many layers of 'cream' – though evidently popular with women. All these were washed down with sherry, cider cup and soft drinks. Apart from cheering Jock on his way, I thought such a party would be of value in promoting more personal relations with the various private secretaries and others with whom we do business, and so it turned out. Everyone quite obviously enjoyed it. I thought it better to draw no line of rank and invited the whole office staff and none of the guests were more obviously appreciative than the typists. Besides our staff and the Private Secretaries of various other offices there were a few outside people, such as Canon Don, the Archbishop's Secretary (with whom we do business over Church appointments and incidentally our parish priest as Rector of St Margaret's, Westminster) with his wife, Brendan Bracken [Minister of Information], Rab Butler [President of the Board of Education], Sir Horace Wilson of the Treasury, Sir Alexander Hardinge [the King's Private Secretary], the Chief Whip etc. Mrs Churchill came and stayed for about an hour and brought the PM with her – very genial and beaming cheerfully on everyone, though of course he couldn't stay very long.

5 *October* Had a few minutes conversation with the King of Greece the other evening, as he arrived to dinner at No. 10 rather before his time and the PM was not ready to receive him. He must have had a pretty bad time. I hear that when he arrived at Alexandria a British officer stepped forward to offer his services to look after his baggage. 'This is my baggage,' said the King, producing a toothbrush from his pocket.

NOVEMBER

Losses from U-boats fell to the lowest level since May 1940. U-boats moved into the Mediterranean: the *Ark Royal* and *Barham* were sunk and there were other heavy Naval losses.

Auchinleck's offensive in North Africa opened, followed by Rommel's counter-move and heavy fighting.

German forces advanced in the Crimea.

General Sir Alan Brooke was appointed to succeed General Sir John Dill as CIGS.

DIARY

November

1 Afternoon walk in Chelsea – gloomy and battered. Railings removed from Eaton Square and other squares, leaving them looking rather squalid.

2 To Windsor for a walk in the park.

3 Dinner with Ronnie Tree at Ritz as farewell to Herschel Johnson [First Secretary, US Embassy, London]; others Hoyer-Millar, Kruger, John Astor, Oliver Harvey, Gen. Lee, Sammy Hood.

7 Lunch with Mrs Churchill.

8 To Chequers. P M arrived back from tour of Hull, Sheffield etc. Heavy RAF losses last night and today.

9 Chequers. Sinking of Italian convoy (to Benghazi) of ten ships plus destroyers.

10 Returned to London. Lord Mayor's Luncheon in Mansion House.

14 To Andover in afternoon.

15, 16 Andover.

17 Returned to London.

18 Battle in Libya began. P M very impatient at absence of news of its progress.

20 Evening party by Trees at Savoy to meet some American Congressmen.

22 Lunch with Jack Churchill [Winston's brother].

28 Various committees all this week on Honours List, now at last ready for P M.

29 In evening to Andover.

30 To Marlborough for John Gulland's confirmation.

DECEMBER

Pearl Harbor and the Invasion of Malaya

Sunday evening, 7 December 1941: The P M's guests were Gilbert Winant, the US Ambassador, and Averell Harriman, the President's Special Envoy; (Mrs Churchill was dining in her room); I was there as Duty Private Secretary. Just before nine o'clock the butler, Sawyers, came in and said that there was something in the news about a Japanese attack on the American fleet. The PM told him to bring in the wireless set and we heard the announcer giving the news of the attack on Pearl Harbor. Immediately the PM said 'Get me the President'. After a word with Roosevelt he handed the telephone to Winant, who (realising that this would bring the United States into the war, a state of affairs for which many Americans had been anxiously waiting, but not yet aware of the extent of the American losses) said 'That's fine, Mr President, just fine' (or words to that effect), while the President was telling him of a heavy attack on the American fleet. The next day, after consultation with the King, Churchill decided to go to Washington as soon as possible.

Also on 7 December the Japanese invaded Malaya, landing first at Khota Bharu on the east coast, where some friends of mine were wakened by noises which they at first attributed to goats invading the beach.

The US declared war on Japan. Germany and Italy declared war on the US. Guam was occupied by Japan.

Japanese forces, during a series of delaying actions, took Penang and thrust down the Malayan peninsula; landings were made in Sarawak and Sumatra. The *Prince of Wales* and *Repulse* were sunk.

The Prime Minister visited Washington and Ottawa after obtaining the King's consent.

Auchinleck's offensive in North Africa was successful: Tobruk was relieved, Benghazi captured and the Axis forces withdrew to Agedabia and Agheila.

Serious Naval losses in the Mediterranean reduced the British East Mediterranean Fleet to three cruisers and a few destroyers. A German air corps was removed from Russia to Sicily and North Africa. A new air offensive began on Malta. The Luftwaffe regained control of the sea routes to Tripoli and made possible a refit of Rommel's armies.

The German autumn campaign to take Moscow failed and their armour was forced back to a line 60 miles from the city.

DIARY

December
1 Returned to town.
5 To Chequers.

67

6   Averell Harriman and Kathleen (her birthday), also Pamela.

7   Chequers. Duchess of Marlborough and Lord Blandford to lunch. Winant to lunch and dinner. During dinner we heard news of Japanese attack on Pearl Harbor and later of landing at Khota Bharu.

8   Returned to town.

9   Statement by PM in House.

10   News of sinking of *Prince of Wales* and *Repulse*.

11   Statement by PM in the House. Later, news of German and Italian declarations of war on USA. 'The stars in their courses are fighting for us.'

12   In evening left with PM for 'Arcadia' [code name for the conference at Washington] – with Beaverbrook, Sir Dudley Pound [First Lord of Admiralty], Portal, Dill, Lt-Gen. Macready [Vice CIGS], Sir Charles Wilson, Harriman, [Brigadier Leslie] Hollis [Deputy to General Ismay], Lt-Col. Ian Jacob [Deputy to Hollis], Poynton [PS to Beaverbrook and PUS Colonial Office], Francis Brown, Tommy etc.

13   Arrived Gourock. Went aboard HMS *Duke of York*. Sailed *c.* 12.30 p.m.

14   At sea. Southerly gale. Unpleasant motion; but I survived the day. Making poor progress in these unhealthy 'Bloody Foreland' waters.

15   At sea. Still stormy and impossible to get on deck. Only half our proper speed.

16   At sea. Much less rough. Increased speed and again possible to walk on deck. Making south towards Azores.

17   At sea. Our destroyers left us in the afternoon.

18   At sea. Gale at night.

19–21   At sea.

22   Arrived at entrance to Chesapeake Bay about 2.15 p.m. Went ashore from HMS *Duke of York* in Hampton Roads to Norfolk aerodrome and flew (in fifty minutes) to Washington. Staying in White House.

23   White House. PM in series of conferences. Press Conference in afternoon.

24   White House. Further conferences. Lighting of National Community Christmas Tree. Short broadcast by PM.

25   White House. With President and PM to Christmas Service at

Foundry Church. Crown Prince and Princess of Norway to lunch. Christmas dinner party.
26   White House. PM's speech to Congress.
27   At White House.
28   White House. PM left for Ottawa after lunch. I remained in Washington. Dinner with Eric Seal.
29   At White House. Dinner with Tony Rumbold [Foreign Service].
30   At White House.
31   Flew to Ottawa in just over two hours. Lunch at Government House. Flew back in afternoon.

NOTES

As great seas swept the decks of the *Duke of York* off Bloody Foreland, Beaverbrook said that he had never travelled in such a large submarine.

We were received with overwhelming hospitality in the White House (where I had the yellow bedroom). The housekeeper delighted in producing enormous helpings of bacon and eggs for breakfast. Sometimes I had lunch on a tray in the room which was our private office, but generally dinner was with the Roosevelts (preceded by gathering in a small room where the President, in his wheelchair, with an array of bottles beside him, dispensed rather potent cocktails). We shared in the family celebrations of Christmas, including the turkey dinner, at which the President carved. Mrs Roosevelt had a room in the White House where she collected throughout the year presents bought at sales of work to which she had to go, for distribution at Christmas.

LETTER

27 December   White House. I wonder if you listened to the PM's speech to Congress and heard the great enthusiasm of his audience. I managed to do a little necessary shopping this morning. The profusion of things in the shops seems like a dream after the rigours of our besieged island. The lights at night are another contrast. Washington's millions of lights as seen from the air the night we arrived were one of the most beautiful sights I have ever seen.

1942

JANUARY

The PM completed his visit to the US. The United Nations Pact was signed.

The US decided to send troops to Northern Ireland. A Combined Chiefs of Staff Committee was set up and the US accepted the principle that the first objective was the defeat of the Axis in Europe.

Rommel made a surprise forward move and Benghazi was given up.

Withdrawal down the Malayan peninsula continued into Singapore. Wavell was made Supreme Allied Commander. Japanese forces invaded Burma.

DIARY

January

1   White House. PM arrived back from Ottawa. Signature of 'Joint Declaration of United Nations' by PM, President, Litvinov [Soviet Ambassador to US] and Chinese Ambassador after dinner.

2   At White House.

3   At White House. Lunch with Childs, the British Embassy Press Attaché. Dinner at Embassy.

4   At White House.

5   Left Washington with PM, Sir Charles Wilson and Tommy, in Gen. Marshall's plane. Arrived West Palm Beach airport. Staying in Stettinius's [US Secretary of State] bungalow at Pompano.

6   Pompano, Florida. Bathing in warm sea. Oysters – for last time, I hope.

7   Pompano. More bathing mixed with some work. Walk with Sir C. Wilson. Mme Balsan [formerly Duchess of Marlborough] to lunch. PM enlarged on the effects of medicine after dinner.

8–9   Pompano. In afternoon drove into Miami.

10   Left Pompano. Lunch with Mme (Consuelo) Balsan at Fort Lauderdale. Left by train for Washington.

11   Arrived back in Washington. Averell Harriman, Bill Donovan [head of US Office of Strategic Services], Jesse Jones etc. at dinner with President.

12–13   At White House.

14   White House. Left Washington by train after dinner.

15   Arrived Norfolk airport. By clipper *Berwick* to Bermuda. Lunch at Government House (Lord Knollys), where we are staying.

16   Left by clipper (Capt. Kelly Rogers), with PM, Beaverbrook, Sir Dudley Pound, Sir Charles Portal, Sir Charles Wilson, Joe Hollis.

17   Arrived Plymouth *c*. 9.45 a.m. By special train to Paddington.

18   Settling down to ordinary work again. Lunch with Tony Bevir and Harvie-Watt.

19   Lunch with Mrs Churchill. Dinner with Cosmo Parkinson.

23   To Chequers in afternoon. Much snow on roads. PM getting worked up for speech in House next Tuesday demanding vote of confidence. To bed 4 a.m.

24   Chequers. Capt. Taylor of *Repulse* to lunch. PM working on speech. To bed 3.20 a.m.

25   Chequers. Sir Stafford and Lady Cripps to lunch (on his return from Moscow as Ambassador). To bed 3.40 a.m.

26   Returned to London after lunch. Following on midnight telegram from President (and phone conversation) arrangement for publication of agreements about shipping, munitions and raw materials.

27   PM's speech opening three days' debate and demanding vote of confidence.

29   PM closed debate. Vote of confidence carried by 464 to 1. Left by night train for Scotland. Sleepers are now scarce, but I got mine through M/War Transport.

30, 31   On leave in Edinburgh.

JANUARY 1942

LETTER

11 January   In the train. We are on our way back from a few days'
break in Florida. The high-up conversations were necessarily
suspended while the Chiefs of Staff on both sides cleared up a
mass of detailed business, and the PM took advantage of this to
escape to the south and the sunshine. It was an opportunity for
him to clear his mind on various things, but we by no means
escaped from the daily conduct of the war, for we were of course
connected with Washington by telephone and a courier once,
and sometimes twice a day, brought down a pouch to us by
aeroplane . . . We were on the coast some way north of Miami –
between that and Palm Beach – in a secluded bungalow on the
beach, an ideal place for a seaside holiday. It wasn't always sunny
or warm, though on our first morning I had to buy some exotic
clothes because my ordinary ones were much too hot; but the sea
was always hot and we had marvellous bathing, sometimes in
surf against which it was hardly possible to stand upright. We
were closely guarded by Secret Service men and, though the Press
soon scented our presence, we were not molested in any way. The
story was put about that a Mr Lobb, an invalid requiring quiet,
was staying in the house and, to explain my untransatlantic
accent when answering the phone, I was his English butler.

We flew down, a wonderfully easy flight of over 800 miles; but
this was not my only long flight for, after holding the fort in
Washington during the PM's visit to Ottawa, I could not resist
the temptation to fly up with the pouch on the last day. Setting off
in a Service plane after ten o'clock I arrived there in just over two
hours, in time for lunch at Government House (Earl of Athlone
and Princess Alice) and, in spite of difficulty in starting, was back
in Washington in time for dinner. It was very cold up in Canada,
but one does not feel the dry cold there nearly so much as a similar
temperature at home. The air is extremely dry and metal objects
are charged with static electricity. I got a shock (and saw the
spark) from touching an iron pipe and someone got a shock
through touching a cat.

NOTES

I think that a main reason for our visit to Pompano was to provide a break for the President, exhausted by the PM's late nights and flow of talk. It was at Pompano that we had the ludicrous affair of the telephone call to Wendel Willkie [Republican Presidential Candidate, 1940] described by Churchill in *The Second World War*, III, 617. Churchill, intending to speak to Willkie, was in error connected to the President – with embarrassing results. I believe the mistake arose from the fact that when I asked the White House switchboard operator, through whom we made our calls even at that distance, to put through a call to Willkie she thought it was meant as a code name for the President. We had been warned to be very careful in talking on the telephone. Hence also the PM's remark on the phone, 'I mustn't tell you on an open line how we shall be travelling, but we shall be coming by puff puff.'

The plan had been that Churchill should return by clipper from Norfolk, Virginia, to Bermuda and then by HMS *Duke of York* to England. But the news from Malaya and the stirring of political opposition, leading to a demand for a vote of confidence, increased the need for a quick return to London, and the speed of the flying-boat (and its comfort) caused him to change his mind. He therefore decided to continue the journey from Bermuda (where he spent the night) by clipper. The Chiefs of Staff were unwilling to agree to this unless they could all accompany him – so the long flight was made with the PM, the Chiefs of Staff, Lord Beaverbrook, Sir Charles Wilson and myself, with Captain Rogers, all on board.

The following is an extract from Lord Moran's diary of 16 January, in *Winston Churchill: the Struggle for Survival*, 23:

In mid Atlantic they brought the PM a bulletin. [Signed by Kelly Rogers, the bulletin ran:

Bulletin at 22.00 hrs G.M.T., 16.1.42	
Latitude	41.05′N
Longitude	41.25′W
Height	9000 feet
Groundspeed last hour	207 mph
Groundspeed from start	199 mph
Distance from start	1440 miles
Distance to go	1890 miles

Time from start   7 hrs 12 mins
Time to go   9 hrs 10 mins
(Using anticipated groundspeed)
Fuel left at present consumption 15 hrs
Note. If present speed is maintained it will be necessary to slow down so as not to arrive too early.]

He read it, and leaning towards me, put his hand on my knee.
'Do you realise we are fifteen hundred miles from anywhere?'
'Heaven is as near by sea as by land,' I reminded him.
'Who said that?' he asked.
'I think it was Sir Humphrey Gilbert.'
He looked at the bulletin again. 'We have still nine hours to go, but we have enough fuel for fifteen.'

That journey was the prelude to some of the most sombre phases of the war. The invasion of Malaya and the surrender of Singapore – where I had spent two and a half very happy years on secondment from the Colonial Office – were cause for great concern; there was the tragic loss of the *Repulse* and the *Prince of Wales*; and in March Rangoon had to be abandoned, increasing the threat to India and Ceylon. The escape of the German ships from Brest; losses in the Atlantic which constituted the most severe threat to Britain's ability to continue the war; and the advance of Rommel to within a few miles of Cairo; all added to the anxieties of the period. But underlying all these calamitous circumstances we had the assurance that our ally across the Atlantic was now fully committed to the defeat of Germany and Japan.

FEBRUARY

The surrender of Singapore was followed by the Japanese continuing to advance in Burma and in the South-West Pacific.

The *Scharnhorst*, *Gneisenau* and *Prinz Eugen* escaped from Brest and successfully passed through the Channel to their home base.

Various Cabinet changes were made. Lord Beaverbrook was appointed Minister of Production but resigned on health grounds (succeeded by Oliver Lyttelton). Sir Stafford Cripps was made Lord Privy Seal and Leader of the House. Sir James Grigg succeeded Captain Margesson as Secretary of State for War. Mr Attlee went to the Dominions Office and was styled Deputy Prime Minister. Mr Greenwood retired from the Cabinet.

DIARY

February

1–3 On leave in Edinburgh.
4   Returned to London.
7   Talk with Mrs Churchill about proposed flight.
9   Rab Butler to dinner in mess.
10   PM in House, explaining functions of Minister of Production.
14   At Andover. Bad news of attack on Singapore all this week.
15   Andover. News of fall of Singapore: PM's broadcast ('Let us move forward steadfastly together into the storm and through the storm').
16   Returned to town.
20   To Chequers in evening. Duncan Sandys also there.
21   Chequers. Chief Whip and Bridges arrived. PM at work on further Cabinet appointments. Walk with James Stuart.
22   Chequers. Sir Charles and Lady Portal and Lord and Lady Portal arrived. Reconstruction of Cabinet completed.
23   Returned to town.
24   Speech by PM on reconstruction of Government, his position as Minister of Defence etc.
25   First speech by Cripps as Leader of the House.
27   In afternoon to Oxford, staying at the Mitre.
28   At Oxford.

MARCH

U-boats sank more than half a million tons, mostly within 300 miles of the American coast. There was a stepping up of Biscay patrols and attacks on U-boat nests, and a Commando raid on St Nazaire.

General Alexander took command in Burma. Rangoon fell. General Wavell handed over command of the Netherlands East Indies to the Dutch and resumed command in India and Burma. The Japanese were in complete control of Java.

General Auchinleck declined an invitation to London (where the PM and Chiefs of Staff were concerned at delays involved in his plans for offensive action).

The announcement was made of Sir Stafford Cripps's mission to India for consultation on the Government's constitutional plans.

R.G. Casey was appointed as Minister of State in the Middle East.

DIARY

March

1   Oxford.
2   Drove back to town with Chief Whip.
3   Completion of junior ministerial appointments.
5   Mr Lowe of Queensland (who is here with Sir Earle Page, Australia's Representative with War Cabinet) to dinner.
6   Dinner with Dr Weizmann. Talk about his fermentation process (supplies for artificial rubber and high octane).
7   Zamoyski [ADC to Gen. Sikorski] brought to dinner in mess a young Pole recently escaped from Gestapo prison.
8   Though still fairly cold, a springlike day at last after a particularly long wintry period. It has been a cold but healthy winter.
13 To Andover in afternoon. Train forgot to stop and took me on to Salisbury.
14, 15 Andover.
16 Returned to town.
20 To Chequers.
21 Chequers.
22 Chequers. Afternoon walk with Mrs Churchill.
23 Returned to town.
28 Day off. Visited John and Mariska Peck at Hatch End.

APRIL

By the end of the month the Japanese stood before Mandalay. There were dive-bomber attacks on Colombo and Trincomalee. The US bombed Tokyo.

Cripps's mission to India to discuss British constitutional proposals failed.

Malta came under heavy air attacks. USS *Wasp* was made available to fly in Spitfires. Malta was awarded the George Cross.

The visit of Harry Hopkins and General Marshall conveyed the President's proposals for joint Anglo-American operations in Europe in 1943, with a possible emergency landing in meantime. They were agreed in principle.

A long statement on the war situation was made by the PM in a Secret Session.

DIARY

April

3   To Chequers.
4   Chequers. News of Japanese fleet approaching Ceylon.
5   Chequers. Japanese air attack on Colombo.
6   Returned to town with Lady Cripps.
10 To Andover in afternoon.
11 Andover.
12 Returned to London.
15 King to dinner at No. 10.
17 To Chequers.
18 Chequers. Raymond Guest to lunch. Lady Cripps and Pamela in evening for weekend.
19 Chequers. Sarah, Mary, Lord Louis Mountbatten and Ismay.
20 Returned to London.
21 Sir Stafford Cripps arrived back from India.
23 St George's Day. Pageant at Albert Hall. Polish reception to welcome Gen. Anders [Commander of Polish forces].
24 Luncheon of American Press Correspondents' Association at Savoy. Next Browne of *Christian Science Monitor* and opposite Mrs Welsh of *Life* etc.
25 Off duty. Walked from Richmond to Kew.
26 Off duty.

MAY

The Japanese captured Mandalay. Alexander's force was finally extricated from Burma and concentrated at Imphal. The Naval battle in the Coral Sea resulted in the Japanese invasion force intended for Port Moresby being turned back.

Diego Suarez in Madagascar was liberated.

Instructions to General Auchinleck to attack were reiterated, but on the 27th Rommel began an offensive in Libya.

Bombing attacks on Malta slackened and daylight attacks were brought to an end. A second flight of Spitfires was delivered by USS *Wasp* (to which PM signalled 'Who said a wasp couldn't sting twice?'). Lord Gort was appointed Governor in succession to General Dobbie.

The Soviet Foreign Affairs Minister, Molotov, visited England. A treaty of alliance with the Soviet Government was signed.

The German spring offensive in Russia opened.

The RAF made a thousand bombers' raid on Cologne (followed by a similar mammoth raid on the Essen region).

DIARY

May

2   News of fall of Mandalay (yesterday).

3   Unusual spell of fine weather continues.

8   This has been the week of Honours Committees.

9   Day off; but much at No. 10 over completion of draft Honours List. Excellent film *One of Our Aircraft Is Missing*.

10   Day off in London.

14   In evening left with PM in his train with Dr Evatt [Attorney-General and Foreign Minister, Australia], W.S. Robinson, Pug, Harvie-Watt and Tommy.

15   Visited RAF stations at Linton-on-Ouse and Leeming, also Ministry of Supply filling factory. Stabled near Ripley Junction by banks of River Nidd.

16   Visit to Leeds – factories, triumphal drive through streets, speech from Town Hall steps to crowd of 25/30,000. Visited 9th Armoured Division, Lakenheath (Newmarket).

17   At Chequers. Brendan and Chief Whip arrived, for Honours List.

18   Returned to town.

22   Luncheon at No. 10 in honour of Molotov and party. To Andover in evening.

23–24   Andover.

25   Returned to town. With [Charles] Barker [No. 10 staff] to ballet and dinner – our annual celebration of appointment to No. 10.

26   Signature of Anglo-Russian treaty in Secretary of State's room at Foreign Office.

27   Stefan Zamoyski to lunch on his departure to USA. News of opening of German attack in Libya.

JUNE

The Battle of Midway marked the turning point of the war in the Pacific.

The effort to supply Malta from both the Eastern and Western Mediterranean resulted in only two supply ships getting through out of seventeen.

Molotov made a second visit on his way back from the USA.

There was continuous discussion of plans for operations against German-occupied Europe.

Rommel's offensive developed in the face of British counter-attacks. Tobruk fell. The Germans pressed on across the Egyptian frontier past Mersa Matruh towards the Alamein position.

The Prime Minister made a second visit to the USA, where discussions took place on future strategy.

The Germans broke through the Russian line on a broad front and began the drive to the Volga and Caucasus.

DIARY

June

5   To Oxford. Staying with Coupland.

6   Oxford.

7   Oxford. Dinner at All Souls.

8   Returned to town with Cherwell.

11 Lunch with Lionel Curtis [Fellow of All Souls] to meet Whitney Shepherdson. Also there John Foster, Ivison Macadam and Michael Balfour.

12 To Chequers. Mountbatten and Mason Macfarlane [C in C Gibraltar] for the night.

13 Chequers. Courtauld-Thompson and Major Gerald Wilkinson (attaché to Gen. MacArthur) to lunch. Gwilym [Minister of Fuel and Power] and Mrs Lloyd-George and Harvie-Watt for the night.

14 Chequers.

15 Returned to town.

17 Left at midday for Stranraer, from which we took off about 11.30 p.m. by RMA *Bristol* (Capt. Kelly Rogers). Party consists of PM, CIGS (Brooke), Ismay, Brig. G.M. Stewart (Director of Plans), Tommy, Kinna [clerk at No. 10] and Sawyers.

18 Crossed Atlantic uneventfully, flying over Gander airport (Newfoundland) and landing on Potomac at Washington about 8 p.m. local time (i.e. after twenty-seven hours' flight). Dined and slept at British Embassy.

19 Flew up, over New York, to Hyde Park, to stay with President Roosevelt. Jimmy R. [President's son] for lunch. 'Tea' with Miss Delano.

20 Hyde Park. In house a.m. Tea in cottage. Sir R. Waterhouse arrived with yesterday's papers from England. Left for Washington after dinner in President's special train.

21 Returned to Washington. Staying at White House. News of fall of Tobruk. CIGS and Gen. Marshall to lunch and in conference with President, PM, Ismay and Hopkins. Dinner with Mrs Roosevelt, Capt. Sedgwick.

22 At Washington. PM in conference with President and saw Admiral King [C in C Atlantic Fleet], Gens Eisenhower and Clarke and M. Leger [former Secretary-General of French Foreign Office].

23 Washington. At White House all day. PM had various conferences and left in evening for Fort Jackson. I stayed behind.

24 In Washington. Lunch with Tony Rumbold and [Isaiah] Berlin.

25 In Washington. Left after dinner by road for Baltimore. Took flight in *Bristol* clipper a little after 11 p.m. Harriman and Jacob added to previous party.

26 Arrived Botwood after breakfast and went ashore for two hours. Thereafter uneventful flight.

27 Arrived Stranraer shortly after 5 a.m. after flight of *c.* twenty-four hours from Baltimore. By special train to London.

28 Got up late and spent an idle day, looking in at the office for a little in the afternoon.

LETTERS

14 June Chequers. Unless anything unforeseen happens I am going off again on other travels and cannot expect to be back in time for Bridge of Lochay. (Please on no account mention the reason outside the family. To anyone else it must be 'he wasn't able to get away'.) . . . I *must* have a holiday soon – and in the Highlands. . . . Unseasonably cold here, which makes one wonder what this big house will be like next winter with austerity in fires. But it is really high summer – with strawberries and 'cream' and all the other signs. Last night we had the film about 'The young Mr Pitt' – interesting resemblances with the present.

26/27 June In clipper *Bristol* over mid-Atlantic . . . (When we arrived in Washington) the President was at Hyde Park, his country estate north of New York, so we were put up for the night at the British Embassy. It was hot and stuffy and we dined with the Ambassador and Lady Halifax on the terrace at the back of the house, where I distinguished myself by stepping backwards in the darkness over the edge and fell some eight feet into the garden, by a miracle landing unscathed on my feet. Detectives sprang from the bushes to pick me up and everyone was astonished to find me safe and sound.

Next morning we flew up to Hyde Park, passing over Philadelphia and New York, where the skyscrapers, reduced to the size of cardboard models, made a rather beautiful panorama. It was half an hour's drive from the aerodrome to the President's house in the valley of the Hudson river – a very pleasant green countryside, vegetation luxuriant in the almost tropical heat. We spent two days at Hyde Park, the PM in constant conference with the President, driving out in the afternoons to tea.

On Saturday night we returned to Washington with the President in his special train, pleasantly air-cooled, where I slept like a log. On arrival we went to our old quarters in the White House, where Mrs Roosevelt was waiting to receive us. Everyone gave us a most kind welcome and we felt as if we were coming home. The next days were fairly strenuous, particularly as this time I had no Francis Brown to help me; but I enjoyed it all enormously and the quantity of nourishment helped to make up for the lack of sleep – three eggs for breakfast every day, delicious orange juice etc. The PM had a very busy time and, as before, got on extremely well with the President. Altogether it was a most valuable and successful visit.

. . . What a rich, spacious country America seems after our little, rationed, strenuous island. Whatever Tobruk may mean, it is impossible not to feel that the tide is setting strong and irresistible on our side. I hope this is not my last visit to the Western hemisphere.

JULY

The Germans captured Sebastopol. The disaster of convoy PQ17 to Russia was followed by a decision not to send the August convoy.

The debate on Sir John Wardlaw-Milne's motion of no confidence ended in defeat by 475 votes to 25.

There was a visit to London by Harry Hopkins, General Marshall and Admiral King for consultation on the conduct of the war. Eisenhower, and C in Cs General Mark Clark, Admiral Stark and General Carl Spaatz were already established here. After reference back to the President it was agreed to abandon plans for 'Sledgehammer' (attack on Brest or Cherbourg in 1942) and to go ahead with plans for 'Torch' (operations in North-West Africa). The PM could not get support for his plan to attack in Norway.

In North Africa indecisive attacks and counterattacks continued on the Alamein front. At the end of the month the PM decided to visit Cairo and accepted Sir A. Clark Kerr's [British Ambassador in Moscow] suggestion that he should meet Stalin. (Stalin agreed to a meeting – in Moscow.) Cadogan recorded in his diary on 30 July: 'Martin tells me PM's doctor, Attlee and Anderson trying to dissuade him from going.'

DIARY

July
1   At House to hear Wardlaw-Milne moving his vote of no confidence. Up late in connection with preparation of PM's speech.
4   Saw Sir C. Wilson about possible Cairo visit.
5   In London off duty.
10 Left for Scotland by night train.
11 To Bridge of Lochay.
12–17   At Bridge of Lochay.
18 In Edinburgh.
19 Returned to London.
22 Fighting flared up in Libya. Went over No. 10 with Mrs Churchill with a view to reoccupation.
23 Meals much more expensive now in spite of 5s limit, e.g. only 1s change out of £1 for our two lunches at Gourmets.
24 In evening down river by barge to Greenwich. Dinner in Painted Hall in honour of Adl King and other American visitors. Sing-song in gun-room, with Alexander (1st Lord) at piano.
25 To Chequers in evening.
26 Chequers. Adl King, Marshall, Harry Hopkins.

27 Returned to London.
29 The King, War Cabinet and [Sir Alexander] Hardinge [Private Secretary to King George VI] dined with PM. PM proposing visit to Cairo.
30 Much discussion of PM's proposed visit to Cairo. Message from Clark Kerr suggesting meeting with Stalin.

LETTER

26 July Chequers. An unusual evening on Friday, when we went down by river to Greenwich to a dinner given by the Admiralty in honour of certain visitors. Fortunately it was a fine day and the river and the Hospital looked their best in the soft evening light. I had not been down that way since before the outbreak of war and saw for the first time some of the blitz damage in the City and East End. Fortunately Greenwich Hospital itself has escaped serious damage and we were able to dine in the fine Painted Hall. I have never seen so many admirals. Their Lordships gave us an excellent dinner, after which we went to the young officers' gun-room, where the PM toasted Admiral (Jackie) Fisher's grandson who was one of them and happened to be celebrating his twenty-first birthday. Alexander, the First Lord, then sat down at the piano and for about an hour thumped out I should think every song in the 'Students' Song Book' and conducted community singing with great gusto. The room was crowded with sub-lieutenants, admirals and Wrens (who have a training course for officers at Greenwich), all singing at the tops of their voices (not excluding the PM), the most cheerful party I have seen for a long time. Altogether a memorable evening, which the Americans obviously enjoyed enormously. It ended with 'Auld Lang Syne' and the two National Anthems. (One of the highlights was Admiral (Betty) Stark, of the USN, singing 'Annie Laurie' solo. Even the grim Admiral King thawed.)

A quiet Chequers so far. The country is still fresh and green. I wish I could find time to get out and enjoy the sunshine.

AUGUST

The PM visited Cairo and Moscow. The decision was made to supersede General Auchinleck by General Alexander as Commander in Chief, Middle East. General Montgomery was appointed to command the Eighth Army.

A costly effort was made to reinforce Malta from the west. Five merchant ships (including HMS tanker *Ohio*) got through. The aircraft-carrier *Eagle* was lost.

General Eisenhower was designated Commander in Chief for 'Torch'.

DIARY

August

1 PM left for Cairo. This time I stayed behind, sending Leslie Rowan as PS.

3 Arthur Galsworthy (at present Captain in Duke of Cornwall's Light Infantry) started as temporary PS. (PM arrived Cairo.)

14 This is apparently to be taken now as Atlantic Charter Day, being the anniversary of publication (not 'signature').

15 At Oxford, staying with Coupland (Boar's Hill).

16 Oxford. Tea with Margery Perham [Fellow of Nuffield College]. Dinner at All Souls (next Col. Swinton).

17 Returned to London.

23 Lunch with Tommy Lascelles [Private Secretary to King George VI].

24 Went down with Mrs C to meet PM and party at Lyneham aerodrome.

28 To Andover in afternoon.

29 Andover.

30 Andover. Cycled over to lunch with Brendan Bracken at Bere Mill, Whitchurch.

LETTER

30 August I went down in PM's special train with Mrs C to meet him at an aerodrome 'somewhere in the south of England'. I used to go and see her most mornings to take the latest news of the travellers, and in the train we had a long heart-to-heart talk. The arrival at the aerodrome was rather thrilling. It was dark, with clouds gathering overhead, and the first we knew was the drone of engines far above. Then a squadron of escorting Spitfires came down into sight and finally the big Liberator. The PM seemed remarkably fit and fresh and so were most of the rest of the party, though they must have had an exhausting time. Now he is back in the old routine again, apparently none the worse – and it is certainly a great relief to have him back.

SEPTEMBER

The final decision was made to have landings at Algiers as well as Oran and Casablanca, and that the date should be 8 November.

In North Africa Rommel's thrust (begun at the end of August) was repelled with heavy loss. 'We had reached the top of the pass, and our road to victory was not only sure and certain, but accompanied by constant cheering events' – Churchill in *The Second World War*, IV, 494.

An argument with Sir Stafford Cripps about the central direction of the war led to his offer of resignation, which he was persuaded was inopportune and (in October) withdrew.

In Russia the Germans reached the Volga. The assault on Stalingrad began.

DIARY

September

2   At Lord Mayor's Luncheon in Guildhall for American troops (the first such function there since its heavy air-raid damage).
3   To Chequers in afternoon.
4   At Chequers. PM had slight tonsillitis.
5, 6   At Chequers.
7   Returned to No. 10.
12   Day off in London. To Richmond.
23   To lunch with Pecks at Hatch End.
17   Rosalind Ross to lunch.
18   To Chequers. Capt. Harold Balfour [Conservative MP] to lunch, with ferry pilots Vanderkloot and Ruggles. Admitted a 'short snorter' [see letter below].
19, 20   At Chequers.
21   Returned to London.
25   Left in afternoon for Andoversford. Staying with Abells, at Foxcote Manor.
26, 27   At Foxcote. Bracing walks on hills.
28   Up at 6 a.m. and returned to London.
30   No fires or central heating supposed to be on till end of October. Evenings in the office unpleasantly cold.

LETTER

20 September Chequers. My turn has come round again already as Peck, though returned after his appendicitis, is not yet up to the succession of 3 a.m. bedtimes (or thereabout). Fortunately there is always a pause in the middle of the afternoon and I have my black eye-bandage with me so as to make the most of any such opportunity.

Are you, like the Queen, going to paint a red line round the bath – five inches, thus far and no further? We have had this idea in the washbasins at my club for a long time, though there the ration is only two inches. The Underground stations have reduced their lighting in a very gloomy way.

A traveller who visited Moscow was struck by the behaviour of the audience at the Bolshoi during the intervals. They marched round and round the foyer in complete silence like prisoners taking their exercise, though during the performance they had shown high spirits and intelligence. The explanation given was that the OGPU [Soviet Secret Service, by then the NKVD] prevented knots of three or more people collecting for conversation.

We had two American Ferry Command pilots here on Friday, who had flown the PM to Moscow in their Liberator. I was admitted a Short Snorter. The qualification is that you must have flown the Atlantic, and the rule is that you must always carry about with you a dollar bill signed by the Short Snorters who admitted you and any others who may be added. If you meet another Short Snorter and challenge him to produce his bill and he can't, he has to pay a dollar to each Short Snorter present. The PM is a Short Snorter and has been caught in this way. All of which must sound, as it is, a little mad.

OCTOBER

Heavy fighting took place in the Stalingrad area. The Battle of Alamein began.

DIARY

October
8   Left for Scotland in PM's train.
9   Arrived Edinburgh 3 a.m. Night in North British Hotel. Home for breakfast.

10, 11 On leave in Edinburgh.

12 PM received Freedom of Edinburgh. Returned to London.

15 My birthday. Only celebration as last year (time off in flat opening letters and parcels), but this time only half hour.

16 Chequers. FM Smuts and his son Jacobus Daniel staying for weekend.

17, 18 Chequers.

19 Returned to London.

20 Smuts' speech to Parliament.

24 To Chequers.

25 Chequers. Mrs Roosevelt and Malvina Thompson [Mrs Roosevelt's secretary] arrived to stay the night.

26 Returned to No. 10.

31 To Andover in afternoon.

LETTERS

14 October There was a surprising accumulation of work here when we got back and since then there has been such a flood that I have had difficulty in keeping my head above water.

I could not discover you in the Usher Hall, partly my own fault because I got into the wrong seat in the back row, hearing the Lady Provost plaintively saying '*Where* is Mr Martin?'. I thought everything went very well, though more might have been done in the way of spreading the news on Monday morning (that the PM was in Edinburgh) and crowds were sparse in some of the streets ... The PM's throat was not quite right; but otherwise he seemed in good form and thoroughly enjoyed himself.

18 October Chequers. For some obscure reason this has been the busiest week for some time and I am still ploughing through accumulated arrears ... There is no opportunity for celebrations in these days and in fact my birthday 'treat' was half an hour at the flat re-reading letters and opening parcels.

Thanks for the various newspapers. The bit about the PM's Scottish ties was supplied by Harvie-Watt and is not quite accurate for Rowan does not come from Edinburgh and in fact only visited it once before, when playing in a hockey inter-national for *England*. The PM brought down his silver casket to Chequers and it has been much admired.

A particularly interesting weekend as we have Field Marshal

87

Smuts in the house and various people have been asked down to meet him. On Friday it was the Edens and Sir Dudley Pound, last night various Air Chiefs and tonight the Crippses and Attlee. Smuts is a remarkable old man – the picture of health and bursting with vitality, though obviously aging. His son is with him as ADC, a nice friendly, slow-spoken young Boer, whom I took for a walk yesterday.

NOVEMBER

The turning of 'the Hinge of Fate' (*The Second World War*, IV, 541).

Victory at Alamein: by 4 November the enemy was in full retreat. Tobruk, Solum, Bardia and Benghazi were recaptured.

Landings were made at Algiers and Oran and on the Moroccan coast. Admiral Darlan, the French C in C North Africa, ordered a cease-fire. The Allies advanced into Tunisia. The Germans invaded Unoccupied France; the French fleet at Toulon was scuttled.

The Russians counterattacked west of Stalingrad: Von Paulus's army was encircled. Four hundred aircraft were withdrawn from the Eastern front.

Operations in Madagascar were concluded and the island handed over to Free French.

The Americans scored a naval victory off the Solomons.

Allied losses at sea were the heaviest of the war – 800,000 tons.

DIARY

November

1 At Andover.

2 Returned to London.

4 In evening arrived news of Alexander's victory in Egypt – Rommel's forces in full retreat.

8 News of beginning of 'Torch' in North Africa.

10 Lord Mayor's Luncheon at Mansion House. PM's triumphant drive to the City. Dinner at No. 10 for King's Speech (over eighty).

11 Re-opening of Parliament. Again no two-minutes silence, the resumption of which had been considered.

13 Left with Rosalind Ross by 6.5 for Oxford – sent via Banbury owing to an accident blocking line and arrived at midnight.

14 At Oxford (Provost's Lodgings, Oriel). Walk with Rozie to Iffley. At start of *Magic Flute*. Evening reception at Rhodes House.

15 At Oxford. With Rozie and Mother to St Columba's. Church bells rung for African victory. After lunch walked up Boar's Hill with Coupland. Dinner in Oriel Hall.

16 Returned from Oxford.

20 To Chequers.

21 At Chequers. To No. 10 for Cabinet and returned to Chequers for dinner. Oliver Stanley [Secretary of State Colonial Office] staying the night.

22 Chequers. Herbert Morrison. Dick Law (for talk about India), Bridges and Cripps arrived. New Government appointments.

23 Returned to No. 10.

24 Honours Committees this week.

26 Rozie to lunch at Jardin des Gourmets.

27 Dinner with Harvie-Watt at Pratt's.

28 Preparing draft Honours List for PM.

29 Off duty in London. St Andrew's Day Service at St Columba's.

30 James Maxton MP and Sir Andrew Duncan [Minister of Supply] to dinner in the mess.

LETTERS

12 November These have been exceptionally active days. I do not remember any more so since the summer of 1940. There have been the operations in Libya and French North Africa, producing floods of telegrams, and the speech in the Mansion House on Tuesday and in the House of Commons on Wednesday, besides arrangements for a dinner of some eighty guests on Tuesday night. For the Lord Mayor's luncheon the PM and Mrs Churchill drove into the City in an open car, while Harvie-Watt and I followed in a closed one behind. On the suggestion of the Remembrancer, loud-speaker vans had announced his coming and we made a triumphal progress along the Strand and Fleet Street, up Ludgate Hill and past St Paul's. There were huge and enthusiastic crowds, with scarcely enough police to control them, and at the last stage we had some difficulty in getting through. The luncheon went very well – an unusually sumptuous repast for these days – and so did the speech. I always enjoy these City functions.

The dinner was a revival of the traditional custom, in abeyance for some years before the war, of a dinner of the members of the Government in the House of Commons on the eve of the opening of Parliament to hear the PM read in advance the King's Speech. The 'Government' means the Ministers, Junior Ministers, Whips etc. and, as I said, these now number over eighty. We never thought we could get them into the big dining room at No. 10 (not used since the blitz and still without its pictures), but somehow we found room for everyone round a large horseshoe table. I was at one of the ends and Harvie-Watt at the other. Following tradition, the speech was read *before* dinner, the doors being closed after all the servants had withdrawn. After dinner – an excellent feast, though the bill of fare (as Winston prefers to describe the menu) had been vetted by Lord Woolton himself – there were speeches by Smuts, Attlee and the PM.

Then, when the guests had begun to go, we escaped downstairs and got to work on the next speech – for the House of Commons the following day. That again was a great success. Altogether it has been a triumphant and most cheering week for the PM – a well deserved triumph.

Bad fogs this week – and worse yesterday than we have had for a few years. In the blackout people get hopelessly lost. Buses went astray and there were all sorts of stories of adventures in the dark. Many people walked into our barbed wire entanglements and we quite expected to recover corpses from them in the morning, like flies in a web.

Aren't you cheered at the thought of the bells? [It was later officially deemed safe enough for the ringing of church bells, which had been stopped earlier in the war, to resume – just too late for our wedding!] Many grim people say it is premature and 'tempting Providence' (as the PM said, it is strange to describe 'thanksgiving' as 'tempting Providence'); but it is a poor heart that never rejoices and we can let ourselves go for once without forgetting all the difficulties and dangers still ahead.

19 November   Safety razor blades simply don't exist. If P is ever in a chemist and can buy I shall gratefully repay.

DECEMBER

Admiral Darlan was assassinated and Giraud took his place as High

Commissioner and Commander in Chief. Harold Macmillan was appointed to assist the American political representative in North Africa (Robert Murphy).

The rainy season in Tunis impeded operations. At the beginning of the month a German counterattack pushed the British back to Medjez. On the 22nd a renewed Allied attack began; but was checked by rain and Eisenhower gave up plans for the immediate capture of Tunis. Meanwhile the Germans grew in strength.

Rommel was dislodged from Agheila and Sirte occupied.

The PM turned again to plans for an invasion of the Continent in 1943. Roosevelt proposed a military conference between Britain, Russia and the US at Cairo or Moscow. Churchill replied that only by a meeting between principals could results be obtained. Roosevelt agreed and invited Stalin. Stalin welcomed the idea but could not leave the Soviet Union. Roosevelt therefore suggested a meeting of himself and the PM with military staffs and this was agreed.

The Beveridge scheme for compulsory social insurance was published.

DIARY

December

5   To Chequers.
6   A young party this weekend for Mary. Also Winant.
7   Returned to No. 10.
11 To Oxford in afternoon to stay with Coupland, travelling with Rozie Ross and Catherine Campbell.
12 Boar's Hill. Walked into Oxford. Tea with Colin and Christian Hardie. Dinner with Prof. Goodhart.
13 Boar's Hill. Rozie with Eleanor and Katharine [Rosalind's sisters] and C. Campbell called and we went for a picnic walk by Bablock Hythe to Eynsham. Tea at Oriel, after which I proposed to Rozie.
14 Returned to No. 10.
15 Rozie had lunch with me at Gourmets.
17 Rozie telephoned, 'I am on your side of the fence'. Lunch with her and her father. Bought ring. Dinner at Carlton Grill and later called on [the] Frank Hardies [Oxford friend, Fellow of Corpus Christi College].

18 (When I told PM of my engagement he said something on the lines of his comment on King Peter's marriage – the whole tradition of military Europe has been in favour of *les noces de guerre* – *The Second World War*, V, 571.)
Lunch with Rozie and Robin Harrison [brother-in-law].

20 Supper with Grants at Ladbroke Grove.

21 To Oxford with Rozie.

22 At Oxford (Oriel).

23 Returned to London.

24 Evening at Marsham Court, R reading aloud the Christmas lessons.

25 With R to early Communion at Westminster Abbey. Day at office. Lunch party there, to which R came.

30 R and I lunched with PM and Mrs Churchill. Also there Neville Lytton [painter friend of Churchill] and Oliphants [Sir Lancelot, Ambassador to Belgian Government in London, and wife]. (From letter of 3.1.1943: 'R made a very good impression when she came to lunch at No. 10, the PM likening her to a gazelle.')

LETTERS

13 December   Boar's Hill. Ten hours sleep on Friday night, a day of remarkable mild sunshine (more like March than December) and a good invigorating walk today have made a great change in the situation. I was much in need of this after a rather strenuous month and a succession of late nights in the last week or more. Coupland hospitable as ever and there could not be a pleasanter place to spend a weekend. Yesterday he took me along to dinner with a neighbour on Boar's Hill, Prof. Goodhart, the Professor of Jurisprudence. He is a clever American Jew, evidently a friend of the Roosevelts and closely connected with the President. We had a most enjoyable and interesting evening. This morning the three Ross sisters called about eleven with a friend and took me off for a walk. We went mostly by field paths and through the usual Oxfordshire mud by Cumnor and Bablock Hythe on the 'stripling Thames' (v. 'The Scholar Gipsy'), where we ate an alfresco picnic lunch washed down with shandy from the pub. It was a beautiful day for December and in the cottage gardens we

were not surprised to see roses and jasmine in flower. Along the
river bank to Eynsham and thence back to Oxford by bus. Tea in
the Provost's Lodgings at Oriel. And so back here. I feel quite
ready now to face the next fortnight.

P.S. I feel fairly sure that there will be before long more than
one Mrs J. Martin.

18 December Rozie gave me her decision over the telephone
yesterday morning, whereupon we both went on strike for the
day, after I had obtained the PM's blessing. We had lunch with
her father, who fortunately was in town for the day . . . Being a
practical as well as learned man, he proceeded to help in drafting
the announcement and then pulled out a diary and we discussed
the date.

Christmas Day: We both had to return last night to duty at
our offices. I was called at quarter to seven this morning and rang
up R to waken her in the first-aid post where she slept. Then at
eight we went to the Communion Service at Westminster Abbey.
Because of the blackout the place was in complete darkness
except for four candles at the altar. The nave was well filled,
though not packed, as I hear it had been for the similar Midnight
Service. We had breakfast at Marsham Court and after short
spells at our desks went to the Morning Service at St Margaret's.

I had arranged a lunch party at the office for shorthand writers
and others on duty. Parry de Winton had given me a turkey from
Wales, a noble bird, and our Swedish cook produced an excellent
meal. Rozie came. Everyone was captivated by her, as I could see
and as Miss Watson, retailing the others' gossip, reported to me
afterwards . . . More work in the afternoon and then we dined at
Marsham Court, where the Dean of Westminster and his wife
(both of whom R knows) and Dr Don of St Margaret's, who had
recognised me at the Morning Service, asked us to join them at
their table. A little time afterwards by ourselves by the fireside
and then I saw her off on the tube and myself returned to another
night at the office.

On 10 December 1942 Lloyd George said to the PM at No. 10,
'I've had my show. This is your show and I don't want to interfere
with it.'

1943

JANUARY

The Casablanca Conference: the Combined Chiefs of Staff agreed on the conduct of the war in 1943 (including the operation for the capture of Sicily); the PM and the President approved. After several refusals, de Gaulle accepted an invitation and arrived on the 22nd. He was prevailed on to meet Giraud and shake hands in front of photographers. At the concluding press conference the President unexpectedly used the phrase 'unconditional surrender', saying that it would be enforced on all our enemies.

After the conference the PM and the President drove to Marrakesh and spent the night in the Taylor Villa as guests of the American Vice-Consul Pendar. The President then flew off and the PM remained for two more days.

After overcoming the strong opposition of the Cabinet the PM went on to Cairo and had a meeting with the Turkish President, Inönü, at Adana.

The Russian offensive continued along the whole front. The Battle of Stalingrad ended with the capture of Field Marshal Paulus and the remnants of his forces.

The Eighth Army captured Tripoli and started the pursuit of Rommel's army towards Tunisia.

DIARY

January

1 To Chequers.
2 Chequers. Gen. Weekes (DCIGS) and Gen. Galloway for night, also Brig. Jacob, back from North Africa.
3 Chequers. Gen. 'Boy' Browning (OC Airborne Division) to lunch.

4   Returned to No. 10.

7   Lunch with Shertok [of the Jewish Agency].

8   In afternoon house-hunted unsuccessfully with Lady Ross.

11 All keyed up for departure, but cancelled owing to weather.
    With R visited flat in Dean's Yard.

12 Goodbye to R after lunch. Left London after dinner and drove
    down to Stanton Harcourt airfield.

13 c. 1.30 a.m. left in Liberator 504 (Pilot Vanderkloot) with PM,
    Sir C. Portal, Sir C. Wilson, Averell Harriman, Tommy,
    Inspector Thompson [PM's detective] and Sawyers. Arrived
    Casablanca 10.20 a.m. and drove to 'Anfa' camp, staying at
    Villa Mirador. Gens Marshall and Clark to lunch. To dinner –
    1st Sea Lord, Adl King, Adl Cooke, Lord Leathers [Minister of
    Shipping and Transport], CCO, and Harriman.

14 President Roosevelt and Hopkins arrived. Sunshine, oranges,
    eggs. Reading Maurois's life of Lyautey. PM spent most of
    morning reading in bed. Later he called on President.

15 At Anfa. Harold Macmillan, Gen. Alexander, Air Marshal
    Tedder and Gen. Eisenhower arrived. Meeting of CCS at
    President's villa.

16 Macmillan and Murphy discussed with PM proposals for
    organisation of French North Africa. Alexander and Harri-
    man to dinner.

17 Anfa. Gens Noguès [Governor General of Morocco] and
    Giraud called. Ismay and Jacob to dinner (PM out).

18 Anfa. Evening walk by sea. Mail from home (including two
    first letters from R). William Stirling and Codrington [from
    Foreign Service] to dinner.

19 Randolph arrived.

20 At Anfa.

21 Visit to Fez by plane with Codrington and Sir C. Wilson.
    Lunch with Glaoui's secretary.

22 At Anfa. General de Gaulle arrived.

23 Final plenary conference at Anfa of combined staffs, President
    and PM.

24 Left Casablanca with PM, President etc. by road for Marra-
    kesh, arriving at Pindar's (Moses Taylor's) villa in late
    afternoon.

25 Marrakesh. President and party left early. Afternoon walking

in market. We left by Liberator 504 *c.* 6.20 p.m., flying over Atlas Mountains at sunset.

26   Arrived Cairo *c.* 7.30 a.m. Staying at Embassy (Lampsons). CIGS also there. Lord Moyne, Gen. Alexander and Lord Lansdowne.

27   At Cairo. General Maitland Wilson and Adl Harwood among others to lunch. Bernard Burrows [of Foreign Service] is looking after us. King Farouk called. Turkish reply received welcoming visit from PM.

28   Cairo. Dined with Sir Arthur Rucker at Mohammed Ali Club.

29   In Cairo.

30   Flew to Adana for conference in Turkish President's special train near Yenidje. President Ismet Inönü, M. Saraçoglu, M. Numan [Foreign Minister], Gen. Çakmak etc.

31   On conclusion of Adana Conference flew to Cyprus. Received by Sir Charles Woolley at Government House, Nicosia. Spent night with Shaws (Colonial Secretary).

William Stirling later sent me the following remarkable extract from AFHQ news bulletin published at Algiers:

> *Nicosia-Cyprus:* It was announced in London today that Primeminister Churchill has vicited Cyprus on his return from his conference with the Turkish president. Churchill was the guest of his excellency the Govonor and Lady Wooley at the govonors house in Nicosia. The Prime minister was accompanied by Sir Allen Brooke Chief Imperial General. Staff General Sir Alexander Cadogan permanent Undersecretary of State, and Foreign Office Secretary Sir Charles Wilhon. Also accompanyong the Primeminister was the President of the Royal College of Physicians Commander Thompson Bumpson, and Royal Navy personal assistant to the Primeminister Jim Martin.

LETTERS

7 January   Life is still pretty breathless . . . We haven't been as austere as we meant to be and have lunched and dined together almost daily – dinner at Marsham Court, where R is able to luxuriate in my hot bath. We are able to have a few pleasant minutes by the fireside and then, according to the calls of the

office, I see her home or to the Underground. One evening I
arrived to find my socks being darned.

16 January We could not spend these January days in a more
pleasant spot. (Paradise enow if I only had my Thou here too) –
bright sunshine, oranges, eggs and razor-blades.

Later: An ideal place had been found for the conference – a
tourist hotel outside the town, surrounded by a ring of very
pleasant little villas. The unfortunate occupants were turned out
at short notice and a wire barrier put round the place, no one let
in or out without special passes and a company of American
infantry put on guard. We used to go down to the sea for a walk in
the afternoon and watch the great Atlantic rollers crashing in, or
occasionally visited Casablanca, where we had one of HM ships
to provide communications; but most of the time we were inside
this internment camp de luxe, so that everyone was within reach
and Private Secretary worries were reduced to a minimum. The
Americans were most efficient and generous hosts, refusing to let
us pay for anything, even for drinks at the bar and for things like
razor-blades, soap, cigarettes and candy, which were there for the
taking. The President was in good form and congratulated me
very nicely (having evidently been told by the PM). The last thing
he said in shaking hands at the end was that we ought to go to the
USA for our honeymoon. I won't say anything about the
conference itself except that very close agreement seemed to be
reached on the final conclusions. Variety was added by the play
within a play of de Gaulle and Giraud.

I took a day off and flew up to Fez. It is a fascinating place –
quarter of a million people, mostly in the old city, an unadulter-
ated Arab city, presumably much as it has been for almost a
thousand years. It belongs to the same Arabs who built the
Alhambra etc. in Spain and has mosques, gateways and colleges
in similar style, with exquisite decoration. There was only time
for a little sight-seeing of that kind; but I was able to see a good
deal of the streets and had lunch at the house of a wealthy Arab
chief, eating with our fingers while we sat propped on cushions,
looking out on to a brilliant courtyard, full of colour and the
sound of running water. The narrow streets were crammed with
people and donkeys, and the shops full of all sorts of exotic
wares.

FEBRUARY

After two nights in Cairo on his return from Cyprus, the PM flew on to Tripoli, where he witnessed the formal entry of the Eighth Army and inspected massed parades of two divisions. He then visited Algiers and returned to England. The PM had a cold and pneumonia. He was given the present of Rota the lion. (For the incident concerning the holding up of his telegram to the Minister Resident in Algiers, see Eden, *The Reckoning*, 367.)

On the 4th the Eighth Army crossed into Tunisia and came under General Eisenhower's command, with General Alexander as his deputy. Alexander's signal reported that the orders given him in August 1942 had been completely fulfilled, with the elimination of HM's enemies from Egypt, Cyrenaica, Libya and Tripolitania. Rommel made counter-thrusts in Tunisia.

The Russians continued to advance, liberating Rostov on the Don and Kharkov.

The reconquest of Guadalcanal was completed.

DIARY

February

1 Nicosia, Cyprus. PM addressed gathering of notables (including Locum Tenens [for the Archbishop]) at Government House. Drive round walls of Nicosia. Left after lunch for Cairo. Boarded out opposite Embassy with Mme de Jong.

2 In Cairo. Lunch with Henry Hopkinson. Col. Dudley Clarke also there. Dined with Capt. Bowlby.

3 PM left for Western Desert. I stayed behind and spent morning with Cadogan and Peter Loxley, being taken round mosques by Sir R. Greig. Lunch with Burrows. Dinner with Lord Moyne.

4 Left Embassy with Cadogan etc. and after breakfast at airfield flew to Castel Benito. Lunch at Montgomery's HQ. Driven round Tripoli in jeep by Lord Jellicoe. Left late for Algiers.

5 At Algiers, staying with Adl Cunningham. Dinner with Roger Makins [Foreign Office adviser to Harold Macmillan]. False start in the evening.

6 At Algiers. Lunch at hotel in town. Walk with Stirling and Jacob, calling on Gen. Smith. Left by Liberator 504 at 11 p.m.

7   Arrived Lyneham (flying up Bristol Channel) *c.* 11 a.m. Special train to Paddington, where R waiting. Visited 25 Pelham Place with her.

8   Left with R in evening for Oxford.

9   At Oriel, looking for furniture, shopping etc.

10 Returned to London.

11 PM's speech in House of Commons on Casablanca and his travels.

12 PM in bed with cold.

13 PM still in bed. Lunch with R. Fulford at Reform.

14 PM in bed all day with cold. R to lunch. Later I walked home with her through Park.

15 Lord Baldwin lunched with PM. After lunch R and I measured rooms at 25 Pelham Place.

18 R and I lunched with Zaranski [Polish Foreign Service] at Écu de France. Labour amendment re Beveridge Report defeated by 335 to 119.

19 Left with R by night train for Scotland.

20 Arrived Edinburgh.

21–24 In Edinburgh.

25 To Peebles.

26 Left Peebles by bus for Galashiels. Walk by Bemersyde to Dryburgh. Train to Edinburgh from St Boswells.

27 Left Edinburgh by night train.

28 Arrived back in London. Breakfast at King's Cross. Spent most of day tidying papers at Marsham Court. Short walk past Pelham Place.

LETTER

14 *February*   Our sleepers are booked for Friday night. R absolutely insisted that we travel third and in the end I yielded – so you see she is a daughter-in-law of whom you will approve.

I have never felt more in need of a holiday and today can hardly keep awake. R too is extremely tired. She has really far too hard a job (at the office from 9 a.m. until often eight at night – and it has been like this ever since she came to the War Office) and added to that has been the excitement of these last few weeks . . .

Carpets are going to be the chief difficulty. There are scarcely any to be had and those that exist are terribly expensive. At the Army and Navy Stores they haven't a single stair-carpet and they don't expect any more until after the war.

MARCH

In Tunisia Rommel made four major attacks, all rebuffed. Battle of Mareth Line: by the end of the month the Germans were in full retreat. Rommel was invalided to Germany.

Very heavy sinkings occurred in the Atlantic.

The March convoy to Russia was postponed. Stalin was informed of this and of the impossibility of continuing convoys after early May until September.

DIARY

March

1 Returned to No. 10. Found PM still in bed but much better. After lunch R and I bought blue Axminster carpet at Selfridges, also lamp.

5 To Chequers. PM taking things quietly, preparing a broadcast (partly about post-war).

6, 7 Chequers.

8 The King drove over from Windsor to visit the PM at Chequers. I shook hands. Returned to No. 10.

12 Left for Andover in afternoon.

13 Andover. Morning in bed. Longish walk in afternoon.

14 Andover. A lazy day.

15 Returned to No. 10. R left for Oxford, beginning her two months' sick leave (anaemia) from W.O.

19 To Chequers.

20 At Chequers. Also Nye [Gen. Sir Archibald, VCIGS], Pile, Mountbatten, [Air Marshal Sir Arthur] Harris.

21 At Chequers. PM's long broadcast about post-war programme.

22 Returned to London.

24 Lunch with Namier.

26 Left for Oxford in afternoon to stay at Oriel.

27, 28 Oxford.

29 Returned to London with Rozie.

30 Visited Pelham Place with R.

31 After lunch bought chairs etc. at Peter Jones with R. She returned to Oxford. Rather bad cold suddenly developing.

APRIL

The advance in Tunisia continued, the Eighth Army meeting the Allied forces from the west, and by the end of the month attacks were launched on the final enemy position defending Tunis. Heavy attacks were made on German air transports.

The PM proposed to the President a meeting to settle future operations – Sicily and Burma.

Germany announced the discovery of thousands of bodies of murdered Polish officers in the Katyn Forest – leading to the Soviet rupture with the Poles.

The success of the anti-U-boat offensive in the North Atlantic resulted in a great reduction in losses of Allied shipping and an increase in sinkings of U-boats.

DIARY

April

1 My cold still troublesome. PM put on his new 'wings' for RAF Birthday.

10 In afternoon to Richmond with R, looking (in vain) for furniture.

14 First furniture arrived at Pelham Place from Oxford.

16 Edinburgh furniture arrived at Pelham Place. Picnic lunch in garden. To Chartwell with PM. Thence to Chequers.

17, 18 At Chequers.

19 Returned to No. 10 via Hatfield, at which we visited display of aircraft, including Whittle [jet engine]. Mrs Ingram installed at Pelham Place.

23 Slept at Pelham Place for the first time.

24 At Pelham Place. Transferred part of belongings from Marsham Court.

28 Rozie dined at Pelham Place.

29 R and I lunched with Gen. Buckley.

30 At No. 10 for a few minutes. Removed last belongings from Marsham Court. Mother and Peggy arrived for breakfast. Went to Oxford with them and Parry de Winton. At Mitre.

LETTERS

22 April   In answer to question – gas masks. I should hardly have thought it necessary to bring one myself; but I hesitate to say so to anyone else, particularly in view of the statement published today. Perhaps you had better put them in if there is room in your suitcases. Of course no one *carries* them now.

25 April   From Pelham Place. The telephone is now installed: such is the influence of No. 10.

I write this in a sunny corner of our garden, the neighbour's lilac on one side and the chestnut tree on the other, both in blossom. I have slept here the last two nights, but as yet have had no meals. Mrs I seems a nice old person, as we first thought, though rather vague in manner. I doubt if we can expect much heavy work from her, but first impression is that in these days she is a lucky find.

Mr Miller, the Minister of the Presbyterian Church in Oxford, is to take part of the wedding service. The Bishop of Oxford . . . evidently does not at all like this and has asked us not to broadcast the fact; but he could not refuse his consent to the combined forces of the Bishop of Carlisle and the Vice-Chancellor of the University.

MAY

Tunis and Bizerta were taken. On the 13th General Alexander signalled: 'All enemy resistance has ceased. We are masters of the North African shore.' Church bells were rung.

The P M visited Washington ('Trident' Conference), followed by a visit to Algiers with General Marshall.

The 'dambusters'' raid was made on the Möhne and Eder dams.

On the Arakan coast of Burma British forces withdrew to the line from which they had set out five and a half months earlier.

The de Gaulle and Giraud factions met to form the French Committee of National Liberation.

Aid to Tito's partisans was started.

DIARY

May

1 Our wedding at St Mary's Church, Oxford. Night in London.
2 Left by night train for Stirling.
3–13 Honeymoon at St Fillans.
14–16 On leave in London. Settled at 25 Pelham Place.
17 Returned to No. 10 (PM away in Washington).
30 Lunch with Jack Churchill, John [Jack's son] and Mary.

LETTERS

3 May Our suite at the Dorchester was waiting for us, but the girl at the reception desk was put out because it had been specially prepared for us (evidently the Churchill connection had impressed) with most lovely flowers but had by mistake been given to another Mr Martin, who arrived first. However, he was ejected and we were duly installed.

11 May St Fillans. We are both rather *piano* today, stiff and weary after a very long walk yesterday. We had set off by Glen Goinan and Glen Artney for Callander, but just as were about to cross over into the Keltie valley we ran into what was apparently a big 'battle'. Bullets whistled past us landing in the heather with little thuds. We beat a retreat and after a council of war decided to walk back to St Fillans over the shoulder of Ben Vorlich and then along the loch side. We didn't get home till eight o'clock, having covered some 20 to 25 miles in sunshine, hail and snow.

JUNE

The PM returned to England. On the 30th he received the Freedom of the City. At this point in his history he observed, 'The hinge had turned'.

Pantelleria and Lampedusa were captured.

Field Marshal Wavell was appointed Viceroy of India.

DIARY

June

2 Received CVO in Birthday Honours.
5 PM arrived back from Africa in early morning. To Chequers with him in afternoon.

6 At Chequers.
7 Returned to London.
12–13 At Pelham Place.
18 To Andover in afternoon.
19 At Andover.
20 Returned to London.
25 To Chequers.
26–27 At Chequers.
28 Returned to London. Called on Lady Mayoress.
29 Called at Guildhall – Remembrancer (Bowker) and Town Clerk (Roach).
30 PM's drive to Guildhall to receive Freedom of the City. Afterwards luncheon at Mansion House.

LETTERS

3 June The CVO was a pleasant surprise. Awards in this Order are a personal affair of The King, not made on the Prime Minister's recommendation like other Honours, and so do not come through our machinery. I only heard on receiving a letter from The King's Private Secretary on Saturday. The award was nicely timed. I wonder if it was meant as a wedding present.

6 June It was a great relief to have the PM and his party safely home, though it was an end to the convenient lull at No. 10. We had a hectic time on Friday night. The special train had been laid on to start for the expected place of arrival and I was about to set out in it with Mrs Churchill at 11 p.m. when at the last moment we got news that the flight had been cancelled. After settling various things I went home to bed at Pelham Place and we were just asleep when (a little after midnight) the telephone rang to say that the party were flying after all but arriving at an airfield near London. I arranged to be called at 4.30 a.m. and R and I tried to fall asleep again, but we were soon disturbed by the sirens and a very small raid. At 5 a.m. a car was at the door and I arrived at the airfield in time to see the great aircraft arrive with its escort, like a lot of small birds round a cuckoo. The PM was in very good form and had thoroughly enjoyed his 'expedition'.

10 June Now that the PM is back I am realising more and more (what I knew beforehand) how ill the duties of a PS and those of married life go together. The usual plan seems likely to be that I go home about seven o'clock for dinner, returning to No. 10 for a couple of hours and back to Pelham Place by, say, twenty to twelve. The worst of this is that it means keeping Rosalind awake rather late; but that seems better than leaving her alone and sleeping at the office.

She is definitely not returning to the War Office, where it would not have been worthwhile picking up the work of a new branch. However, she refuses to be entirely idle and has started going daily to the WVS Headquarters, where they were evidently glad to have her. True to the reputation of the WVS she finds herself in a room with three 'Ladies'. All I know of the work so far is that she was helping with the evacuation of young children – which still goes on.

She has bottled some gooseberries – a method without sugar, which we hope works.

18 June Rosalind has planted some tomatoes, which we attend with anxious care, also some rows of lettuces and dwarf beans.

JULY

Allied landings were made in Sicily and Syracuse, Gela and Palermo taken. Allied decision was taken to attack the west coast of Italy and seize Naples, but the Americans refused to send reinforcements and insisted on withdrawal of three of the heavy bomber groups.

The first use of the 'window' anti-radar device in a raid on Hamburg was followed by other massive raids.

Mussolini fell. Marshal Badoglio was entrusted with the formation of a Cabinet.

The German eastern offensive, near Kursk, failed before the end of the month and the Russians took the offensive near Orel.

DIARY

July

3–4　At Pelham Place.

14　Indoors 'Garden Party' at No. 10 for Ministers, Chiefs of Staff etc. and wives.

17–18　Weekend at Pelham Place. To *Arsenic and Old Lace*.

22　R and I dined with Lord and Lady Woolton.

23　To Chequers.

24 At Chequers.

25 At Chequers. In the evening (while watching *Sous les Toits de Paris*) we received news of Mussolini's resignation and the proclamations by the King of Italy and Badoglio.

26 Returned to town.

30/31 Cabinet at 1.30 a.m. To bed 4.20 a.m.

31 Idle day at Pelham Place. Great heat.

LETTERS

18 July The Party at No. 10 was a big affair – about 230 guests – originally intended to be a garden party, but the day was cold and sunless, so we had it indoors instead. A buffet tea and a band. All the Ministers with their wives were invited, plus the Chiefs of Staff and all the private staff at No. 10 with their wives. It went very well and I think most of the guests thoroughly enjoyed themselves, such a party being unknown in these days. [R, who had been expecting a baby for some weeks and had a good deal of sickness in consequence, was unable to come to the party or to the Investiture when I received my CVO.]

We had Mrs B to lunch – an excellent meal almost entirely supplied from Andover – duck and green peas and stewed raspberries. Our tomatoes are rewarding the attention lavished on them – quite a number of babies forming.

25 July On Thursday we dined with Lord and Lady Woolton in their flat just off Whitehall. When we met at Lady Churchill's party the other day Lady W said she wanted to see R. Robin Harrison, who till recently was Lord Woolton's PS, was there too, the only others being the new PS and his wife. The Wooltons are very easy, genial people and we had a very pleasant evening. Dinner was not notably austere – potato soup, chicken with many vegetables and stewed plums and custard. No second helpings. No bread.

The famous black cat at No. 10, the Munich Mouser, was found dead the other day in a room in the Foreign Office – most sinister. We are avoiding publicity for fear of being flooded with black cats from all over the country to take his place. I don't love Nelson, the Chequers cat, which flopped in at my window and woke me up at 4 a.m. after I had only got to bed at 3 a.m.

(There is a reference to the death of the Munich Mouser in Eden's *The Reckoning*, 339: 'He died in the F.O. this afternoon. Winston says that he died of remorse and chose his death-bed accordingly. He feared he had been thrown on the ash can. He would have been ready to give him burial in the garden of No. 10. Yes, I said, R.I.P. Munich Mouser would have looked well there. We laughed a good deal about the poor cat.')

AUGUST

By the 17th the whole of Sicily was in our hands.

The 'Quadrant' Conference took place at Quebec, followed by a visit to Hyde Park. There was discussion on future strategy in Italy and against Japan; and on plans for 'Overlord', with a target date of May 1944. It was agreed to appoint an American commander for 'Overlord' and Admiral Mountbatten as Supreme Commander in South-East Asia. Private talks took place on 'Tube Alloys' (atomic bomb). The French National Committee in Algiers was recognised by Britain, the US and Canada.

German forces withdrew along the southern Russian front. The Russians recaptured Orel and Kharkov.

DIARY

August

1 At Pelham Place.

4 Left with PM's Quadrant party at midnight for the north.

5 Arrived Faslane (Gareloch) 2.30 p.m. Taken out on SS *Maid of Orleans* to *Queen Mary*. Sailed *c.* 6 p.m. (off Greenock).

6 In SS *Queen Mary* at sea. At dinner with PM – Brigadier and Mrs Wingate etc. Others on board include Mrs C, Mary, Averell and Kathleen Harriman, Pug, Pound, Brooke, Portal, Mountbatten.

7 At sea. Overcast. Lunch with PM – Lord Leathers, Sir Ralph Metcalfe [Director of Sea Transport], Gen. Riddell-Webster (QMG).

8 At sea. Mostly overcast, but some sunshine in afternoon. At Church Service. After dinner Sqn Ldr Gibson VC ('the dambuster') described his experiences.

9 Arrived at Halifax in the afternoon. Met by Malcolm Mac-Donald [UK High Commissioner in Canada], Vaughan [Presi-

dent of Canadian National Railways], Admiral Neller etc. Left by train.

10 In train. Arrived Quebec afternoon. Staying at Citadel. Met by Mackenzie King, Lt-Governor and Premier etc. Mackenzie King to dinner.

11 Quebec. Rain. Left in afternoon with PM, Mary and Tommy for Niagara.

12 Niagara. After breakfast visited Falls. Came on south by Rochester, Syracuse etc. to Hyde Park, staying with Roosevelts. Harry Hopkins there. Grey [Irish representative in USA] to dinner.

13 Hyde Park. Oppressively hot. Swim. Picnic lunch at Mrs R's cottage (hot dogs).

14 Hyde Park. Visited Naval Museum and Library. Swim. Picnic lunch at cottage on hilltop. Judge Rosenbaum. 'Rolly' Hambley. Left by train after dinner.

15 Troy. Arrived back in Quebec. The Governor General's ADC Col. Willis O'Connor rather a character and a great help.

16 Quebec.

17 Quebec. Governor General (Earl of Athlone) and Princess Alice arrived (with Redfern and Eastwood). President Roosevelt arrived later. Sherry party and dinner party at Citadel. Sat next Sheila MacDonald [sister of Malcolm].

18 Quebec. Tummy upset; banting. Eden and Bracken arrived, with Cadogan, [Nicholas] Lawford [Private Secretary to Eden] and Sendall [Private Secretary to Minister of Information].

19 Quebec.

20 Quebec. A quiet day, as President and PM are away fishing. With Miss Layton [PM's secretary] visited Montmorency Falls and Ste Anne de Beaupré. Cordell Hull [US Secretary of State] arrived.

21 Lunch with President. Short walk in old town with Turnbull, Mackenzie King's PS. Dinner with Garner at Chateau Frontenac.

22 Quebec.

23 Quebec. PM's drive through the streets. With Mary dined with Saul Rae [Private Secretary to Canadian PM], John Baldwin etc. in Citadel mess.

24 Quebec. Conference ended with press conference. Dinner with

President, who left afterwards for Ottawa. Rough telegram from U.J. [Uncle Joe, Stalin].

25 Quebec. After lunch left with PM etc. and Col. Clarke for latter's fishing camp, La Cabane, on River Montmorency.

26 Drove up from La Cabane with Mary to Lac des Neiges. Fished. Returned after dark to La Cabane.

27 At La Cabane. Eden, Cadogan, Brooke and Portal to dinner.

28 Returned to Quebec. At Mrs C's YWCA luncheon at Citadel. Afternoon walk on Cape Diamond.

29 Quebec. To St Andrew's Presbyterian Church.

30 Quebec.

31 Quebec. PM returned from fishing. Broadcast. Luncheon with Canadian Ministers. In afternoon left by train from Wolfe's Cove.

LETTERS

1 August As a cat enthusiast you would have enjoyed my visit to the Zoo with the PM to see his lion with four young cubs. It was given a bunch of catmint which it sniffed with obvious relish. There were large hot crowds which jostled us wherever we went. Inside the bars in the swan enclosure the PM turned to them and said, 'I suppose you would like to feed me.'

5 August In the train near Linlithgow. We have with us Wingate, seized last night on arrival from Assam, with little but a bush shirt and a toothbrush – an interesting and striking person, not unlike my idea of T.E. Lawrence.

9 August At sea. We expect to land in Canada this afternoon, but how soon there will be a chance of sending a letter to you I do not know. My style is cramped by the ban on mention of the means by which we crossed the Atlantic and there is little to write about except the orange juice and bacon and eggs which always seem to loom so large on these occasions. Fittings and facilities of all sorts are not what you would expect in peace-time, but we have plenty of space – e.g. a cabin of my own with private bath, apart from an office shared with Rowan – and are extremely comfortable. There has been little work beyond reading up the papers brought with us and we have shared the late hours . . . We were taken out to our ship at the port of embarkation in one of the familiar old Channel steamers that made the most exciting beginning for a holiday. It seemed haunted by the ghosts of green-faced passengers.

We have had grey skies most of the way, often with mist or rain and a strong wind, so any visions of basking in deck-chairs have been disappointed; but there has been little more than the mildest roll and creaking and very slight vibration to remind us down in our cabins that we are at sea.

10 August In the train. We reached Halifax yesterday and I was thrilled to get your letter dated only two days earlier. Malcolm MacDonald met us, with various Canadians, and we were led to a massive train that was waiting by the quay. The PM has the most sumptuous coach imaginable, the private coach of the president of the Canadian National Railways. I have a very comfortable 'Pullman' coach to myself. We had a regular banquet for dinner and I have just returned from an equally gargantuan lunch – fruit salad, soup, salmon, lamb, lobster salad, ice in cantaloup, coffee and cream, dessert and the usual extras. You will have to let out all my clothes when we get home . . . It is a most pleasant countryside, little fields in strips (subdivision for large families), with neat wooden houses and churches. There is something Hebridean about the lush brightness of the hay crops seen against a background of distant blue mountains. Crowds collect wherever we stop and wave and cheer the PM and return his V sign. Rather ludicrous to see a priest give the sign: I felt like shouting back 'et cum spiritu tuo'. Rumour that there was a distinguished passenger had evidently spread quickly; but it is said that expectations were divided as to his identity, some saying that the Pope was coming to take refuge in his faithful Quebec. I suppose such a warm and apparently unusual welcome in this province is of some significance.

13 August Hyde Park. There is an interval before the main conference begins and the PM has taken advantage of it to pay a short visit to the President here at his private estate on the Hudson River (where we stayed for a few days last summer). Mrs C is thoroughly tired out and stayed behind at Quebec, but Mary has come. She is so nice and a great success with everyone. We travelled in a most comfortable special train with observation cars and long baths, air conditioned.

14 August   I am now finishing this on the return journey in the same train. We had a very pleasant visit to Hyde Park in spite of rather oppressive heat. Picnic lunches at cottages in the woods and a swim daily in an open-air pool. The President looks wonderfully well and so does Eleanor.

16 August   The Citadel, Quebec. The other day at Hyde Park (I am told) I was walking in a wood by some water when the PM pointed me out to some people sitting beside him and said, 'Look at John Martin wandering among the trees thinking about his wife.'

We had a twenty-hour train journey from the ocean port to Quebec, a very pleasant countryside, not unlike parts of Scotland. News of the arrival had already got about (though some said it was the Pope, others Stalin) and little crowds were collected at the stations, who waved in a very friendly, though stolid, way and returned the benediction of the V sign, liberally bestowed on them from the platform of the observation car at the rear of the train.

The staffs etc. are staying in the Chateau Frontenac Hotel, requisitioned for the purpose; but our little party is in the Citadel, the Governor-General's summer residence, a very pleasant place, inside very solid battlements on a height overlooking the St Lawrence. We have the ground floor and the President's party, when it comes, will be upstairs, very convenient to be all under one roof.

We went off for a couple of nights to visit the President and Mrs Roosevelt at Hyde Park, stopping at Niagara Falls. It was another twenty-hour journey in a very luxuriously appointed train, complete with long baths and proper beds and vast meals. Hyde Park was excessively hot – damp, sticky heat – but it was a very pleasant visit thanks to the kindness of the Roosevelts and the attractive surroundings. Each day we had a picnic lunch at a cottage in the woods – hot dogs and hamburgers cooked on the spot, corn on the cob, fish chowder, huge slices of water melon etc., and had a refreshing swim in an open-air pool. The journey back was more direct and much shorter, overnight. We stopped at such storied cities as Syracuse and Troy. Quebec, thank goodness, is cool and we have settled down again to work in more reasonable conditions.

18 August The Governor-General and Princess Alice came to Quebec yesterday to receive the President, who arrived in the afternoon with his usual squad of security men.

Double interruption at this point as Attlee rang up from London and at the same time the plane bringing Eden and Brendan Bracken appeared in front of the Citadel and circled round before coming down. Attlee's voice was quite drowned by the roar of its engines.

There has been a succession of junketings to celebrate the Governor-General's visit and the President's arrival. We had a dinner of twenty last night which I only just managed to survive. I sat next to Sheila MacDonald, Malcolm's sister, very good looking and intelligent. Rather regal – curtsies and gloves.

The President's dog Falla trots about very happily.

Mary Churchill is so nice. I always thought so, but have seen more of her on this expedition. She is wonderfully unspoilt, ready to be excited and interested in everything.

22 August Quebec. We are fairly hard at work all the time, with the usual late nights, and quite often a day passes without my going outside the Citadel. The Citadel is on a height overlooking the St Lawrence and much of the city of Quebec. From the top floor and particularly from an outside decked terrace on the ramparts there are magnificent views, most pleasant in the bright sunshine we have had lately and wonderfully coloured at sunset . . . Among Governors-General of recent memory I gather that none was more popular than Tweedsmuir. He seems to have been a particularly good speaker.

I wonder if you realise how completely French this part of Canada is – in language, in appearance, in everything. There is something about Quebec that reminds me of Edinburgh. I suppose it is the mixture of French architecture, steep streets, distant views and hilltop citadel.

22 August I have been pretty well tied by the leg in the Citadel, except one day when the PM and the President went off fishing and I managed to drive in the country, visiting the Montmorency Falls – a tremendous tumble of water, higher than Niagara – and Ste Anne de Beaupré, the local Lourdes, a large modern basilica on the site of older churches. Have just been having lunch with the President – Stimson and Brendan there, besides the Churchills, and some good stories told of the kind I enjoy at the time and forget afterwards.

24 August   Quebec. The conference has come to an end, but there are various things left to do before we return. We are going off tomorrow for a very short holiday at a fishing camp, but will be in constant touch with our base.

On Monday the PM made a triumphal progress through the streets of Quebec in an open car – crowds all along the way and a tremendous reception. In the evening I dined in the officers' mess in the Citadel as guest of some of Mackenzie King's staff, followed by a cinema show and a sing-song until a late hour. Mary astonished everyone by singing all the favourite French songs and knowing all the words.

29 August   Quebec. I went up with the Churchills on Wednesday to a fishing camp on the Montmorency River. It was a most lovely place on the river bank, a fair-sized fast-flowing river, with thickly wooded hills all round. We lived in comfortable log houses, complete with electric light, sanitation, hot baths and a blazing wood fire to sit round at night. In the evening the PM went up to another camp on the Lac des Neiges, while Mary and I followed the next morning. It was a beautiful ride, full of skids and steep ascents, up a frightful road, but we had an extremely skilful driver, one of the scarlet-coated mounties who have been guarding us. After a large lunch we went out fishing. It rained a little and there was disappointingly little sunshine and I haven't felt so cold for a long time; but it was a beautiful place and I enjoyed it enormously – even though I only caught three trout. We returned after dark to the lower camp, where we spent Friday working away on papers brought up by courier and wandering about by the river. It is a rather wilder version of Speyside. Anthony Eden and Cadogan came up for dinner, at which we were joined by the CIGS and the CAS on their return from an independent expedition to the Lac des Neiges, where they had caught fabulous draughts of fishes. On Sunday morning I changed guard with Rowan, who had meanwhile been holding the fort at the Citadel. I drove down with Mrs C and Mary, who were going to a luncheon party for leaders of the YWCA. One other and I were the solitary males, but I think I have been rewarded by some nylon stockings from my neighbour at table.

One of the YWCA women had the boldness to tell me that I didn't look as if I had suffered from lack of food, to which I replied that after all I had been in Canada for a fortnight.

SEPTEMBER

The PM visited Washington, Harvard and Hyde Park, returning to the UK in HMS *Renown*.

The Eighth Army crossed the straits of Messina. Taranto was seized and an armistice made with the Italian Government. A landing was made at Salerno and German forces evacuated Sardinia. The French landed in Corsica.

The Germans were in retreat along the whole Russian front from opposite Moscow to the Black Sea.

Admiral Pound resigned after suffering a stroke.

DIARY

September

1 Arrived Washington in afternoon. Met by President. Staying in White House. Col. Hobby at dinner.
2 In Washington. Lunch with Stefan Zamoyski.
3 Washington. Biddy Wylie had lunch with me and afterwards helped to shop. Italian rep. signed Armistice terms.
4 Washington. At Press luncheon for PM.
5 Washington. Left by special train in evening.
6 At Harvard. PM's speech – alliance with US, Basic English. Lunch in Art Museum – President Conant, Secretary David M. Little.
7 Arrived back in Washington.
8 Washington. Italian surrender announced.
9 Washington. Lunch with Eric Seal.
10 Washington. PM's meeting with heads of missions etc. at Embassy.
11 Packed up at Washington and left after dinner by special train.
12 At Hyde Park. Picnic lunch in President's cottage. Tea with Mrs Hall (ex-Mrs Vincent Astor). Left after dinner.
13 In train all day, travelling through Maine and Quebec. At St John at midnight. A fine country of lakes and forests.
14 Arrived Halifax. At 3 p.m. left in HMS *Renown* (Capt. Parry).

A day of brilliant sunshine. We have Brendan, Ismay and Moran in our party.

15 At sea. Gun practice in morning. Mary Churchill's 21st birthday. Sunny all day.

16 At sea. Destroyer left us with signals for despatch. Verses from A.P. Herbert in HMS *Orwell*. Stormier in evening, but threatened hurricane passed us. Poker with PM etc.

17 Fairly rough but ship steady. Sherry with Capt. Parry. (The Commander is Conder.) Poker again at night. Read *Thirty Seconds over Tokyo*.

18 At sea. Joined by USS *Ranger*.

19 Arrived at Greenock about 9.30 a.m. Short Service on quarterdeck. By train to London. Rosalind meeting at Euston.

20 Rosalind is now working at WVS Headquarters in afternoons.

21 PM's long speech in House – over two hours interrupted by luncheon interval.

24 Cabinet reshuffle following on death of Sir Kingsley Wood. John Anderson chosen as Chancellor of Exchequer.

25 Day off. Idle morning.

26 At Pelham Place. Crowded St Columba's Service at Imperial Institute for 'Battle of Britain Sunday'.

27 Cocktail party by Lord and Lady Mountbatten before Dickie's departure for South-East Asia Command.

28 Lunch with [Sir Alan/Tommy] Lascelles.

29 R and I had lunch with the Dean of Westminster and Mrs de Labilière [his wife]. Major Eastwood [of Government House, Ottawa] to dinner in mess.

30 Left by night train for Edinburgh.

LETTERS

4 *September* The White House, Washington. This place at this time of year has a most foul climate – hot and humid, though much heavy rain has cooled the air a little in the last two days. My tuxedo for dinner is a cruel penance. The PM has a beautifully cool air-conditioned room, but we work next to him (and sleep) in the atmosphere of a hot-house and the constant transition from one to the other is a Bad Thing. Mrs Roosevelt has been away in the Pacific and there are no guests.

7 September The White House, Washington. We have just returned from a most successful day at Harvard (Boston), where the PM received an honorary degree. You probably heard his speech on the wireless – a particularly good one.

Here it is twenty hours' journey by train from Quebec and as we are so much further south it is correspondingly hotter. The humidity on Saturday was ninety-nine per cent. This combined with high temperature is rather overwhelming.

Harvard is an attractive place – red-brick buildings spaciously set out on both sides of a river. The proceedings were very like those on any similar occasion at home. The PM in Oxford doctor's cap and gown looked like a genial Henry VIII. He was received with the greatest enthusiasm and everywhere in the streets there was the usual welcome of cheers and waves. Lunch in an Art Museum. I sat next a professor's wife who was married in Oxford, so we had something in common.

9 September The White House, Washington. The visit to Harvard was a great success. We used our special train and travelled overnight, arriving at Cambridge (Boston) at eleven o'clock in the morning. President Conant and the Governor of Massachusetts were there to meet the party and we drove with them in a slow procession to the Conants' house and then on to the local equivalent of the Sheldonian (a building of the worst Victorian period, about which everyone was most apologetic). There had been no advance announcement of the visit, but as usual the news spread quickly and there were crowds along the way with the usual smiles and cheers. The general impression is of pleasant brick buildings spaciously laid out on both sides of a wide river. There is a remarkable similarity in the academic face on both sides of the ocean. Anyhow the platform party looked as if they might have been in Oxford. Perhaps it was because of the robes – including more than one Oxford doctor and the PM among them as DCL, looking just too Henry VIII by Holbein. (I hope he really is a DCL. There was some difficulty in raising the robes but in the end they were borrowed from New York.) Old Whitehead [philosopher] was there – a most distinguished looking figure but aged. The speech went down very well.

13 September On the train from Hyde Park. It is the most lovely country of lochs and forests, everything looking as if it was the first day of the world in the sparkling sunshine. Here and there we pass a splash of autumn colouring, almost unbelievably red and gold. It is a great relief to get away from the heat of Washington, which seemed at times as oppressive as any ever known in Malaya. We had a perfect day for our visit to Hyde Park yesterday – the Hudson valley looking its best. Across the river from the President's property is Father Divine's house.

NOTE

The following extract is from Sir Alexander Cadogan's diary for 2 September: 'Summoned to White House at 10.30. Went round and found PM not available. He was not available at 11.30. I told Martin I would wait till 12 and then go home. I don't know what sort of message he gave to PM, but latter turned up at 11.58, with apologies which I received in silence. It's really too much. What he wanted was to give me instructions about drafting two messages to Stalin about the Mediterranean Commission and the Three Power meeting.' I well remember the occasion. The PM was watching a film with the President and would not come out, though he had summoned Sir Alec. The latter said that none of his predecessors would have put up with that sort of thing.

The following signals were exchanged with HMS *Renown*, which was being escorted across the Atlantic by HMS *Matchless* and HMS *Orwell*. The Prime Minister and his wife and daughter Mary were in *Renown*, and Sir Derrick Gunston MP and A.P. Herbert MP were in *Orwell*:

With respectful salutes and greetings from Derrick Gunston and A.P. Herbert:

> 'Return ULYSSES and soon to show
> The secrets of your splendid bow,
> Return and make all riddles plain
> To anxious ITHACA again.
> And you Penelope the true
> Who have begun to wander too,
> We're glad to greet you on the foam
> And hope to see you safely home.'

Reply from the Prime Minister:

> 'Ulysses and Penelope too
> Return their compliments to you,
> They too are glad to wend their way
> Homewards to Ithaca after a stay
> With friends from where the land is bright
> And spangled stars gleam all the night.
> And when he's mastered basic Greek
> Ulysses to the world can speak
> About the plots and plans and bases
> Conferred upon in foreign places.
> We thank you from our hearts today
> For guarding us upon our way.
> To chide these simple lines be chary.
> They are the first attempt of Mary.'

From all in *Orwell* to Miss Mary Churchill:

> 'Telemacha, the sailors send
> Their greetings to a fighting friend.
> The major adds a smart salute
> To any lady who can shoot.
> And I, poor scribbler, must give place
> To one who writes with such a grace.
> Why not (when Mister Masefield's past)
> A lady Laureate at last?'

On parting company, from the Prime Minister:

> 'Thank you MATCHLESS. Thank you ORWELL.'

From *Orwell* to the Prime Minister:

> 'It has been a great honour. May we wish you
> Good Luck, Sir.'

OCTOBER

Naples was captured.

Sir Andrew Cunningham was appointed First Sea Lord. Admiral Pound died on Trafalgar Day.

The PM made speeches on the coal mining industry and on plans for rebuilding the House of Commons.

The Russian advance continued.

Discussions took place with the Russians about the resumption of convoys, including an offensive message from Stalin which the PM refused to receive.

Italy declared war on Germany.

An unproductive correspondence was exchanged with the President about the desirability of announcing the commander for 'Overlord'.

In correspondence with the President and Stalin about a meeting of the 'Big Three', Stalin insisted it should be at Teheran.

There was heavy American bombing of Schweinfurt; but losses of flying fortresses led to the suspension of unescorted daylight raids pending the production of long-range fighters. The decision was taken to change over to aluminised explosives, which greatly increased the effectiveness of our bombs – a fruit of Cherwell's 'roving eye' (Churchill, *The Second World War* V, 464).

DIARY

October

1–2 In Edinburgh.

3 Edinburgh. Left by night train.

4 Arrived back in London. Day off.

5 Day off. R and I dined with Dr and Mrs Weizmann.

6 Farewell dinner for Lord Wavell on departure to take up appointment of Viceroy. Sat next to his PS, Jenkins.

8 To Chequers. Averell and Kathleen Harriman staying.

9 Chequers. FM Smuts and Jan [his son] arrived.

10 Chequers. Eden called on departure to Moscow conference.

11 Returned to London. R is at Oxford this week, helping her mother to entertain in succession Archbishop of Thyateira, Queen Marie of Yugoslavia and the Queen of the Netherlands.

15 Left in afternoon for Oxford. Staying at Oriel.

16, 17 Oxford.

18 Returned to London. Jock [head of British Colonies Supply Mission in Washington] and Joan Macpherson to dinner on their way from Jerusalem to Washington.

20 We have been having small air raids these last few nights – nothing much, but enough to waken us up, which is a nuisance.

21 Jock Colville to lunch. PM spoke to CAS about releasing him from RAF to return to No. 10.

119

24   Jack Churchill and Parry de Winton to lunch. Jack Churchill took me in the evening to see the 'Churchill Club' in Ashburnham House.

29   Left with R by 6.05 to Andoversford, staying with Abells at Foxcote Manor.

30, 31   At Foxcote.

LETTERS

10 October   We had a noisy evening on Thursday. We were dining with the Pecks when the sirens went and in a lull in the gunfire started to walk home; but the guns opened up again on the way, with a lovely fireworks display right above our heads. We thought it better to go down into a basement shelter and sat on a bench there (with Hector beside us), quite like old times. Fortunately this didn't last long and we had no bombs anywhere near.

14 October   Four nights out of the last six I haven't got to bed till 2.30 a.m. and it is perhaps not surprising that the cold is not yet shaken off, but I hope to have a refreshing weekend at Oxford.

24 October   Here I am on duty over the weekend and, as Bevir is still away sick, I can't leave the fort to sleep at home, although I go along each day for breakfast and lunch. Fortunately the last two nights have been free from gunfire, though there was a brisk little raid after dusk on Friday. I took an extra hour off at lunchtime on Saturday and we did some very enjoyable gardening. I wish there was time for more.

Yes, I have met the other John Martin. He went out to South Africa from Scotland, where his home was at or near Stirling, so no doubt we are distant relations. Last year Brendan Bracken had us both to lunch, with no one else, and John Martin was introduced to John Martin. I gather that he is a very important person in South Africa.

NOVEMBER

In the continued Russian offensive Kiev fell. Convoys to Russia were resumed.

In Italy the Eighth Army closed up to the River Sangro and at the end of the month attacked across it.

Disturbances in Lebanon followed the arrest by the French of the

Leslie Rowan and I step down from the train after the Churchills on arrival in Quebec, August 1943.

A press conference given by Churchill, Mackenzie King and Roosevelt in Quebec, August 1943. (I am standing on the far left.)

Churchill meeting a group of Wrens. Catherine (Judy) Love, later Lady Rowan, is standing behind Churchill's right shoulder.

A Mounty showing Wrens the sights in Quebec, August 1943. Catherine (Judy) Love is standing on the bench (left).

With the Churchills on a special train, Quebec Conference, August 1943.

A meeting with Ibn Saud near Cairo, November 1943. (I am standing behind

Chiang Kai-shek, Roosevelt, Churchill and Madame Chiang Kai-shek in Cairo, November 1943.

Carthage, Christmas Day 1943. Left to right, front row: Eisenhower, Churchill, Gen. 'Jumbo' Wilson; back row: Maj. Gen. Whiteley, Air Marshal Tedder, (?), Adm. John Cunningham, (?), Alexander, Adm. Power, Gen. Gale, Gen. Hollis, Gen. Bedell-Smith.

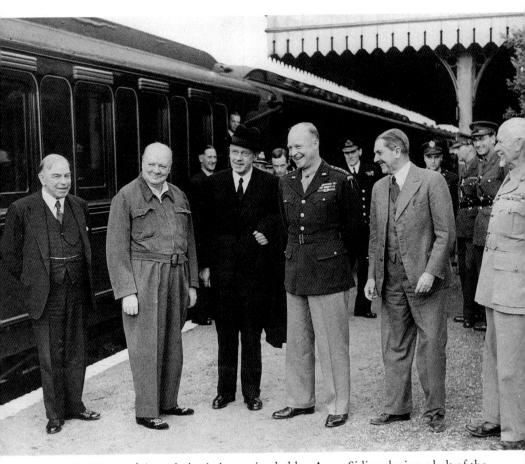

'In Fraternal Association'. A meeting held at Ascot Siding during a halt of the special train in which their party was travelling, 12 May 1944. Left to right: Mackenzie King, Churchill, Peter Fraser, Eisenhower, Sir Godfrey Huggins, Jan Smuts.

Prime Minister's train

Ascot Siding

Inspirational Association

10, Downing Street,
Whitehall.

12 May 1944

Winston S. Churchill

[several signatures]

'In Fraternal Association'. Downing Street letterhead bearing the signatures of those on the Prime Minister's train at Ascot Siding.

Montgomery and Churchill survey a line of jeeps on the beach in Normandy, June 1944.

Churchill (centre, next to jeep) in a crowd of troops, Normandy, June 1944. (I am in civilian clothes, in front of the jeep.)

A picnic in Normandy with officers from HMS *Kelvin*. On my left is Jan Smuts junior.

Watching enemy planes being pursued by Allied fighters over the Normandy coast, June 1944. Left to right: Lt Gen. Dempsey, Gen. Smuts, Churchill, FM Brooke, Montgomery, Lt Gen. Sir Richard O'Connor.

A second visit to the Normandy coast, 1944. Left to right: Gen. Marshall, Churchill, Gen. Arnold, me, Tommy Thompson.

Churchill giving his famous salute to the troops at the field bakery, Normandy, July 1944.

With FM Dill at the
Citadel, Quebec, August
1944.

The Prime Minister's staff on RMS *Queen Mary* on the way to Quebec,
September 1944. Left to right: Brian O'Brien, Marian Holmes, Inspector
Hughes, Dorothy Pugh, Sgt Davies, Frank Sawyers, Jo Sturdee, Charles
Barker, Elizabeth Layton, me.

Churchill in Yalta,
February 1945.

A visit to Athens on return from Yalta, February 1945. Left to right: Sarah
Churchill, Alexander, Churchill, Lt Gen. Scobie, Macmillan.

Official War Office photograph, Yalta, February 1945. Left to right: Leathers, Churchill, Eden, Stettinius, Roosevelt, Cadogan, Molotov, Stalin, Harriman.

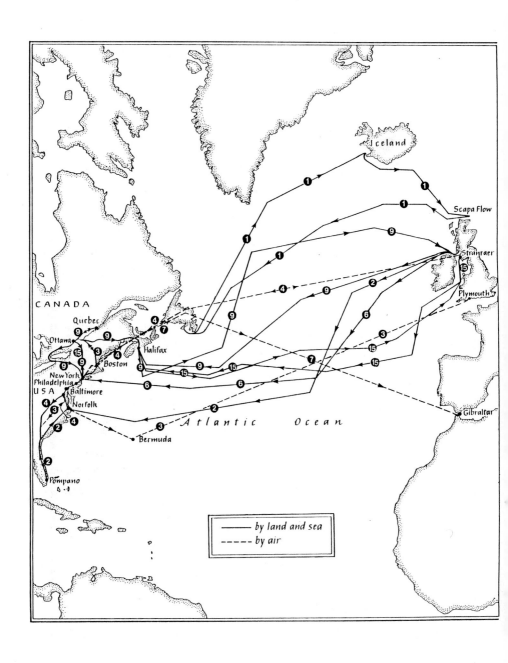

Maps depicting the journeys undertaken by Churchill 'in defence of the British
Commonwealth and Empire'. Route key on page vi.

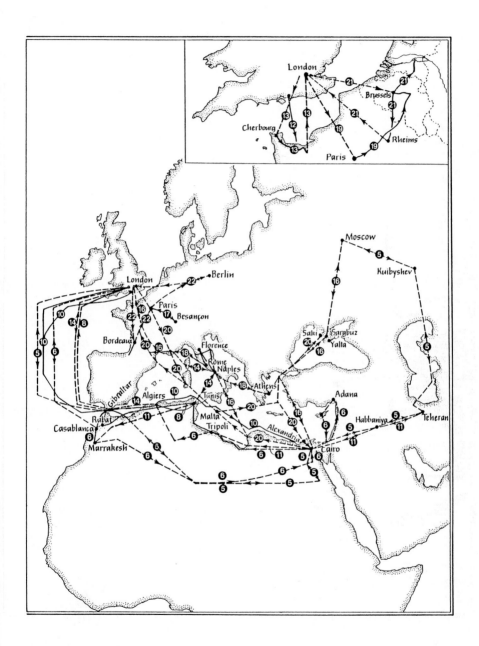

Allied leaders around the conference table in Yalta, 1945.

President and most of the ministers. General Catroux (from Algiers) mediated, prisoners were released and negotiations were begun for the ultimate independence of Syria and Lebanon.

Leros fell, 'our first really grievous reverse since Tobruk, 1942' (Churchill).

The PM departed for Malta, Cairo and Teheran, where the conference with Stalin and Roosevelt began on the 28th.

Tito set up a provisional government in Yugoslavia.

DIARY

November

1 Returned to London.

5 To Chequers.

6 Chequers. Also Brendan, Bridges, Randolph and Chief Whip – reshuffling.

7 Chequers.

8 Returned to London.

9 Lord Mayor's Luncheon at Mansion House.

12 Travelled down to Plymouth in PM's train and embarked in HMS *Renown* at sunset.

13 At sea. PM's party includes Sarah, Admiral Sir Andrew Cunningham [C in C Mediterranean], Pug, Desmond Morton, Moran, Hollis, Tommy and Francis Brown.

14 At sea.

15 At sea. Called at Gibraltar. Harold Macmillan and his PS, Wyndham, joined us.

16 Arrived Algiers, but did not go ashore. Various callers during the day – Gen. Bedell Smith [Eisenhower's Chief of Staff], Admiral Sir John Cunningham, Gen. Georges [Commander of Operations in North-east France, 1939, and recently come out of France], Roger Makins etc. Left in *Renown* after dark.

17 At sea. Making 29 knots in bright sunshine. Passed Cape Bon and Pantelleria. Arrived Malta after dark. Staying with Lord Gort, the Governor, at San Anton Palace.

18 Malta. Others here are Alexander, Eisenhower, Brooke, Portal, Tedder. In afternoon drove with Tommy into Valletta and saw blitz damage.

19 Malta. In afternoon PM visited Royal Dockyard and Palace, appearing on balcony. Met Campbell, Lieutenant Governor.

Governor's staff are Major Geddes, Major Woodford, Major Gordon Duff, Capt. Holland. Left.

20 Sailed in *Renown* shortly after midnight. At sea.

21 Arrived Alexandria about midday. Flew on by Dakota to Cairo. PM's party in Casey's villa. Met by Capt. Stonor.

22 In Cairo. At villa all day. Among callers Capt. Maunsell (Security), Ryan and Malet (Press), Burrows and Charles Johnston (Embassy), Clarke Kerr, Yates etc.

23 Cairo. Lunch with President Roosevelt, PM, Harry Hopkins, [Admiral William D.] Leahy [President's Chief of Staff], Sarah and Tommy. Visited Sphinx and pyramids.

24 Gilbert Yates to lunch. Macmillan and Desmond Morton arrived from Algiers, and Eden, Cadogan etc. from London. PM's party for Chiang Kai-shek.

25 Cairo. President's Thanksgiving dinner. Besides PM others included Harry, Averell, Winant, Steinhardt, Ross McIntyre, Pa Watson.

26 Cairo.

27 Left Cairo West airport at 8.15 a.m. in PM's York, with PM, Eden, Sarah, Moran and Tommy. Arrived Teheran 5½ hours later. Staying at Legation (Sir Reader Bullard).

28 Teheran. Bright autumn sunshine. Molotov fearing 'scandal', President moved from American Legation to Soviet Embassy.

29 At Teheran. Presentation of Stalingrad sword to Stalin at Soviet Embassy. Molotov and Voroshilov there, besides many Americans. Lunch with Somers Cocks.

30 Teheran. Lunch with Cumberbatch (Commercial Secretary). PM's 69th birthday. Dinner party – Stalin, Molotov, Voroshilov, President Roosevelt, Hopkins, British and American Chiefs of Staff, Eden, Winant, Harriman etc.

LETTERS

7 *November*   Chequers. No dull November today. The very pleasant landscape seen from my office window is looking particularly bright with brilliant sunshine on the red and gold of the few remaining leaves. Unfortunately there is too much going on to let us go out and enjoy this morning sunshine, which I fear is 'too bright to last'.

It would amuse you to see the cat here sitting demurely on its chair at the dinner table on the PM's right.

15 November This will have to be a very dull letter, saying nothing of whereabouts, destination or company, beyond the fact that we have been at sea. A very rough sea it was on Saturday night, with the deck of my cabin half awash and my tummy most unhappy. Somehow lunch was surmounted – though the noble lord fled suddenly from table with a face the colour of parchment. A change of course in the afternoon brought much improvement. Since then all has been well and we have enjoyed a pleasant weekend of occasional work, a fair amount of sunshine, much fresh air, plenty of food and more than the usual ration of sleep, all with a seasoning of Trollope.

21 November This is written before landing to say that we have reached our destination. I hope our news will break soon officially (as it has already on the Axis radio) . . . Meanwhile it is only possible to repeat that we are well and have had a very pleasant and interesting journey, and revel (as usual on these parties) in the sunshine and escape from Wooltonian (or should I now say 'Llewellinian'?) rigours. [Col. Llewellin had just been appointed Minister of Food.]

23 November There is to be no release of our news for several days. I can at least say that we are very comfortably ensconced in a pleasant villa and enjoying warmth and sunshine. A fountain splashes in a tessellated marble courtyard. The rooms open off it on two sides. A garden surrounds us, with barbed wire fences and an armed guard. Things have begun well and prospects are good.

26 November It has been decided to continue our silence for some days longer. All absent husbands are in despair to think what they can say to their spouses. Great joy among these last night when an accumulation of mail arrived from England. At a cheerful Thanksgiving Day dinner last night with one who has been our host before. An immense turkey and an Army band. All very *gemütlich*.

NOTE

Lord Moran wrote on 29 November (*Winston Churchill: The Struggle for Survival*, 141): 'The PM is appalled by his own impotence.' The PM himself wrote in his history (V, 358):

'Surveying the whole military scene, as we separated in an atmosphere of friendship and unity of purpose, I personally was well content... The political aspects were at once more remote and speculative.' Cadogan shared this optimism at the time. (*Diaries*, 586).

DECEMBER

On conclusion of the Teheran conference, the PM flew to Cairo, where there were further discussions with President Roosevelt, unproductive talks with the Turkish President and a visit by Field Marshal Smuts. The PM and the President visited the Sphinx. 'She told us nothing and maintained her inscrutable smile' (*The Second World War*, V, 371).

The PM flew on to Tunis, where he developed pneumonia and for several days was seriously ill. 'I did not at any time relinquish my part in the direction of affairs, and there was not the slightest delay in giving the decisions which were required from me' (V, 373) is rather an exaggeration. Mrs Churchill (with Jock Colville) flew out to join us.

In Cairo the President decided to nominate General Eisenhower as Commander in Chief for operation 'Overlord'. While the PM was at Carthage (Tunis) it was decided to appoint General Wilson as Supreme Commander for the Mediterranean, Alexander to command the whole campaign in Italy, Tedder to be Eisenhower's deputy in 'Overlord' and Montgomery to command the cross-Channel invasion force until Eisenhower could transfer his HQ to France and take over (Leese taking over the Eighth Army).

In Italy some advances were made by the Eighth and Fifth Armies, till wintry weather brought operations to a close. Plans were discussed for a landing at Anzio, south of Rome.

The American campaign in the Solomons was successfully completed.

After Christmas the PM went on to Marrakesh for convalescence.

DIARY

December

1 Teheran. Bright autumn sunshine continues. Lunch party at Legation. Drove with Hollis and Major Buckley up to hills and walked up gorge (near summer legation). Dinner with Holmans.

2 Left Teheran 9.30 a.m. Uneventful flight to Cairo, flying over Baghdad. Returned to Casey's villa.

3 Cairo. Lunched at Embassy – Killearn [Sir Miles Lampson, 1st Baron Killearn, Ambassador to Egypt], Eden, Cadogan, Norman Smith and Millard.

4 Cairo. Arrival of Turks (President Inönü, Numan etc). Dinner with Francis Keenlyside [PPS to Minister of Shipping and War Transport], Burrows and his fiancée at the Auberge des Pyramides.

5–7 Cairo.

8 Cairo. Dinner at Embassy. Next Bill Deakin [first British Liaison Officer with Tito in Yugoslavia].

9 Cairo. Shopping.

10 Cairo. To Embassy in morning, where PM saw King Peter of Yugoslavia and Regent of Iraq, and afterwards held press conference. Goodbye dinner at Embassy.

11 Left Cairo in PM's York about 1 a.m. Arrived Tunis for breakfast. Staying at 'The White House'. Lunch with Eisenhower's naval aide, Cdr Butcher.

12 At Carthage. PM in bed all day with temperature. Gen. Alexander here from Italy. He and Tedder to dinner. CIGS is staying with us. Consul General (Moneypenny) called. Visited ruins.

13 Carthage. After lunch drove with Tommy to Bizerta to meet Hollis (off *Penelope*) in Naval Office.

14 Carthage. X-ray and blood tests show that PM has pneumonia. Besides Moran we have Brig. Pulvertaft and two nurses. Gen. Wilson arrived from Cairo.

15 Carthage. Brig. Bedford (heart specialist) and Col. Buttle (M & B specialist) arrived. PM had 'auricular fibrillation' and pulse all over the place. First bulletin.

16 Col. Scalling arrived. Owing to this influx of doctors and their equipment I have moved my bedroom to guesthouse in Sidi Bou Sayid. PM distinctly better.

17 Alas, detained at Carthage and not home to celebrate our anniversary. PM's condition further improved. Mrs Churchill with Jock Colville and Miss Hamblin [Personal Secretary to Churchills] arrived.

18 Carthage. PM again better, though pulse irregular. Drove into

Tunis with Lt Garris, visiting German military cemetery, shops and bombed area of port. In evening Lady Tedder took me with Sarah to RAF mess in Tunis.

19 Carthage. PM's condition continues to improve. Sunny and warm again after several days of rain. In afternoon drove up to Sidi Bou and walked back with Moran.

20 Carthage. With help of Mme de Cevens bought Mergoum rug in Kasbah.

21 Carthage.

22 Drove to ruins of Dougga.

23 Carthage. PM out walking on terrace. Gen. Alexander arrived.

24 Carthage.

25 Morning Parade Service. Military Conference – PM, Ike, Jumbo. Alex, John Cunningham, Tedder, Gale [Lt-Gen. Sir Humfrey, Deputy Chief of Staff and Chief Administrative Officer under Eisenhower] etc. Festive lunch with toasts à la Russe. Called on Coldstream HQ. Fork supper.

26 Carthage. Brilliant sunshine. Afternoon walk by ruins on shore.

27 Left Tunis c.8 a.m. by PM's York. Flew through Atlas mountains, arriving Marrakesh c. 2 p.m. PM staying at Taylor villa. I have room at Mamounia hotel.

28 At Marrakesh. Afternoon walk in medina with Jock. Lord Beaverbrook arrived with young Max.

29 Marrakesh. Bright sun. Lunch out of doors. Drive up into hills beyond Asni. Hollis has been promoted Major-General.

30 Marrakesh. Picnic near Souk el Tnine. Bright sun.

31 Marrakesh. Gen. Montgomery arrived with his ADC, Chavasse. Eisenhower also at dinner. 'Auld lang syne' round a bowl of punch.

LETTERS

2 *December*   Cairo. I am writing in the air on the way back from Teheran (not alas on a magic carpet, the price of magic carpets being prohibitive).

The veil will have been lifted a little today with the announcement of the conversations with Chiang Kai-shek, so I can at last give some account of our travels.

The sea voyage was comparatively uneventful. It was very pleasant to find ourselves among our old friends in the familiar ship and, as always, the Navy looked after us marvellously. As we got south and continued along the Mediterranean the weather rapidly improved and we had several days of glorious sunshine. Various interesting landmarks on the way – Tangiers, Cape Bon, Pantelleria. We stopped at Gib, but it was at night and we did not go ashore. We spent two days in Malta, staying with the Governor (Lord Gort) in his country palace at San Anton, an uncomfortable big place with most lovely gardens – big bougain-villaeas and other flowers even in November. Facilities for carrying on our work were rather poor and there was a frightful flap one day when it appeared that, owing to leakage about our rendezvous, the conference might have to be in Malta. It would have meant housing the American staff in a place with a single tap and a single lavatory, and a great sigh of relief went up when the decision came to proceed on our journey.

The town of Valletta is a sad sight, though the place has been thoroughly tidied up and they have had no raids since the early summer; but the people look none the worse for their ordeal and the children in particular struck us as remarkably plump and healthy – attractive kids, with the most engaging smiles. The PM visited the Naval Dockyard, where he received a tumultuous welcome from hundreds – or thousands – of Maltese. We drove from there up to the Governor's (town) palace, where Winston appeared like Mussolini on the balcony and beamed upon a large cheering crowd in the square below.

We left our ship at Alex and flew to our conference place, the whereabouts of which is still supposed to be confidential. There isn't much to tell about the conference beyond what will have appeared in today's papers. I have been shut up most of the time in our closely guarded quarters and have had no opportunity for shopping or sight-seeing – beyond a visit to the Sphinx with the PM and the President, 'the two most talkative people in the world meeting the most silent', as Winston is said to have remarked. I never saw the Generalissimo or the Missima except for a glimpse when they came to dinner, there being no room for the staff that night at the dinner table.

We flew up to Teheran in perfect weather in five and a half

hours, passing the Dead Sea and the Tigris and Euphrates and over ranges of fairly high and exceedingly rocky mountains. You couldn't imagine more desolate, barren looking country. Teheran itself is in a beautiful situation, surrounded by mountains, several snow-capped and one giant of almost Himalayan height (18 or 19,000 ft, I think). The secret was well out of the bag and we drove past considerable crowds on the way to the Legation. We were all put up in the Minister's house or other houses in the compound, a frightful invasion, particularly for the Minister (Sir Reader Bullard), who was only too obviously miserable. (He is one of Smith of Balliol's sons-in-law.) Poor man: he had a hard time. He kept asking people to meals to meet the PM and the PM regularly cried off at the last moment and fed outside. We had the most lovely bracing weather – brilliant sunshine but a cold nip in the air and we were glad of the piled up coal fires in our rooms at night.

The President and Stalin stayed in the Soviet Embassy, in a large compound almost next door to ours, and most of the conference meetings were there. I can't add anything about these to what you will read in the communiqué. I only went into the Russian compound once, for the presentation of the Stalingrad sword, which had lived in my bedroom and attracted many callers to admire it. The affair was indoors and not as impressively arranged as it might have been (Voroshilov dropped the sword); but I can leave that story to the press account. The highlight of the conference was the dinner party given by the PM in our Legation on his birthday. We sat down over thirty, including Stalin, Molotov, Voroshilov, Roosevelt, Harry Hopkins, Eden, Cadogan, Winant and the American and British Chiefs of Staff. At a very early stage in the meal the PM gave the toast of the King, President Roosevelt and President Kalinin, and after that toast followed toast in the Russian manner, the PM, Stalin and Roosevelt making frequent speeches with contributions from most of the others I have mentioned. There could not have been greater cordiality and Uncle Joe enjoyed himself as much as anybody. When the PM talked about the different degrees of redness in various countries and said that even in England our complexions were becoming quite pink, Stalin interjected, 'That is the colour of good health.' Everyone felt that it had been a most memorable occasion – among my own experiences, on the level of that Service on the deck of the *Prince of Wales*, and equally significant. I think it will be judged a momentous conference and well worth the journeys involved.

(In an earlier letter, I 'wondered if the world will realise what a momentous conference this has been; not so much for the agreement on military plans for the immediate future as for what it has achieved in welding together the three Great Powers.')

4 December   Cairo. There have been no startling events since we got back and little to record outside the official round apart from lunch at the Embassy and lunch at the Gezira club today with an old Malayan friend. It is a very pleasant time of the year in Cairo. I try to get a few minutes free in the morning to sunbathe on the roof.

8 December   Cairo. I daresay Mrs Warden [code name for Mrs Churchill] has told you that she has been promised return before Christmas. That at least seems certain, barring unexpected developments; but I must admit that hopes of celebrating our anniversary with you are beginning to fade, though not quite gone.

By now most of our secrets are published and you will have seen that after the Chinese and Russians came the turn of the Turks. Now even the Americans have gone and we are left with the Yugoslavs, the Greeks and the like. I have seen most of this only from the wings and have not been having a particularly exciting time. We are shut up in our defended villa, rather a long way from Cairo, and I have been very little outside except to one or two meals. It is however quite a pleasant place and the daily sunshine is a great joy. Cairo itself is not very attractive – a sprawling, untidy town, with a great deal of dirt and squalor. There are far too many generals and the war seems rather remote from them; but I believe it was so even when the enemy was at the gates.

10 December   Cairo. We are leaving Cairo this evening; but alas not direct for England, home and beauty. I overdid the sunbathing and have not felt very bright these last two or three days as a result. This isn't a healthy place in spite of the deceptively sparkling sunshine; but I have escaped 'Gippy tummy', which has been no respecter of persons and smites the highest with the lowest. I tried to do a little shopping one day but had to do it in a rush and was singularly unsuccessful, so please don't expect me to return with rich treasures of the Orient.

12 December   Tunis. Here we are, some 1500 miles nearer home, and enjoying a different variety of Mediterranean sunshine. We flew overnight from Cairo, leaving after a farewell party at the Embassy, and arrived here in time for breakfast. [Our journey had been complicated by arrival at the wrong airport, and I well remember the pathetic sight of the PM, already exhausted by the punishing schedule of the last few days, sitting on his official boxes for about an hour in a bitterly cold wind until the journey to General Eisenhower's 'White House' near Carthage could be completed. Later I was not surprised to learn that he was running a temperature.]

I share a bedroom with Moran, with a camp bed of my own, and a bathroom with the CIGS, and, though arrangements generally are a little sketchy, we are really very well looked after. My master is not in very good health and the prospect therefore is that we shall be detained here for a day or two; but if the pleasant sunshine of this morning continues the delay will be easier to bear. There is a distinct possibility that it may result in reducing excursions and actually speeding the return home. We are more or less on the site of Carthage – I walked over the neglected ruins of the theatre yesterday – on the seaside, looking over the blue waters of the Bay of Tunis to the Cape Bon peninsula.

13 December   My master is still unwell and future movements remain uncertain. Meanwhile we remain like Marius among the ruins of Carthage; some of which I visited yesterday. The French have neglected them scandalously. Mosaic pavements are completely exposed and unprotected and naturally in process of disintegration and everywhere bits of broken columns and half-covered brickwork lie about in confusion as if the Vandals had just gone.

16 December   Here's a how d'you do, and for obvious reasons I must be careful what I say. First, the illness is serious. Secondly, the doctors' latest indications are that probably we shall be here (the place from which I last wrote) a fortnight and possibly (for convalescence) as much as four weeks. I need not say how sickening it is to be away from you so long and miss not only our private anniversary but also our first Christmas in our own home. Besides, each day is selfishly precious for me as this is the last section of the period when I shall have you entirely to myself and also I don't want to leave you alone at such a time. Clearly I could not leave my post here at the moment and all private inconvenience has to be accepted; but if all goes well perhaps in ten days or so (when convalescence begins) I might fly home and send out John Peck or Jock Colville in exchange. What do you think? Then there is another worry. Now that it comes to the point, do you think that it is wise to have your baby in London, where the intermittent blitz evidently still continues? I don't know what to think. Of course I want to have you in London, but is that merely selfish?

No special news. The treatment and condition of the patient is the one and only interest and I had better keep off that. We have quite an assembly of medical talent and everything possible is being done for him.

18 December   North Africa. I ought to have more time now for my own letters, but somehow the day seems to be as crowded as ever, and I am again caught with a bag closing and several distractions competing for attention. It is clear that I can't leave my post till W is out of the wood, which he certainly is not yet. Jock Colville (who has now returned to No. 10 from the RAF) flew out with Mrs C yesterday and I don't see why he should not hold the fort with Francis once the process of convalescence begins, especially as we hope to have Brig. Hollis [General Ismay's No. 2] in the party, so I hope to return in a week or so.

19 December   We have had an anxious time and things would have been easier if the illness had happened at home. Fortunately there is a galaxy of medical talent in the Middle East and Lord Moran assures me that he could not ask for a better team to look after him if he were ill and in London. We are guests of the Americans here and are being treated with their usual hospitality. The PM is in a pleasant villa by the sea, where I spend the day. At night I go up to a very attractive house in an Arab village on top of a neighbouring hill. It is built in Arab style, with courtyards, tiled walls, trellis windows and so on, most picturesque.

22 December   North Africa. Our courier who takes this was delayed several days on his outward journey by foul weather in

England and may arrive rather late for the role of Father Christmas . . . A final *terminus ante quem* seems to be the opening of Parliament on 18 January, but if all goes well and there is no setback I shall try to seize the first opportunity to escape once the final stage of convalescence begins . . . This is certainly not a bad prison. I write by the terrace window, looking out on a sea of deepest blue, with sharp-cut hills across the bay and blue sky above. A few sprays of bougainvillaea peeping over a wall add a touch of more exotic colour . . .

Christmas Day. You mention the Honours List. That was one of my headaches because it had to be got through the PM by a certain date and he wasn't fit to be troubled by such things. However it was managed in the end and is not too bad. Tony Bevir did all the spade work. The PM is remarkably well and has begun doing a good deal of work in the last two or three days. The doctors are quite unable to control him and cigars etc. have now returned. I was amazed to find him dictating their bulletin. As Lord Moran said, they have the benefit of an excellent consultant – the PM himself.

This has been a business as usual day, with a large conference of generals etc.; but I got away in the morning for an open-air parade Service of the troops who are guarding us. At the Early Service, held indoors in a sort of shed, everyone had been struck by the dramatic ending of the proceedings when the Cathedral bells (on a hill top nearby) broke into a wild peal and at the same time a dove flew in at a window and alighted in front of the altar. The troops took it as an omen of peace.

We have just had a soporific lunch of turkey and plum pudding. The PM was up for it and in good form, proposing a whole series of toasts. General Jumbo Wilson was there, also Air Marshal Tedder, Admiral John Cunningham, General Alexander and others . . . No time for more. Now for next Christmas.

26 December   North Africa . . . (On Christmas Day) the house was filled with generals, admirals and air marshals and their hangers-on for a big military powwow. Some of them stayed on for a festive lunch of turkey and plum pudding, to which the PM came for the first time since his illness. In the evening we had a bigger party for a fork supper, to which several officers of the guard and others outside were invited.

28 December   In North Africa. Tomorrow's newspapers will publish a message from the Prime Minister which will show you that we have moved our camp; but I mustn't say where the tents are pitched beyond telling you that it is a place where we have been before. We came by air and at one time had to fly at 12,000 feet, which was rather a worry to the doctors, but Winston took oxygen and was none the worse. The days are short here and it is apt to be cold out of the sun; but in general the scene is gayer than in England and the heavily laden orange trees look almost too good to be true. We have a particularly good French chef, who, though temperamental (last night he flung two pies on the floor and one at an American army cook), produces the most marvellous meals. Our first nearly finished us – delicious ham (which we all guzzled, imagining it to be the main course), followed by steak, followed by chicken salad. Today he restrained his exuberance, but even so there is no risk of growing thin.

   Jock and I went for a stroll yesterday through some 'native' streets – scarcely a European and everything as it must have been in any such town for the last two or three thousand years. It is endlessly picturesque.

1944

JANUARY

The Prime Minister continued his convalescence at Marrakesh until the middle of the month. He held a conference on Anzio plans attended by Lord Beaverbrook and the British and American generals and Naval officers concerned. He had talks with President Beneš, General de Gaulle ('now that the General speaks English so well he understands my French perfectly') and Brigadier Fitzroy Maclean [commander of the British Military Mission to the Yugoslav partisans]. Returning by Gibraltar, he arrived back in England on the 17th.

There was bitter fighting on the Cassino front. The Anzio landing took place.

The Russians reached the 1939 Polish frontier.

General Alan Brooke was promoted Field Marshal. General Eisenhower arranged to establish his HQ at Bushey Park.

DIARY

January

1   At Marrakesh. Picnic near Amismiz. Visited cooperative olive oil factory.
2   Marrakesh. Visited Medina with Lord Beaverbrook.
3   Marrakesh. Picnic and magnificent drive by Tadment holiday camp.
4   Marrakesh. Afternoon walk with Moran. Beneš to lunch and dinner. Smutny to dinner.
5   Marrakesh. Picnic (joined this time by Consul Nairn with his wife and daughter Judy). Beneš and Smutny again to dinner.
6   Marrakesh. Glaoui Pasha to tea (walks barefoot through the

streets of London). Dinner with Nairns. Also there Gen. Astier La Vallette, his wife and his brother, Capt. La Vallette.

7   Marrakesh. Conference of PM with Generals Jumbo Wilson, Alexander, Bedell Smith, Timberlake, Adl John Cunningham, Capt. Power etc.

8   Marrakesh.

9   Marrakesh. Picnic by river.

10 Marrakesh. Mr Duff Cooper [British Representative with Free French] and Lady Diana arrived.

11 Marrakesh. After dinner went to party at Gen. de Villate's to meet the Resident General and see Berber dances etc. Met Gen. de Gaulle's second secretary, Cmdr de Courcelles.

12 Marrakesh. Gen. de Gaulle to lunch (with Palewski and Capt. Burin des Roziers). Walk with Boggis Rolfe.

13 Marrakesh. Review by Gen. de Gaulle, PM also taking salute. Picnic at Pont Naturel. Goodbye cocktail party at villa with Arab (?) and Berber dancers.

14 Left Marrakesh at quarter to one. Arrived Gibraltar about two hours later, flying over Casablanca. While PM had conference with Jumbo and John Cunningham at The Convent (residence of the Governor), Mrs C, Sarah, Jock and I were taken on a tour of the Rock and tunnels. After dinner (next Miles Clifford and Capt. Redshaw) went aboard HMS *King George V* – Captain Halsey, Commander Wellby.

15 Sailed I think *c.* 3 a.m. At sea all day. Sunny and mild, but considerable swell. Dinner party in Ward-room.

16 At sea. Church Service in morning. New Russian National Anthem broadcast.

17 Arrived Plymouth shortly before midnight. Peck waiting, with PM's train.

18 Arrived at Paddington 10 a.m. PM in House to answer his questions. To Pelham Place, where I found Rosalind looking extremely fit.

19 A great joy to be home again. R and I at Leslie Rowan's wedding at Holy Trinity, Brompton.

21 There being signs of David's arrival I stayed at home in the morning and did various chores with R. In afternoon took her to Westminster Hospital. Returned after dinner. Blitz. David Ross Martin born.

22 Day off. Visited R and D in hospital twice: both very well. At 'Carnet de Bal'.

23 Day off. Visits to hospital. At Westminster Abbey.

24 Lady Ross to lunch, after which I took her to see R. R not so well later.

25 R had four ups and downs of temperature.

26 R had temperature of 104 in the morning. Given 'M and B'. X-ray taken, later found to be negative for pneumonia.

27 Searle [the surgeon] says R has signs of pyelitis. She is still not well, but David makes steady progress.

28 R found to have streptococcal infection. Isolated in her present room. Called on her.

29 Rosalind much better now. David (6 lb 4 oz at birth) now weighs 6.8. Noisy blitz at night.

30 Communion at St Columba's. Mild sunny morning. After-noon at hospital seeing Rosalind.

LETTERS

4 January   In Africa (*we are bidden not to say whether N, E, S or W*). We had Montgomery here on New Year's Eve on his way back to England to take up his new command. He is an impressive person, with of course a sense of his own ability (and apparently ready to receive flattery), austere and a bit of a martinet. This he illustrated in his manner towards his very nice young ADC, a Chavasse, son of the Bishop of Rochester formerly of St Aldate's, with whom I was able to talk about the Rosses of Oxford. An *obiter dictum* was 'My chaplains are more useful to me than my artillery'. As he wanted to go to bed early we celebrated the arrival of the new year an hour ahead of the clock, all linking hands and singing 'Auld Lang Syne' round a bowl of steaming punch, after which we drank to Monty and Eisenhower (who was also there) and to the PM.

On New Year's Day we had lunch out of doors, wearing sun spectacles and almost preferring the shade of a tree. It is the most luscious sun, with a bright blue sky and everything bright and gay – not least the oranges, looking absurdly artificial, on trees lining the roads . . . We have had several picnic lunches, each time in a most lovely place, generally by running water, with a view of the snowy mountains beyond us. The best of all was in a place of indescribable beauty, by a river bank, looking up the valley, a village perched on the hills on each side, and all about us cultivated fields and olive groves.

6 January ... I can't pretend there is much work to do here and we don't keep abnormally late hours. Every other day or so we go for a picnic lunch and every day the sun pours down on us. Even if we lunch at the villa it is out of doors ... We have had Beneš here on his way back from Russia, an interesting talker on both past and present. Various other visitors are in prospect and meanwhile the Beaver [Lord Beaverbrook] has become an established part of the household. I went shopping with him one day in the native market and he insisted on buying you a long garment, complete with belt, buckle and shoes. I'm not sure what you can do with it – perhaps a piece of evening négligé for the house ... Coldish for a change this morning, but I have just revived life with a glass of butter rum.

13 January I am writing this in the sunshine on the roof, trying to thaw after a very cold hour (for the mornings until the sun is up are bitterly cold), watching a review by General de Gaulle. The PM in RAF uniform stood by him at the saluting base and they both got a very warm welcome, though the 'Vive de Gaulle' claque was too obviously organised. The French coloured troops made a picturesque display, particularly the mounted Spahis. The Sultan's brother sat beside us with expressionless face ... I am able to rave about Singapore to a fellow enthusiast here as we have Duff Cooper staying at the hotel with Lady Diana and she says her heart is there.

17 January At sea. The enclosed letter written at Christmas time was never finished. The day after it was begun we flew over the Atlas mountains to Marrakesh in Morocco, where we stayed in the same most lovely villa where we spent a night last year after the Casablanca conference. It is 1500 feet up, with fine bracing air and brilliant sunshine almost every day, though cold at night ... I can't tell you the beauty of the landscape or the brightness of the colours in that sparkling sunshine. The newspapers will no doubt tell you of our various visitors. The native city at Marrakesh – we lived outside in the modern French quarter – is the most fascinating place – endless narrow streets of little shops, all of the same kind together, very little changed from what it must have looked at any time in the last five hundred years.

Interruption. I have just been called away to the gun-room, where the midshipmen have been giving a party. We hope to land this evening at Plymouth, where we arrived from Bermuda two years ago to the day. This time I have more to come home to.

23 January You can imagine my joy and excitement . . . Rosalind's date was January 29 and I did not really expect anything to happen for some days after that, so you could have knocked me down with a feather when she told me at breakfast time on the 21st that she had indications that morning that the baby was about to arrive . . . So we rang up the sister at Westminster Hospital, who advised us to come in after lunch. I took the day off and we had a very happy morning together doing various chores, scrubbing the cot etc. After lunch we drove along to the hospital in a taxi and I saw her comfortably installed in her bed . . . I returned to the hospital about eight o'clock. I was allowed to go and sit with R . . . The air raid began and was pretty noisy, with guns firing near. It was the worst for many months, but R did not worry, having other things to think about . . . The pain soon became more than she could bear and she was taken along to the labour room, while the matron took me downstairs to a large sitting-room. There I spent what seemed a long time with the raid banging away outside, talking for a few minutes to the matron and then to the secretary of the hospital – both of whom had had letters from me at different times offering them Honours, which made a good introduction. Searle, the surgeon, looked in for a few minutes to report that all was going well. Eventually, after eleven, he came back to report that David had arrived and R was quite well . . . At the last stage R was under an anaesthetic. When she came to, her first remark was 'My poor husband', apparently pitying my anxiety, whereat Searle, who is a New Zealander, asked 'Are you Scotch?', because only a Scottish wife would care for her husband in that way. I think the baby was born at 10.30, so R and I didn't have too long to wait . . . I must say I think he looks an excellent baby, with much more individuality in his face than I expected. When she sleeps he is taken out to a little room with a lot of other babies: if there is a raid they are wheeled into the corridor. Many thanks for your telegram. Among others we had, 'Many many congratulations from Winston and Clementine Churchill'.

FEBRUARY

The situation at Anzio was disappointing: the landing could not be consolidated. 'I had hoped we were hurling a wild cat ashore, but all we had got was a stranded whale.' But repeated German attacks were repelled and by 1 March Kesselring accepted his failure.

Attacks failed at Cassino, where the monastery was bombed.

The Russians crossed the Estonian frontier; 100,000 Germans were encircled west of the middle Dnieper.

Successful American attacks were made on the Marshall Group and a US task force attacked Truk in the Carolines.

There were many air raids on London and a fair amount of damage was done round Whitehall. On the 23rd the US Air Force began a week of concentrated attacks, assisted by long-range fighters – 'a turning point in the War against Germany' (*The Second World War*, V, 462).

DIARY

February

1 Rosalind not so well again.
2 Rosalind (still in Westminster Hospital) ill.
3 R's illness still obstinate.
4 Rosalind having a different treatment, a little better.
5 Rosalind much better.
6 Rosalind again better.
7 Lunch with Professor Glaser (Polish Minister to Allied Governments).
8 Rosalind now much more normal: injections stopped.
9 R up for the first time, for a few minutes.
10 Dinner (with Jack Churchill) at the Rowans' flat.
11 Francis Brown left on return to Army.
12 Day off. Short walk in park. Visited R in hospital.
13 Day off. A sore throat. A little gardening. Visits to R. One of the noisy but fairly harmless evening raids we have been having lately.
14 Murphy, editor of *Fortune*, dined in Mess.
16 Nurse arrived. Fetched Rosalind and David home to Pelham Place.

18 To Chequers in afternoon.
19 At Chequers. Very cold. Gen. [Robert, Chief of Combined Operations] and Mrs Laycock arrived for dinner and to stay. Adl Cooke and Gen. Hull (US) to lunch. Gen. Doolittle [Commander, US North-west African Strategic Air Force] to dinner.
20 Chequers. Gen. Montgomery to lunch with ADCs (Henderson and Chavasse). PM working on speech.
21 Returned to London and saw damage at No. 10 from last night's raid. Almost all windows broken. Up late on speech.
22 Speech by PM in House.
24 We have been having a succession of bad blitzes for the last five or six days and this afternoon I decided to evacuate Rosalind and David.
25 Took day off, packing at Pelham Place and in afternoon drove with R and D and Miss Cressey (the nurse) to Oxford, where R will stay at Oriel.
26 At Oxford. Very cold.
27 Oxford.
28 Returned to London, leaving Rosalind and David at Oriel. In afternoon visited Pelham Place, now shut up, Mrs Ingram having gone off.
29 I am now living at the Annexe and will no doubt visit Pelham Place from time to time in the afternoon. Lunch with Shertok.

LETTERS

3 *February* The last few days have been rather worrying. After getting back almost to normal for a day or two and being taken off her M & B, Rosalind has had rather a relapse and, though her temperature has been lower than last week, she has had several wretched days. A slightly different form of the drug and it may be this which has made her terribly depressed. She burst into tears when I called on Tuesday and is quite unlike her usual self. It is tantalising for her not to be able to handle the baby freely (she always has to wear a mask) and unpleasant to be treated as a victim of the plague, though the hospital staff have all been very kind. Fortunately David has made excellent progress. He only showed a gain of half an ounce at the last weighing, but he can

afford to go slow after reaching ½ lb above his birth weight (i.e. reaching 6 lb 12 oz) in the first ten days. I feel helpless and the doctors too are baffled by the slow progress; particularly as she was so well when she went into hospital. Today they propose to try one or two transfusions and if these fail will call in further advice. They tell me there is no cause for anxiety, but how can one not be anxious? ... I am on duty at the office this weekend, so will have plenty of opportunity to visit the hospital, which is only about ten minutes walk away. Alas there appears to be no immediate prospect of return to Pelham Place, though the nurse's suitcase has already arrived. She is coming for a month.

13 February   Great joy – Rosalind and David are coming home on Wednesday. It is disappointing not to have them here when this is my weekend off and next weekend I shall be at Chequers; but at least it is something to have a definite date to look forward to. Christopher Eastwood came to lunch yesterday, which was followed by a walk in the Park. He is expecting his fourth child next month. Why all this talk about 'the empty cradle'? Any cradles I know of seem to be full ... David saves us £25 of Income Tax this year.

17 February   The family is now at last established at Pelham Place. I took Wednesday morning off to help in the arrangements. The nurse, Miss Cressey, arrived shortly after breakfast and, after giving her an hour or so to get things ready, I set off with her to the hospital and fetched R and D home in a taxi.

27 February   We are wondering how much longer it is reasonable to maintain our home here if these loud nightly blitzes are to continue; but it will be hateful to have to separate. When the guns begin David is taken downstairs in his cot and is put under one of the tables in the kitchen against a wall, with another table turned on its side in front. Fortunately the noise has not, so far, wakened him. There we sit by the light of a candle till the all clear.

MARCH

The weather brought a deadlock in Italy. There was fierce fighting in an unsuccessful attempt to take Cassino monastery.

Chindits were flown into north Burma. General Wingate was killed.

The Russians advanced in the Ukraine and reached the frontier of

Romania. The German Sixth Army was routed in the battle of the Dnieper bend.

There was continued debate on the role of British and US bombers in the pre-Overlord period and a decision made in favour of attacks on communications in France as a priority.

The PM made a world broadcast, including extensive references to the Government's social measures and plans. After the Government defeat on an amendment of the Education Bill requiring equal pay for men and women, the PM made this an issue of confidence, when the Government won by 425 to 23.

The plan for a meeting with the President in Bermuda was abandoned.

DIARY

March

1   Afternoon Party at Buckingham Palace.
2   The last few days have been fine and bright, with ice over part of the lake. President [spoke] on transfer of Italian ships to Russia.
4   In afternoon dug for an hour in the garden.
10   To Oxford in afternoon, taking pram.
11   At Oxford. David now occasionally gives a half-smile.
12   Oxford.
13   Returned to No. 10.
14   King and War Cabinet dined at No. 10 and we all went into the shelter during raid.
15   A little digging at Pelham Place in afternoon.
16   Lunch with Lord and Lady Marchwood.
17   Hoppy [Sir R. Nind Hopkins] dined with PM to talk about 1939/44 Star etc.
18   To Chequers in evening.
19   Chequers. Sir Victor Mallet [Foreign Service] and Oliver Stanley to lunch. Returned to London at midnight.
23   Lunch with Dr Weizmann.
24   To Oxford in afternoon. David can now manage a sort of laugh accompanied by various odd sounds.
25   At Oriel. Lady Ross very ill. R and I dined with Sir William and Lady Beveridge at Univ. Lord David Cecil among others there.
26   Oxford.

27 Returned to London.
28 In afternoon dug at Pelham Place. Government defeat on Education Bill, followed by evening Cabinet.
29 More digging.
31 To Oxford in afternoon.

LETTERS

2 March There have been two raids this week so far – one (after dinner on Tuesday) was very light, but last night's (*c.* 3 a.m.) is said to have been of the noisier variety, though in my shelter I slept peacefully and heard nothing. It is such a relief to have Rosalind and David out of all this. I have been along to Pelham Place each afternoon for a few minutes. It is most painful to see the empty nursery and all else like some abandoned Pompeii. Fortunately the days are passing quickly: life at the office is very tolerable and the PM certainly has a more assiduous PS. Yesterday I was at the Afternoon Party at Buckingham Palace. It lost its point without Rosalind but I quite enjoyed it all the same – about two hundred people in a long narrow gallery, with tea buffet down one side. The King and Queen and the two Princesses are most charming, such very pretty colour; but I'm afraid I can't tell you what they had on. I was surprised to find how many people I knew, but the most surprising thing was when (surely by mistake), the Lord Chamberlain shouted out the name of the middle-aged woman who came in just behind me as 'Mrs Martin'.

5 March The worst of living at the office all the time is that one also tends to work all the time – morning, noon and night – which is a good thing from one point of view but tends to make Jack a dull boy. There has been little inducement to go out these last few days, for, though sunny, it has been piercingly cold, with a sheet of ice over part of the lake. Yesterday afternoon I spent an hour digging at Pelham Place. This was begun as a preparation for a lawn, but I am rather at a loss as to how to proceed next. The old man who used to do a little work occasionally in the garden has now collapsed and in any case there is the difficulty of letting anyone into the garden with the house shut. The first blush is beginning to appear on the almond tree.

I have been looking up the Christening Service in the Book of

Common Order of the Church of Scotland – a much more real service than that in the Prayer Book. The infant is 'received into the membership of the Holy Catholic Church, and is engaged to confess the faith of Christ crucified, and be His faithful soldier and servant unto his life's end'.

14 March   The King dined at No. 10 with Ministers. All had to go down to the air-raid shelter when the Jim Crow warning went, with sundry of the domestic staff in their night attire, and spent a rather amusing half hour or so. I was posted at the telephone getting the latest news every few minutes. At one point I was told that there had been an enemy aircraft over Oxford, whereupon the PM informed the King of my special reason for concern.

19 March   Chequers. Still little sign of spring here apart from some primroses in the garden, but it is at last warmer and I was too hot last night in the warm pyjamas bought for protection against the usual rigours of Chequers. Pelham Place looks sad with no one to admire the almond blossom and the afternoon sunshine in the nursery. All the same, having inspected the damage done in Tuesday's raid, I am relieved to have my family in a safer place. The recent bombs are of a kind with a much greater blast effect and seem to destroy windows over a considerable area. The district round Graham Terrace looks pretty battered.

Have just been having my clothes ration book explained to me. Not a single coupon has been used.

APRIL

The Cabinet was anxious about civilian casualties arising from the bombing of French railway centres in the plan to create a 'railway desert' round the German troops in Normandy. Eisenhower was convinced that the bombing would increase the chances of success in the critical battle and believed that the estimates of casualties were exaggerated. While discussions continued, bombing began on a limited scale.

There was a crisis in the Greek Cabinet in Egypt and mutinies in the Greek Army and Navy. Vigorous action by British forces led to the surrender of the Greek brigade and the mutinous ships. The King of Greece flew to Cairo and announced the formation of a representative government. Venizelos became Prime Minister, but was replaced by Papandreou.

In Burma Kohima was successfully defended against the Japanese and the garrison relieved.

The Russians reached the borders of Czechoslovakia. Odessa was recaptured.

The PM was in charge of the Foreign Office for a week or two while Eden took holiday.

DIARY

April

1–8 At Oriel.

9 Easter. At Oriel. Communion Service in Lady Ross's room. Christening of David Ross Martin at St Columba's.

10 Returned to London. Spent an hour or two in the garden at Pelham Place before returning to No. 10.

14 To Chequers in afternoon.

15 Chequers. Stettinius to lunch – also Mr Winant, Mr Pratt, Dr Bowman (of Johns Hopkins) and Mr and Mrs Dick Law.

16 Chequers. M. Jean Marin to lunch.

17 Returned to London.

19 At Lord Mayor's Easter Luncheon for Diplomatic Corps at Mansion House.

21 To Oxford in afternoon.

22 Oxford. Shopping with R. We spent an hour or so in Christ Church garden with David.

23 Oxford. a.m. – walk with R through parks and along Cherwell. p.m. – basking on roof. Dined in Hall with Provost.

24 Returned to London.

25 Tea with Hoppy. Gardening at Pelham Place. PM has nominated me as one of Courtauld Thomson trustees for Dorneywood.

26 Lunch alone with Mrs C. At Stettinius's cocktail party. Shane Leslie dined in mess.

28 At Government luncheon in honour of Indian representatives at War Cabinet – Maharaja of Kashmir and Sir Firoz Khan Noon.

29 Gardening for an hour or so in afternoon.

30 Lunch with Rowans to meet Turnbull, Mackenzie King's PS.

LETTERS

9 April Oxford. I have had such a happy week here . . . [At David's Christening . . .] When the Minister said he was to be a faithful soldier of Christ he waved his arm as if brandishing a sword. [In connection with the Communion Service in Lady Ross's bedroom . . .] The Provost produced a box which had been handed to him by his predecessor and was said to contain a small set of Communion cups etc. to be used on such occasions. Search failing to discover a key, it was taken to a shop to be sawn open, when among other objects it was found to contain a calling card with a Corrennie Gardens, Edinburgh, address [where my mother lived] and an account to George MacLeod [Lord MacLeod of Fiunary] for physical training lessons in Glasgow.

16 April Chequers. The benefits of my holiday are quickly undone by such nights as that of Friday/Saturday, when we got to bed at 3.30 a.m. Protests by Mrs C improved this to 1.30 a.m. last night. We had Stettinius, Winant and two other Americans to lunch yesterday. Conversation lasted so long that we did not rise from the dining room table until after 4.30, when it was already tea time.

27 April Fortunately Anthony Eden has resumed charge of the FO, but the PM is still overwhelmed with work and on top of it all we shall have for a week or more the conference of Dominion Prime Ministers. I had lunch alone with Mrs C yesterday – a very pleasant meal, starting with some delicious fat asparagus.

MAY

The PM and Cabinet continued to be unhappy about French casualties in the bombing of the railways; but accepted the President's view that no restrictions should be placed on military action by responsible commanders that in their view might militate against the success of Overlord or cause additional loss of lives to the invasion forces.

A Greek administration was set up in Cairo in which all groups could be represented under the premiership of Papandreou, while in Greece a united military organisation would continue to struggle against the Germans. Thus 'a dangerous episode came to a satisfactory conclusion' (*The Second World War*, V, 488).

In Italy an Allied offensive was launched. Cassino was taken and by the 24th Alexander could report that the Adolf Hitler Line had been smashed in front of the Eighth Army. There was a break-out from Anzio beachhead.

The Red Army captured Sebastopol and completed the liberation of the Crimea.

(This month there are various references in the memoirs of Brooke, Eden and Eisenhower to the PM's exhaustion.)

DIARY

May

1 Opening of Conference of Dominion Prime Ministers.

5 To Oxford in late afternoon.

6, 7 At Oxford. David weighs just over 14 lb.

8 Mrs Ingram is at Pelham Place this week, cleaning and waging war with moths.

9 Government dinner at No. 10 for Dominion Prime Ministers. Speeches by PM, Mackenzie King, Curtin, Fraser [New Zealand], Smuts, Firoz Khan Noon and Huggins [Southern Rhodesia].

10 At Guildhall for conferment of freedom on Curtin and Fraser. Lunch afterwards at Mansion House.

11 Government cocktail party for Dominion delegates. Dinner with Weizmanns. Offensive in Italy began.

12 Left with PM in his train for Lydd (Kent), with Mackenzie King, Smuts, Huggins and Col. Carver. Saw 'wasp' and various Army demonstrations, ending at Hastings. Eisenhower and Fraser joined for dinner at Ascot 'in fraternal association'. [The reference is to sheets of paper signed by the diners, to which the PM appended the words 'in fraternal association'. See illustration page 21.]

13 Left train at Cosham and visited Navy at Spithead and in Southampton Water. Arrived at Chequers for tea. Curtin, Sinclairs and Brendan staying for weekend.

14 At Chequers.

15 Returned to London, visiting Dorneywood on the way, where Courtauld-Thompson showed me round. Afternoon Party at Buckingham Palace. Conversation with Queen.

16 Up late, getting to bed at 4 a.m.

17   Beaver – 'Honours should be put on sale at Christie's'.
19   To Oxford in afternoon.
20, 21   At Oxford. Dined with President at Corpus.
22   Returned to London.
24   PM's speech in Foreign Affairs debate.
26   To Chequers in afternoon.
27   Curtin and Averell and Kathleen Harriman to stay the night.
28   Chequers. Gen. Donovan and Fitzroy Maclean to lunch. Gen. Pownall [C in C Persia-Iraq, 1943] and Moiseiwitsches [celebrated pianist and his wife] to dinner.
29   Chequers. Drove over to Oxford with Cherwell in afternoon and spent an hour or so at Oriel. Great heat.
30   Returned to London.

LETTERS

7 *May*   Oriel. It has been a most wearing week, but I managed to get the Honours List finished in time to get away on Friday evening. I don't think I could have endured another day.

14 *May*   Chequers. We arrived yesterday after a day's expedition in the train, visiting the Army in Kent and Sussex and in a launch seeing something of the Navy. Smuts, Mackenzie King and Huggins [of Southern Rhodesia] came with us all the way and Fraser (who had flown down from Edinburgh after receiving the freedom of the city) joined the party on Friday evening. It was a particularly successful trip. The country was looking its best, the men everywhere seemed the picture of health and tremendously keen and we saw a great many interesting things. Now we have Curtin of Australia here for the weekend.

14 *May*   We had a particularly interesting expedition in the PM's train, partly the Army and partly the Navy. Smuts, Mackenzie King and Huggins came all the way and Fraser [described in another letter as 'a pet . . . speaks like a Highland minister'] joined them on Friday evening, when I dined with them and Eisenhower. A long, interesting talk till after midnight, when there was an exchange of autographs 'in fraternal association'.

21 *May*   Oriel. Yesterday we took David in his pram and spent part of the afternoon sitting in the garden of All Souls, with chestnut blossom falling on us like snow.

28 May Chequers. The PM suggested I should ask Rosalind to come over here or myself take one of the cars and visit her in Oxford for lunch; but *she* couldn't very well manage and I don't think my conscience will let me go on such a joy-ride. Perhaps the conscience will weaken: it is a heavenly summer day and I long to see my family again.

28 May Chequers. The PM asked if I would like to send a car to bring you over here. On my mentioning the difficulty of deserting David, he said – bring him too. But I thought you wouldn't want to encourage this, apart from the fact that young Winston here has German measles. Then I was offered a car to visit you. At the moment conscience has rejected this as sheer joy-riding and 'unnecessary' use of petrol.

NOTE

At Chequers on the 28th Moiseiwitsch played the piano. The PM startled us by saying that what mattered in music are the silences between the notes. Moiseiwitsch recalled this some years afterwards when I met him at a dinner in the Embassy at Lisbon.

JUNE

On the 4th Allied forces entered Rome. The advance in Italy continued northward.

On the 6th Anglo-American landings were successfully made in Normandy. The PM accepted the King's wish that he should not go to sea on D Day; but he landed in Normandy six days later. On the 27th Cherbourg surrendered.

Russian offensives opened on the Leningrad front and central front. The Russians broke through the Mannerheim Line.

Tokyo was bombed by US bombers flying 1,000 miles from China. Flying bomb attacks on London began.

There was disagreement with the Americans about the choice of future operations in the Mediterranean theatre.

It was agreed that the Russians should have responsibility for Romanian affairs, while leaving Greek affairs to HMG.

DIARY

June

2 To Oxford in afternoon.

3 At Oxford.

4 At Oxford. Rome captured.

5 Drove back to London with Lord Cherwell.

6 Invasion of France began. Successful landings in Normandy. PM with Tommy Lascelles accompanied the King to Allied Air HQ [Leigh-Mallory] and SHAEF [Supreme Headquarters of Allied Expeditionary Force].

9 To Chequers in afternoon. Field Marshal Smuts and his son Jan staying for the weekend.

10 At Chequers. Winant, Gen. Marshall, Eden and Lawford arrived.

11 At Chequers. Left by train in afternoon. Joined at Ascot by Marshall, King, Arnold, Cuter, Kirkpatrick, MacCarthy and Good. Slept on train.

12 Embarked in HMS *Kelvin* at Portsmouth for France, landing at Courseulles. Lunch at Montgomery's HQ at Creully. In launch and *Kelvin* up and down coast Arromanches to Orne. Returned to Portsmouth. Train to London.

15 Pilotless aircraft attack at night.

16 To Oxford in afternoon.

17 At Oriel. Archbishop of York arrived to spend weekend.

18 At Oxford. University Sermon by Archbishop of York on need for Prayer Book reform. Lowe of The House, Carpenters of Keble and Miss Plumer of Society of St Anne to meet him. Dined with Radford at Trinity.

19 Returned to London. More pilotless aircraft.

23 At present we are working at the Annexe because of the 'doodle-bombs'. To Chequers in afternoon. Brig. Bruce White reported on damage to harbour gear on beachhead.

24 At Chequers. PM meditating and producing a large egg on alternatives before us – 'Anvil' etc.

25 At Chequers. Harold Macmillan to lunch. Duncan and Diana Sandys etc. In afternoon walked with Mrs C, visiting field where flying bomb fell yesterday.

26 Returned to London.

27 Visited Pelham Place to see damage by blast by flying bomb which hit Thurloe Court in the night. All windows broken in front and some at back. Bedroom ceilings partly down.

30 To Oxford. Crowded train, two standing in compartment from Reading. At lunchtime saw flying bomb falling at Piccadilly Circus.

LETTERS

1 June A long weekend at Chequers as we did not return till Tuesday. I still feel sleepy after such a run of late nights (3.30 on Monday); but it was certainly best to be in the country for these very hot days. Things were quieter owing to the bank holiday and I was able to go over to Oxford on Monday afternoon (taking advantage of the fact that Lord Cherwell had to drive across on official business) and spent over an hour at Oriel. Moiseiwitsch and his wife came to dinner on Monday and afterwards he played to us. Very enchanting it seemed after such a long starvation from concerts, though the more expert said he was not in his best form.

8 June It is a great relief to know that the 'invasion' (here we are always told to call it 'the liberation of Europe') has started at last. It had been like counting the days to the end of term at school and then as we got to the last day or two I could think of little else, particularly on Sunday night, when the wind rose, with heavy rain. As you know, there had to be one day's postponement, but after that the weather improved and the attack was successfully launched. In the afternoon I went with the King and the PM on their visit to Allied Air HQ and the Supreme Commander's HQ, where the latest position was shown on large maps. It is betraying no secret to say that the landing was accomplished with less difficulty than had been expected; but of course there is harder fighting now and there will be more as the enemy rushes more troops to the battle. How little we thought as we sat dolefully on the beach at Bernières [we went for a family holiday there in the summer after my father's death] and ate our tea in the pâtisserie at St Aubyn that these would be the scenes for such events.

I wonder if you listened to the King's broadcast. I thought that the matter could not have been better and I hear that the rest of the BBC programme that evening was good too.

15 June Luckily we had a perfect day on Monday, with not a cloud in the sky until evening, for our expedition to France. We had spent Sunday night on the train (with the American Chiefs

151

of Staff – Gen. Marshall, Adml King and Gen. Arnold) and embarked in a destroyer after early breakfast for the Channel crossing. This took about three and three-quarter hours, in almost perfect conditions. I was on the bridge all the time and there was always something to watch – shipping passing or being overtaken, and aircraft overhead, swarms of Fortresses, Liberators and others. There was a little excitement at one moment as ack-ack fire was sighted ahead, but this turned out to be simply a ship practising its guns.

We went ashore in a duck (a swimming tank), landing on the beach at Courseulles, the town next to Bernières. Monty was waiting with two or three jeeps, into which we crowded. I shared one with an admiral, three other naval officers, Smuts's son and the driver, a very tight fit. Thus we drove off through the town and into the country. The houses on the seafront had been badly damaged by bombardment, but inland we were astonished by the general peaceful aspect of the countryside. Here and there buildings had been knocked about or there was a crashed plane or burnt out car, while German signs with 'Minen' and skull and crossbones showed where there were mine-fields, possibly bogus; but generally speaking the landscape was little changed. Crops were ripening for harvest. I even saw fat cows munching contentedly, and the people on the roads, friendly and happy, showed no obvious marks of privation.

The PM with the CIGS and Smuts had a conference and lunch with Monty at his HQ. Meanwhile with the rest of the party I hurried through some sandwiches and then went for a stroll in the nearby village. It was full of military patrols, but some of the inhabitants were also going about or looking out of their windows. German placards were still on the walls (full of 'Verbotens') and there was one amusing one of the PM, shown as a hideous cigar-smoking octopus, with tentacles over half Europe.

From this HQ we drove to another and while there saw a German bomber come over. There was a burst of ack-ack fire ('quite like London') and we heard that the plane had been brought down. Meanwhile the larger barks of the bigger guns (chiefly naval) had been going on all the time.

On return to the beach the PM was mobbed by the troops and there was some difficulty in clearing a way to his launch. We then cruised along the shore, watching the ships disembarking troops, lorries, tanks etc. in great quantities. As far as the eye could see the water seemed to be covered with a stupendous mass of craft of all sizes for miles to the horizon on both sides. There can never have been such a sight in the history of the world and I doubt if there ever will be again.

Eventually we returned to the destroyer and passed back along the beach to the end of the British line (the end near Caen), where the smoke of battle could be seen ashore. Before turning away we fired two or three rounds at the enemy's position.

We weren't back in England till ten o'clock at night, after one of the most memorable days I have ever spent. It was a thrilling tour and everyone was immensely impressed . . .

On reading this I see I have scarcely mentioned the troops, of whom we saw a great many. They looked fit and in very good heart and gave the PM a great welcome when they recognised him.

21 June   The doodle-bugs or whatever it has not yet been decided to call them have been a bore, but on a much diminished scale since our counter-measures took effect. Sleeping underground we aren't much worried by the noise at night.

22 June   The flying bomb has been a nuisance here, but I personally have escaped the worst nuisance, the noise at night, through sleeping in my burrow at the office, where we hear nothing. The counter-measures have taken effect and there are many fewer visitations than at first.

Had another tête-à-tête lunch with Mrs C the other day and showed her the photographs of David, which she much admired.

I go to Chequers this weekend. It should have been Dodds, the new PS, but the PM, who is always very difficult with new faces, has not yet quite taken to him.

25 June   Chequers. The chief subject of conversation this week has been the flying bomb (variously named bumble-bomb, doodle-bug etc.). They are a nuisance and have done a fair amount of damage, but little serious, and altogether they are better customers than bombers. You hear them coming over and you have the comforting knowledge that when they have passed they don't come back. There have been a few bumps round us in Westminster, but nothing in the immediate neighbourhood. One fell in a field four miles from here yesterday in the middle of the night and made a surprisingly loud noise. Mrs C and I went to visit the place in the afternoon, quite a big crater, and walked home. We trespassed into a farm and were turned back by a fierce woman, then got lost in a wood, but it was a lovely bit of countryside and we arrived back late and a little weary but (myself at any rate) much the better for the fresh air and exercise.

28 June   Alas a flying bomb burst on top of a block of flats near Pelham Place on Monday night and blew in all the front windows besides some of the glass at the back. I only heard of it on Tuesday morning because a friend of Miss Watson's telephoned to say that she had passed along the street and seen our windows smashed and the front door blown in. I went along at once and found the place in a great mess. Windows, with frames and shutters, are badly smashed and part of the ceiling in our bedroom had collapsed. I organised a party of cleaners in the afternoon and once the glass, plaster and soot had been swept up the house didn't look so bad. Fortunately the furniture had been covered and I didn't find any real damage to the contents of the house beyond one lampshade smashed and our bedroom carpet filthy. The main structure of the house is undamaged. I got in touch with a builder at once and he has promised to start emergency repairs as soon as possible. When I called today I found a slater examining the roof, but otherwise no progress has yet been made. The whole street is looking rather derelict. Yesterday it was roped off, with a policeman on patrol.

Altogether we feel we have got off lightly. The damage can be repaired and I think repairs will be paid for by the War Damage Commission. I cannot be too thankful that Rosalind was not in the house with David. Either she would have been in the bed, on which the ceiling descended, or taking refuge in the kitchen, where floor and tables were covered with a shower of glass.

JULY

Caen was liberated. Montgomery began a new offensive and in the American break-out Avranches was taken.

An unsuccessful attack was made on Hitler's life.

The President insisted on the launching of 'Anvil' [Allied landings in the South of France, 1944] at the earliest possible date and

General Wilson was instructed accordingly. Meanwhile Alexander's advance in Italy continued: Arezzo, Leghorn and Ancona were taken.

The Russians captured Minsk and the Vistula was approached. The Americans landed on Guam.

DIARY

July

1   At Oxford. Tea with Powickes [F.M. Powicke, Regius Professor of Modern History, and his wife].
2   Oxford.
3   Returned to London. A detestable day of torrential rain, November gloom and flying bombs. Dinner with Ronnie Tree.
6   PM's statement on flying bombs. At last warm and summery.
7   To Chequers in afternoon.
8   At Chequers. Subasič, Yugoslav PM, Stevenson (our Ambassador) and Adl Alan Kirk, USN, to lunch. Afternoon walk with Mrs C.
9   At Chequers. Eisenhower called. Maharaja of Kashmir and Col. Rawat to lunch. Gen Alexander to dinner. Walk with Mrs C and Prof.
10 Returned to London in afternoon.
12 Dined with Sir John Hunter, Governor of British Honduras, and Roland Turnbull.
13 This is a detestably wet summer. One dull day after another.
14 To Oxford in afternoon.
15 Oxford. Walk with R along Cherwell and by Marston Ferry.
16 At Oxford.
17 Returned to London. Crowded train: had to stand.
20 After lunch flew with PM, Gen. John Lee, Pug, Tommy etc. from Heston to Normandy. Visited Cherbourg. By motor torpedo-boat from Utah beach to Arromanches. Night in HMS *Enterprise* (Capt. Peachey).
21 Visited Gen. Montgomery's HQ near Blay. Lunched with Gen. Naylor at Line of Communication HQ. Visited General Hospital. Saw William Stirling's guns in action near Tilly. Visited field bakery. Night in HMS *Enterprise*. Alarm of human torpedoes.
22 Walked round Arromanches (NOIC Hickling). Visited Port-

en-Bessin. Drove to Bayeux. Night in HMS *Enterprise*. German aircraft dropped leaflets – 'Why are you dying for Stalin?'

23 With Pug and Tommy taken by Capt. Chavasse to Caen and on to neighbourhood of Bourguebus, 4000 yards from German lines. Visited Second Army HQ (Gen. Dempsey) and Gen. Ritchie's HQ. Flew back to Northolt. On to Chequers.

24 Returned to No. 10 in afternoon.

25 Zaranski dined with me.

26 Drove down to Windsor and spent the night with Tommy Lascelles.

27 Returned to No. 10.

28 To Oxford in afternoon, standing in crowded train.

29–30 At Oxford.

31 Returned to town.

LETTERS

2 *July* Oriel. With us the unsummery weather has the extra disadvantage that the clouds make things easier for our plague, the flying bomb. I saw one of these fall on my way to lunch on Saturday – very spectacular, but I am quite content not to see any more. At Pelham Place the slates have been replaced and the roof is watertight again, but the windows were still gaping when I last saw them . . . Oxford is full of people who have come away from London. On Friday coming down in the train they were standing in the compartment as well as the corridor. Meanwhile the war is going well on all fronts and it is difficult not to be wildly optimistic.

24 *July* Chequers. On Thursday we went to Cherbourg and drove round the port, seeing the German demolitions and the great progress already made in restoring the place for Allied use. Away from the port the town is not too badly damaged and there were a great many people about, some of whom recognised the PM as we drove past. It was wonderful to see how their faces lit up with pleasure and the enthusiasm of the crowd at one place where we stopped. A few miles out of the town we visited one of the flying bomb sites – an elaborate erection of concrete only 60 per cent complete and apparently intended for launching bombs in the direction of Bristol. Then from one of the American beaches we went out in a 'duck' to a motor torpedo-boat in which

we travelled along to the British area. It was very rough and the voyage took two and a half hours (which gives you some idea of the size of the area liberated in Normandy). The PM went below and took Mothersill, but I remained on the bridge and just managed to survive.

Friday, Saturday and Sunday were spent in the British area, where we drove about a lot and saw a great deal, visiting Monty and some other headquarters. The troops look extremely fit and happy and certainly must be encouraged by the scale and efficiency of the organisation behind them. The French people too are remarkably cheerful, though they are said not to have been badly treated by the Germans and we alas have brought great destruction on their towns and villages. Bayeux fortunately has survived with little damage; but Caen, which I saw yesterday, is very badly knocked about. We went beyond Caen towards Bourguebus, where we were among our guns shelling the Germans, whose front was only about 4000 yards away.

AUGUST

Allied landings took place between Cannes and Hyères. By the end of the month the Americans were beyond Valence and Grenoble. By the same time Marseilles and Toulon were fully occupied.

On the Normandy front the Germans counter-attacked near Mortain but US forces swept on and turning north to Argentan in the direction of Falaise encircled large numbers of them, while the 21st Army advanced from the north to close the gap. In Brittany the Americans swept forward and rapidly exploited their success. Paris was entered on the 24th: other cities liberated during the month were Rennes, Le Mans, Chartres, Orléans, Rouen, Rheims, Verdun and Amiens.

The Russians advanced into Romania and a *coup d'état* took place in Bucharest.

There was an insurrection of Poles in Warsaw.

In Italy the Germans abandoned Florence and General Alexander's general offensive began.

The Americans gained complete control of Marianas.

The Dumbarton Oaks talks on future world organisation opened.

The PM visited General Montgomery and General Bradley. From the 11th to the 28th he was away on a visit to Algiers (where de Gaulle refused an invitation to meet him), Naples (meeting with Tito), Corsica (for embarkation in a destroyer to see troops landing in the south of France), the Italian front and Rome. On the 29th he returned home with a temperature of 104 – a mild attack of pneumonia.

DIARY

August

4   Polish Ambassador called to press for dropping of supplies from Italy on insurgents now holding part of Warsaw.

5   News that Russians are now fighting in East Prussia.

10   After dinner drove to Northolt to see PM off on his visit to Italy. (I did not go with him this time.)

11   To Andover in afternoon (R being at Swanage). Great crowd at Waterloo and queue in tunnel.

12   At Andover.

13   Returned to London in crowded train.

14   Jock Colville returned to Private Office. Dodds has gone back to Admiralty.

15   Landing on Riviera.

18   News that some Americans have reached the Seine.

19   Newspapers full of news of decisive victory in France, the 'gap' at Falaise being now closed.

22   Bombs in Harrington Road interrupted Underground through South Kensington for a time; but Pelham Place not affected.

23   At lunchtime left for Basingstoke, where I met R and David. Accompanied them to Oxford, where we spent the night.

24   Left in afternoon for Birmingham, where we changed to LMS night train for Edinburgh.

25   Arrived Edinburgh.

26–31   In Edinburgh.

SEPTEMBER

The Allied advance from the south of France joined hands with the American Army advancing from Normandy. In the north the rapid advance of British and Canadians overwhelmed the flying-bomb launching sites and on the 6th Herbert Morrison announced 'The Battle of London is won', but two days later the first V2s (rocket bombs) were launched against the city. During the month Brussels was taken and Antwerp entered. The south of Belgium and Luxembourg were cleared. The Moselle was reached. The Battle of Arnhem took place.

Romania and Bulgaria were overrun by the Russians, who drove on up the Danube to the Hungarian frontier.

In Italy the Eighth Army crossed the Rubicon.

The agony of Warsaw continued throughout the month. (At the beginning of October the remaining Poles surrendered to the Germans.)

The PM attended a conference in Quebec and visited Hyde Park.

DIARY

September
1–3   On leave in Edinburgh.
4   Arrived back in London. After breakfast at Paddington saw off R and D to Oxford. Preparing for departure for 'Octagon'.
5   Left with PM etc. in his train for Greenock, where we embarked in *Queen Mary*, sailing at dinner time. Party includes Mrs C, three Chiefs of Staff (Brooke, Portal and Cunningham), Cherwell, Leathers, Pug, Hollis, Jock.
6–7   At sea.
8   At sea. In Gulf Stream, warm and sticky.
9   At sea.
10   Arrived Halifax at lunch time. Disembarked and proceeded by train for Quebec.
11   Arrived Quebec. President and Mrs Roosevelt were already at Wolfe's Cove when we arrived. Mackenzie King meeting. Drove to Citadel. This time Major Eastwood is Controller.
12   At Quebec. Dined with Joe Garner [UK Deputy High Commissioner in Canada] at Chateau Frontenac.
13   At Quebec. Sir William Glasgow (Australia) and Firth (New Zealand) called on PM. Evening party at Chateau.
14   At Quebec. PM's conversation with President, Morgenthau [US Secretary of the Treasury] and Cherwell about Lease-Lend. Eden arrived. Norman Robertson [Canadian Under-Secretary for External Affairs], Murray Hume and Heeney to dinner.
15   At Quebec. Zones of occupation. Eric Speed [Permanent

Under-Secretary of State for War], Ince and Joan Bright [Gen. Ismay's secretary] to dinner.

16 Final plenary session of Octagon Conference. President left.

17 At Quebec. Archduke Otto [Hapsburg heir] to lunch. Left after dinner by train for Hyde Park.

18 Arrived Hyde Park. Anna and John Boettiger [Roosevelts' daughter and son-in-law] staying. Duke of Windsor to lunch. President, Harry Hopkins and Adl Leahy had long talk before dinner. Morgenthaus to dinner.

19 At Hyde Park. Picnic lunch at cottage. PM's conversation with President and Leahy about 'Tube Alloys'. Left by train after dinner.

20 Left train after breakfast at Statten Island and embarked on *Queen Mary*. Fog blotted out view of New York.

21 At sea. Hot and sticky.

22–24 At sea.

25 Arrived Greenock about 6 p.m. and left by train for the south.

26 Arrived back at Euston 10 a.m. The usual crowd meeting PM. Telephoned R, who is still at Oxford.

29 To Oxford in afternoon.

30 At Oxford.

LETTERS

10 *September*   At sea. It has been a very pleasant voyage – the usual mixture of sunshine, fresh air and overeating ('One egg or two, Sir?'), with enough work to keep us from being bored.

12 *September*   Quebec. We are back here in the familiar surroundings, everyone very kind and welcoming, and the weather quite perfect. I am very fit in spite of much over-eating. On the train from our port of arrival they gave us a ten-course dinner.

14 *September*   Quebec. Here all has continued to go well. There have been so many of these conferences now that the machinery has been made more or less perfect and the people concerned, having changed remarkably little in these last four years, know one another very well. It has been an added advantage to return to such familiar surroundings, so that we feel as if we had only been away for a week or two since the last visit and everything is where we left it. We couldn't have better hosts. Nothing is too

much trouble for the Canadians and they seem genuinely pleased to see us back. At past conferences some of my worst troubles have been about the press; but this time Brendan has given us Cruikshank, head of the American division of the Ministry of Information and formerly editor of the *Star*, and there could not be a better man for the job.

Otherwise much the party as before – Pug and the three Chiefs of Staff (the latter almost inseparable even at the cinema), the Prof, Lord Leathers and Jock, as the other PS. We have as usual attracted various visitors – Dick Law on his way to the UNRRA [United Nations Relief and Rehabilitation Administration] meeting at Montreal, Cadogan from Dumbarton Oaks, Anthony Eden and others from England. We live as before in the Citadel, shared between the President and Mrs R and the PM and Mrs C and their personal staffs. The PM and the President have their meals together and can have constant conversations without any fuss about arranging meetings. We also have a cads' party downstairs, with the most delicious food.

19 September Hyde Park, Dutchess County. Everyone seems to be pleased with the results of the conference and certainly a very pleasant time was had by all. The President left on Saturday after a 'colourful' ceremony at which an honorary degree of McGill was conferred on him and the PM in the open air (speeches drowned by the hum of movie cameras). We then had Sunday in which to clear up (and see the Archduke Otto and others) and came on down here by train. The Hudson valley is much pleasanter at this time of year, without the oppressive heat we met on previous visits. The Duke of Windsor came to lunch yesterday, looking oldish but in quite good form. He is an interesting talker, with a pronounced American accent.

OCTOBER

The Americans landed at Leyte (Philippines) and won the naval victory of Leyte Gulf.

Calais was occupied. Fighting continued to clear the Scheldt estuary and approaches to Antwerp. The Americans captured Aachen.

The Russians took Belgrade and Riga, and advanced into Hungary.

The Polish patriots in Warsaw capitulated.

The Italian campaign bogged down.

Commandos occupied Patras and liberated Athens.

The PM visited Moscow.

The Committee of National Liberation under General de Gaulle was recognised as the government of liberated France.

DIARY

October

1 At Oxford. Dined in Oriel Hall.

2 Returned to London.

6 Appointment of Swinton as Minister for Civil Aviation and Sir W. Jowitt as Minister for Social Insurance.

7 Left after dinner for Northolt.

8 Left Northolt just after midnight with PM in his York (Sqn Ldr Fraser). Arrived Pomigliano in time for breakfast at Naples (Rivalta Villa). Arrived Cairo 6.15 p.m. Staying in Moyne's villa.

9 Left Cairo West 1.30 a.m. Arrived Moscow *c.* noon. Drove out to dacha. Zinschenko liaison with NKVD [People's Committee of Internal Affairs; precursor of KGB]. Ershov in charge of dacha.

10 Luncheon 2.30–6 p.m. in Reception House of NKVD – Stalin, Molotov etc. I sat next Novikov. Returned to dacha for the night.

11 Moscow. Sir Arthur and Lady Abrahams and Miss Johnson [of British Red Cross] to lunch at dacha. Reception to Diplomatic Corps. Dinner at British Embassy (Sir A. Clark Kerr) – Stalin etc. Fireworks for Szeged.

12 Moscow. In town house all morning. Drove out to dacha in afternoon.

13 PM's meetings with Russians plus London and (separately) Lublin Poles.

14 Moscow. More Polish meetings. Went with PM to Kremlin for private talk with Stalin (I waited with NKVD men). Concert in Bolshoi Theatre.

15 In town house, Moscow. PM developed fever in evening. Celebrated birthday by going to *Swan Lake* at Bolshoi Theatre (after cocktails at Balfour's).

16 PM back to normal. In town house, Moscow (Ostrovskaja Street), in charge of Guskov.

17 Quiet day in town house, Moscow.

18   Moscow. In afternoon visited Embassy with PM for talk to Press. State banquet in Kremlin, next to Petrov [interpreter].
19   Left Moscow by air *c.* 10.45 a.m. Arrived Sarabuz in Crimea *c.* 3.30 p.m. Met by Krabanov, Chairman of Crimean Soviet, and Gen. Yermetchenko of Soviet Naval Air Force. Drove to Simferopol (where we dined).
20   Left Sarabuz 12.45 a.m. Arrived Cairo West 8 a.m. Staying in Moyne's villa. Mountbatten also there. Dinner party.
21   Left Cairo after breakfast. Arrived Naples late afternoon. At dinner – Gens Wilson, Alexander, Harding, Clark, Gammell etc. and CIGS (who travelled in PM's plane), Adl John Cunningham and Morse.
22   Left Naples after breakfast. Uneventful flight across France. Arrived Northolt 5.30 p.m. Drove to Chequers and on to Oxford for the night. David can now crawl and has one tooth.
23   Returned to No. 10. Lascelles to dinner in mess.
24   Very sleepy after many late nights in last fortnight.
27   Lunch with Weizmann. To Oxford in afternoon.
28   Caviare and vodka party. [See Gerald Pawle, *The War and Col. Warden,* 325.]
29   Oxford.
30   Returned to town. Saw official of Kensington Borough Council about stage two air-raid repairs.
31   Lunch with Lord Marchwood.

LETTERS

5 *October*   Yesterday we had a sudden thunderstorm with drenching torrents of rain. Everyone thought the thunder was the noise of the arrival of rockets.
7 *October*   On setting off for Moscow. It is an anxious journey for my master's sake, but in some ways it is one of the most important he has undertaken. It may make all the difference to the peace of the world in which David will grow up.
9 *October*   We took the air just after midnight on Sunday and arrived near Naples a little after seven o'clock in the morning. I slept most of the time in my bunk, with the Moran underneath and Tommy and the detective alongside. The PM and Sawyers made up the party. At the Italian airfield there was quite a little

163

crowd – Jumbo, Alex, Harold Macmillan etc. – and after shaking hands we were driven away (about half an hour) to Naples, then through the streets to a villa outside, high up overlooking the bay. Torrential rain helped to make the Naples streets look even more wretched. Particularly down by the sea there is a great deal of war damage and very little seems to have been done to tidy it up. The swarms of people looked happy enough and regarded the British cavalcade with friendly expressions.

After breakfast there was a short conference and then we set off again a little after eleven, Eden this time joining the party in our plane. We flew down past Vesuvius, with a long black stream of lava from the latest eruption still smouldering, across the toe of Italy and down over the Mediterranean to strike the African shore about Benghazi. It is strange to see the desert still criss-crossed with thousands of tracks of tanks and trucks and bearing other marks of a war that has so completely passed on, leaving only emptiness and ghosts. On over Mersa Matruh and then darkness came on and when we landed at Cairo it was by the help of flares and landing-lights and we came down with rather a bump. Moyne with others was waiting and took us to the villa where we stayed last December. It was pleasantly warm in rather a humid way. After midnight we returned to the airport and there found that our plane was not the better for its bump on landing, so we changed to another, which is much more comfortable for all except the PM, who doesn't have his private cabin. I slept solidly and woke up this morning to find ourselves in bright sunshine over South Russia.

At Moscow we were received with a guard of honour, with national anthems – Molotov, Maisky etc. We are living in a villa about forty minutes drive out of town, not a convenient arrangement but comfortable.

12 October A plane brings us every afternoon the day's London newspapers.

Next morning when I woke up after a most solid night's sleep it was 10.30, but the PM slept even longer so all was well. The chief event of the day was Stalin's luncheon party – in an ornate house (once owned by a rich sugar merchant) used à la Lancaster House for official receptions. The party began at 2.30 and lasted till after 6. First a string of hors d'oeuvres – caviare, smoked salmon, various forms of other fish and meat, including delicious sucking-pig, and then, just when you thought the meal was over, soup – and you know that fish, meat, pudding and dessert etc. are to follow. It has been the same at every lunch and dinner since we arrived here: only this time it was more festive and went on longer, accompanied by a great many speeches and toasts, all with the greatest *gemütlichkeit*. About five o'clock we adjourned from the lunch table to another room, where we sat down again and continued with coffee, liqueurs, chocolates, cakes and fruit. At length it was all over and, after a short visit to the Embassy, we drove out in the dark to our country house. How we faced dinner that night (menu as above) I can't think.

Wednesday morning was deliciously bright and sunny, with the most exhilarating champagne air, when I went for a walk among the pine trees around our house. We had some of Mrs Churchill's Red Cross people to lunch. Then in the afternoon we went into town to a large reception given by Molotov for the diplomatic corps – once more caviare, smoked salmon etc., only this time taken standing up. Then to our town house, a smaller place, for a short rest until it was time to go to the Embassy for dinner. This was a big affair – twenty-six guests – the first time Stalin has dined at a foreign mission. All the usual crowd – Molotov, Maisky, Vyshinksky [Foreign Minister], Litvinov etc. and Eden, the Ambassador, the CIGS etc. Again many toasts and speeches. The meal was interrupted by a salute in honour of the capture of Szeged. The curtains were drawn back and we all crowded to the windows to watch the star-shells bursting over the Kremlin, a fantastic display of fireworks and not at all what I had imagined 'a salute of 112 guns' to be like. After the dinner the PM, with Stalin, Eden and Molotov, withdrew into a private room and the party slowly melted away. I waited for the PM at the town house and did not get to bed till 4 a.m.

16 October Letters from Edinburgh dated Friday caught the plane that reached us on Saturday afternoon. The arrangements laid on for our communications have made a great impression here. Every day we have the same day's London newspapers. My birthday celebration on 15 October was an evening off at the ballet – *Swan Lake*. The Bolshoi Theatre is a huge place with five tiers of boxes and a big stage. One sees the perfection of ballet here. I thought it enchanting and was quite carried away. I enjoyed the intervals too, watching the crowd in the foyer parading round and round in an orderly ring. By contrast with what one sees in the streets they looked remarkably well dressed and they were mostly a very pleasant-seeming people, with bright, open faces.

But we were at an even more thrilling show the day before at the same theatre, especially arranged for the PM, who sat with Stalin, Molotov and co. in the central box. The first half of the programme was part of *Giselle*, superbly done. At the interval everyone turned to the central box and cheered. Stalin had drawn back out of sight when the lights went up, so as to leave the PM to receive the applause, but Winston got him to come back and there was a greater burst of cheering than ever, which kept on for some minutes with obviously genuine cordiality. The second part of the programme began with some solo songs – the women in exquisite gowns, the men in tails, followed by the Red Army Choir, mixed with some astonishing dancing, wildly extravagant and athletic.

Earlier in the afternoon I had gone with the PM to the Kremlin, where he had a long talk alone with Stalin (with an interpreter). I waited in an anteroom, but twice went into the marshal's room with messages (through a secretary's room, where there was the largest collection of telephones I have ever seen).

Stalin has paid the PM every courtesy and today gave him a charming brooch for Sarah (whom he met at Teheran) – the Red Flag and the Union Jack in enamel, with the Russian for 'Victory' below.

Expect no presents. There is little to buy and prices are extravagant; e.g. at the theatre last night the price of an apple was the equivalent of £1 and two of our clerks in an interval ordered themselves soft drinks and found that the price was the equivalent of 30s.

20 October We wound up with a long dinner party in a magnificently regal hall in the Kremlin; 8 p.m. to 2 a.m. Fortunately the meal was not as vast as we feared; but there must have been well over twenty toasts (I lost count). After coffee and dessert etc. in another room we went on to a cinema, where we sat at little tables partaking of more fruit and champagne and saw a rather long programme – a news reel followed by two full-length feature films, one Russian and one American. Back at the house I found some work to clear up and had to pack, so that for the second night running I didn't get to bed till 4.30 a.m.

We went off by air after breakfast (at which I was almost made sick by being offered sucking-pig again), seen off by the Marshal himself (a unique honour). After an uneventful flight mostly above the clouds, though at one point we had a glimpse of the Dnieper, we landed at Sarabuz in the Crimea in the afternoon. The local Commissar and the Naval Air Force CO met us on the field and took us to a buffet, where a long table was groaning with the usual caviare and cold meat etc. and bottles. We had just had a hearty lunch on the plane and even politeness could not enable us to do more than drink toasts, which they pressed us to do in the local vintages. We then drove along an exceedingly rough road to Simferopol, where a house had been got ready for our reception. While the PM rested some of us drove south towards the mountains between us and the Black Sea. It was a beautiful evening and the country looked most attractive in the soft lights of sunset. It is a remarkably Grecian landscape: I am sure Iphigenia must have felt quite at home in the Crimea. The peasants are an extremely comely and pleasant looking crowd. They gave an appearance of well-being much superior to that seen in the streets of Moscow. In Simferopol they were well dressed and seemed relatively prosperous and happy, in spite of the ravages of war, visible on every hand.

Dinner at Simferopol was the usual immense affair, not omitting the sucking-pig. The Commissar and Commander dined with us and there were the usual toasts. Lord Moran, who maintained tea-totality to the best of his ability in these some-what adverse circumstances, threatened to report me to you.

25 October   10 Downing Street. I have never felt more sleepy in my life. We had far too many late nights at Moscow (4.30 a.m. the last two) and no chance to make up on the journey. I always find these long journeys wearing mentally, perhaps because of the unusual readjustments of ideas involved when e.g. (as happened on Sunday) one has breakfast in Naples and supper the same day in Oxford. The PM himself is remarkably well and in excellent spirits.

Still no word of completing repairs to Pelham Place. A special licence is required for anything over £10: this has been applied for but not yet approved. Meanwhile sirens continue at night, though bombs are now few and far between, and I think Rosalind and David are better in Oxford; but I need not tell you how we pine for our own home.

29 October   Oriel. A very pleasant weekend here, to which I have been looking forward so long. David is much advanced and now *stands* in his play-pen, holding on to the sides, though he seems to find it easier to stand up than to sit down . . . He is very fond of Hector and 'bow-wow' is the only firmly established word in his vocabulary. Yesterday there was a party to consume some caviare I had brought from Moscow – the Warden of All Souls and the Dean of Christ Church with their wives and some others. After a little preliminary hesitation the caviare went like hot cakes, also a bottle of vodka.

NOVEMBER

Operations in the Scheldt estuary continued. The first convoy reached Antwerp. In the south the Allied advance towards the German frontier continued. The Rhine was reached between Mulhouse and the Swiss frontier and crossed near Strasbourg. Metz and Belfort were taken.

The Russians reached the outskirts of Budapest.

Sir John Dill died and was succeeded in Washington by General Wilson, General Alexander taking over as Allied Supreme Commander in the Mediterranean theatre.

The PM visited Paris.

Lord Moyne was assassinated.

Roosevelt was victorious in the Presidential election.

(The PM told me he had said to Smuts, 'It is not as easy as it used to be for me to get things done.')

DIARY

November

2   Rozie up for the day and came to Pelham Place (first time since February).

3   To Chequers in afternoon.

4, 5   Chequers.

6   Returned to London, stopping at Northolt to see PM's new C54 (Skymaster).

9   At Lord Mayor's Luncheon.

10   In afternoon left with PM, Mrs C, Mary and Eden by Dakota for Paris, arriving Villeneuve-Orly. Installed at Quai d'Orsay. Duff Cooper [Ambassador in France] and Lady Diana to dinner.

11   In Paris. To Champs Élysées for Armistice Day procession, PM and de Gaulle driving in open car. Lunch at Ministry of War. Parodi [Minister of Labour] spoke to me. Sat between Chauvel [Foreign Ministry] and Alphand. Dinner with Lévis-Mirepoix.

12   In Paris. Short walk in morning to Rue Royale. Luncheon (Bidault) at M. des Affaires Étrangères. With PM to Hôtel de Ville. Dinner with Duncannon at Cercle Interallié. Left Gare de Lyon in presidential train with de Gaulle.

13 . A day of snow. Arrived Besançon 10 a.m. Drove to Maiche. Lunch with de Lattre de Tassigny's HQ. Review at Valdahon. Dinner on train with de Gaulle etc., Palewski, Diethelm, Rancourt.

14   Arrived Rheims 10 a.m. Drove to Eisenhower's advance headquarters. Tedder and CIGS. After lunch returned by air to Northolt.

15   Visited Pelham Place, where signs of progress with repairs, but annoyed to find that windows are being reglazed with not entirely transparent glass.

16   To Oxford in afternoon.

17, 18   At Oxford.

19   Returned to London after lunch.

24   Dinner with Parkinson, also Jock Macpherson.

25   Honours List to PM.

30   Floods of telegrams etc. for PM's 70th birthday.

LETTERS

2 November   This is already my seventeenth official birthday. It has also been a red letter day as Rozie returned to London for the first time since February. She met me for lunch at the club, after which we went along to Pelham Place. The water board man was waiting for us and we turned off the water, now considered a greater danger than incendiaries. By a lucky chance our landlord's representative called too and went over the house to see the damage, finally deciding to reduce the rent for a period, since we were blitzed until repairs are complete, from £130 to £75 per annum – a very generous allowance.

All the repairs in the street have been assigned by the Kensington Borough Council to a single firm. This was annoying as we should have preferred to deal with our regular firm (who are very reliable and have done the work at 25 for some years), but we have had to bow to the local bureaucracy. We are told that repairs will begin in about three weeks. They will be confined to ceiling, woodwork and glass, no 'decoration' being allowed at this stage. We thought our home looked so attractive, with the sunshine coming in at the back, and it looks as if only a little hard work will be needed to restore it to a fairly normal state.

We walked across the park and I left R in the Oxford train.

5 November Chequers. The family life of the Private Secretaries grows. Yesterday Leslie Rowan's first child arrived at the Westminster. Meanwhile I have no further news of David except that he has fifty per cent fewer teeth than Christopher Eastwood's several weeks' younger boy. (The latter has two.) . . . I didn't get out at all yesterday and seemed to have occupation all day. Dr Weizmann, the Zionist, came to lunch and in the afternoon Mr Eden arrived on his return from Italy. Both on Friday and last night, repeated because it was so good, we saw the film of *The Mikado*, in colour.

6 November 10 Downing Street. A quiet weekend, with comparatively early nights – to bed by 2.30 a.m. or 2.45 a.m. every day.

7 November We have discovered too late that the lavish supplies of caviare, vodkas and other liquor that arrived with our luggage from Moscow were after all not a present from Uncle Joe but were intended for the Russian Embassy Red Army Day celebrations.

10 November At the Lord Mayor's Luncheon at the Mansion House, the fourth of these annual festivities I have attended. They are quite amusing, with pleasant traditional pomp and circumstance – though (like the meal itself) much reduced in wartime.

12 November I wish you were here to enjoy Paris in this lovely autumn sunshine. I had forgotten how beautiful it is, so much more beautiful than London, and now the comparison is unfair because there is none of London's wartime drabness, and the scars are few and far between. There are still enough leaves to make a mist of gold all down the boulevards.

At lunch at the Ministère de la Guerre Alexandre Parodi, the Minister of Labour, looked me out and spoke of himself as a friend of the Rosses and talked to me for several minutes – full of interest in you all and evidently sharing my opinion of Rosalind.

The food is not thrust on us in such quantities as at Moscow, but it could not be more delicious. The omelette at dinner last night was a dream.

15 November We flew to Paris on Friday and returned by air yesterday. In Paris we stayed at the Quai d'Orsay in the rooms prepared for the King and Queen when they visited Paris before the war, a most palatial place . . . On Armistice Day I was with Mrs C and Mary in a stand on the Champs Élysées, where we watched the long march-past and saw the PM and de Gaulle drive along in an open car. There were immense crowds, kept back by the police with the greatest difficulty, and wild enthusiasm. Of all the troops none were given a louder cheer than the Highland pipe band in kilts. We were entertained at various formal meals, with the most delicious food. On Sunday afternoon the PM drove to the Hôtel de Ville, again past cheering crowds, and was given a great reception by the Paris Committee of Liberation. His impromptu speech in fluent but ungrammatical French was a remarkable *tour de force* and clearly made a great impression.

Paris was looking more beautiful than ever, particularly by contrast with drab, war-torn London, and in the absence of coal fires there is no smoke to spoil the autumn sunshine. The people seemed very happy and well dressed, many of the women in the curious high hats they affected during the German occupation.

On Sunday night we left by train from the Gare de Lyon for Besançon. It was good to see again the pleasant wagon-lits coaches, though this was the presidential train and unusually comfortable inside. On Monday morning we found the world covered with snow and more falling. This curtailed the programme, but did not prevent us going on a long and rather adventurous drive to lunch at a French Army headquarters. We had to get out more than once to shove the car when it stuck in the snow. On the way back to Besançon there was a review of French troops, in the dusk with driving snow and cold slush at our feet. By a miracle the PM was none the worse.

30 November I feel completely deflated – perhaps a very mild touch of the flu that is going about. The last straw was a 3.30 a.m. night on Monday, followed by another latish night on Tuesday, when the PM gave an eve of session dinner to ministers in the House of Commons. We sat down seventy-nine to a meal of broth, pheasant and plum pudding, followed by speeches – an unusual affair in these days. I sat next an MP from East Lothian, Buchan-Hepburn. The PM as usual wanted Irish stew, but this time forgot to add pineapple chunks. Speeches by the PM, Attlee, Eden, the Speaker and Bevin – the latter very good.

In the House on Wednesday for speeches on the Address. The seconder was a young Scottish miner from Hamilton – Tom Fraser. I very much liked his looks and he made a most excellent speech. Today we are swamped with Birthday – floods of messages and gifts. We couldn't think of a present from the Private Office, having turned down the idea of a cat, and ended up by sending only a message.

I have been to inspect Pelham Place and found it now completely habitable, with the bedroom ceiling at last repaired. I am afraid the 'decoration' looks rather the worse for wear in several rooms, but we must just put up with that for the time being. I'm afraid however that I can't have R and D up here till the rockets cease.

DECEMBER

The American Third Army crossed the Saar and came to a halt facing the Siegfried Line. The German counter-offensive in the Ardennes was halted by the end of the month.

Also by the end of the month the Russians had completely surrounded Budapest.

In Italy the Eighth Army captured Ravenna.

In Burma Kalewa was taken.

The PM made a Christmas visit to Athens.

DIARY

December

1   To Oxford in afternoon.

2, 3   In Oxford.

4   Returned to London.

8   PM's speech on Greece.

9   Began Honours List with PM and Chief Whip. To Chequers in

time for dinner. Field Marshal Alexander and Lady Margaret to dinner.

10   Chequers. Munster [Under-Secretary, Home Office] to lunch, on return from welfare mission to 14th Army. Duncan and Diana Sandys to dinner. American LSTs [Landing Ships, Tanks] for Greece.

11   Returned to London. To film of *Henry V*.

14   Lunch with Rowans seeing Sarah for first time.

15   To Oxford in afternoon.

16, 17   At Oxford.

18   Returned to London.

22   Dined tête-à-tête with PM, who had delayed departure for Chequers.

24   PM decided to fly to Athens with Anthony Eden tonight. Glad I am not going on an expedition of which I disapprove, the prize not being worth the risks. To Oxford in evening. David obstreperous at night.

25   In Oxford. In the morning at St Mary's. Big lunch and tea parties at Oriel. David much enjoyed his first Christmas, receiving his presents with loud crows of delight. Lady Ross in bed.

26   Morning at Oxford. Bitter cold but sunny. Trees thick with white frost. Walked in parks and by Cherwell. Returned to London in afternoon.

29   In afternoon drove through fog to Bovingdon airfield to meet PM on return from Athens.

30   To Oxford in afternoon.

31   At Oxford. We took David in his pram to see skating on Port Meadow.

LETTER

31 *December*   My last letter to you in 1944. It has been an unsatisfactory year in many ways, but David in himself is enough to make up for all the disappointments and I can't call it a dull year in which I travelled to Quebec, Moscow and Paris (after seeing it in at Marrakesh in the company of Montgomery, Eisenhower and Winston). It was a relief to have the PM safely back from Athens, apparently none the worse for his adventures. He celebrated by staying up till 4.30 a.m.

1945

JANUARY

Montgomery launched the northern counterattack. By the end of the month the Germans were back behind their frontier.

The Russians captured Warsaw. By the end of the month they were in complete possession of East Prussia, except Königsberg. The Russians recognised the Lublin Committee as the provisional government of Poland. There was a helpful reply from Stalin to the PM's message asking for information about offensive plans.

The decision was taken to meet at Yalta. Harry Hopkins visited London. The PM left for Malta on the 30th.

In Greece the armistice came into force, under which ELAS withdrew from Athens and Attica.

There was progress in Burma. The Irrawaddy was crossed and Akyab reoccupied.

General MacArthur invaded Luzon.

DIARY

January
1 At Oxford.
2 Returned to London.
4 Lunch with Cruikshank (MOI). To *Love in Idleness* (Rattigan) with Mrs Churchill, dining with her afterwards.
5 In afternoon drove to Northolt to meet PM returning from short visit to Eisenhower and Montgomery.
6 To Chequers in afternoon. First snowdrops.
7 At Chequers. Very cold. Gen. Carton de Wiart [British Special Representative to Chiang Kai-shek] to lunch.
8 Returned to London.
9 Saw Nind Hopkins about selection of his successor.
12 Left for Edinburgh by night train.

13–15 In Edinburgh.

16 Edinburgh. Left for London.

17 Arrived back in London. Found daffodil shoots showing at Pelham Place.

18 PM's speech on Greece etc.

22 Went to see Bridges to congratulate him on appointment as Secretary of Treasury, of which PM told him today.

23 Feeling rather the worse for wear after TAB inoculation yesterday. Vaccination today.

26 To Oxford in afternoon. Bitterly cold and no sign of heating in train.

27 At Oxford. Hard frost. Afternoon walk along towing path with R.

28 At Oxford. Colder than ever. Pipes frozen. Morning walk in meadow and by river. Alexandre Parodi with his sister Jacqueline and his *chef de cabinet* to lunch.

29 Returned to London. Long waits at Oxford and Didcot in bitter cold. Arrived two hours late. Lunch with Peter Brooke, Rajah Muda of Sarawak. Left with PM in his C54 from Northolt at 9.30 p.m. Party includes Sarah, Sir E. Bridges, Moran and Tommy.

30 Arrived Malta (Luqa airfield) at 4.30 a.m. PM had fever and we did not leave the field till 10.30, when he was a little better. Drove to our quarters in HMS *Orion* (Capt. Gornall). Afternoon walk in dockyard area near French Creek.

31 At Malta. Dinner at Government House.

LETTERS

7 January Chequers. The first snowdrops have already appeared under a tree outside the window where I work . . . A small party here – just Winston, 'Clemmy', Jack Churchill and me at dinner, but there will be one or two more today. On Thursday evening, while the PM was in France – he did without a PS this time – Mrs C took me to a play, my first theatre since May (except Moscow) – the Lunts in Rattigan's *Love in Idleness*, most amusing and brilliantly played. Afterwards we had a quiet tête-à-tête dinner, conversation eventually settling on death-bed scenes. It is bitterly cold – thank goodness I have a hot water bottle.

22 January   We had a very profitable weekend here with the PM, clearing off all arrears of work and in particular settling my chief worry of the last few weeks (the selection of a new head of the Civil Service) in the way I wanted.

25 January   The carpenter repairs are now done at Pelham Place, i.e. shutters are up again, so 'stage 2' is complete and more isn't allowed at present.

31 January   Just a line to report all well though I am not at the moment in London. Oxford at the weekend was frightfully cold. Most of the pipes froze and by Monday morning there were very few taps still functioning. On Monday Eleanor [Ross] and I had one of the worst journeys I ever remember, arriving in London two hours late, most of which we spent standing on platforms at Oxford or Didcot.

FEBRUARY

The Yalta Conference. The PM visited Athens and Egypt on the way home.

The Colmar pocket was cleared. Montgomery began the advance to the Rhine north of Cologne. The Ninth Army launched an attack.

The British forces in Burma reached Meiktila.

General MacArthur entered Manila.

DIARY

February

1   At Malta. Afternoon drive with Capt. Gornall to St Paul's Bay and back by Mosta.

2   At Malta. President Roosevelt arrived in USS *Quincy*. Bright sunshine. Afternoon walk in Valletta. Visited *Quincy* for drinks with Anna Roosevelt. Left HMS *Orion* for airfield late.

3   Left Malta (Luqa) in PM's CR54 at 3.30 a.m. (Sarah, Moran, Bridges, Tommy etc.) Arrived Saki in Crimea 12.20 p.m. local time. Met by Molotov etc. Drove over mountains through Yalta to Vorontsov Villa at Alupka.

4   At Alupka. Sunny. At work in villa with occasional stroll in grounds running down to sea. Leslie Rowan joined party yesterday. We have meals with Bob Dixon [PS to Foreign Secretary] and Nicholas Lawford. Stalin called on PM in afternoon.

5   At Alupka. Duller day. Afternoon walk with Nicholas Law-ford in park and village above villa.

6   At Alupka. Brighter day. Afternoon walk with Moran and FM Alexander.

7   At Alupka. Sunny. Afternoon walk with Leslie. Col. Frank McCarthy and Cmdr Dornin to dinner.

8, 9   At Alupka.

10   At Alupka. Drove by Livadia to Yalta to visit Chekhov's house. Stalin dined with PM.

11   Last day of Crimean Conference. Left Alupka and drove to Sebastopol, where we went aboard SS *Franconia*.

12   At Sebastopol. Drove to Balaclava. Brig. Peake pointed out scene of charge of the Light Brigade. Sebastopol completely devastated.

13   At Sebastopol. Went ashore with Bridges for short walk through ruins, visiting Cathedral and another wrecked church.

14   Left Sebastopol after breakfast and drove (3½ hours) to Saki, from which we flew to Athens. PM drove with Regent (Archbishop Damaskinos) to Constitution Square, where he addressed a vast crowd. Dinner with Leepers [Sir Reginald, Ambassador in Athens, and his wife] at Embassy. Visited flood-lit Parthenon.

15   Flew from Athens to Alexandria, where PM took leave of President. Lunch in HMS *Aurora* (Capt. Barnard). Flew on to Cairo, where we are staying with Sir Edward Grigg in the 'Casey' villa.

16   At Cairo. Jordan, the retiring, and Graffety-Smith, the new Minister at Jeddah, called, also Howe, Minister at Addis Ababa. Haile Selassie in afternoon.

17   Drove to Fayoum. PM's meeting with Ibn Saud. Tea at Killearn's place in the desert. King Farouk and Shukri Kuwatly called at villa.

18   At Cairo. In afternoon visited Museum, where Mr Lucas guided us round the Tutankhamen exhibits. PM planted palms in villa garden.

19   Left Cairo by air at 2 a.m. Flew non-stop to England, arriving Lyneham at 3 p.m. BST (14-hour flight). By bus to London.

20   Visited Pelham Place. Dined with Lascelles.

23   To Oxford in afternoon.

FEBRUARY 1945

24, 25 At Oxford. R is not able to get out as she is nursing her mother, who is still in bed. David can now walk, staggering in a ludicrous way. Vocabulary includes 'no' and 'more'.

26 Returned to London.

27 PM's speech in House on Crimea Conference (Poland etc.). Farewell Treasury party for Hoppy.

28 Almond blossom in park.

LETTERS

5 February 'Not from Downing Street'. There would be plenty to tell about our doings and surroundings here if the censorship were lifted, but at the moment it seems better to say no more than that all is well and progress is being made. I do wish you could share these jaunts, which are great fun even when (as here) they involve various minor personal discomforts.

5 February Vorontsov Villa [to J.R. Colville at No. 10]. Many thanks for all the news of London in your letter of January 31. Since then, to judge by all the evidence, a stupor has fallen on the Private Office, and it has gone to my heart to hear Colonel Kent calling again and again for news and being offered only caviare. No doubt your answer is 'tu quoque', so I am sending you this short account of our doings to supplement the official Diary, which has been modelled so scrupulously on the style of the Deputy Prime Minister. Please show it to any of the others who put in at least a daily appearance at the office.

The flight to CRICKET was uneventful. Our arrival, as you have doubtless heard, caused the maximum of inconvenience to the highest personages in the island, owing to circumstances directly attributable to the negligence of Master —, which will be suitably punished on our return. The Prime Minister gave us all rather a fright by running a temperature, and the night was much disturbed by the comings and goings of Lord Moran and his consultations with local medical opinion. A bed was prepared in the Military Hospital and we had all but summoned Sir Lionel Whitby when fortunately the Colonel took a turn for the better, and a little after breakfast time it was decided to proceed to our cruiser.

We were immediately installed in most comfortable quarters and overwhelmed by the characteristic hospitality of the Royal Navy. All concerned, from the Captain down, left nothing undone

178

for our convenience, giving up the best cabins in the ship.

Colonel Kent spent most of his time at CRICKET aboard and chiefly in bed. He was able to have long and useful conversations with Field Marshal Alexander, General Marshall, Admiral King, Harry Hopkins and 'Ed' Stettinius. Randolph also put in an appearance. The Colonel did not make any public appearance ashore, but one evening we went to a dinner with the Governor at San Anton Palace. After dinner (a large party) the company were entertained with parlour tricks by the CAS.

The President arrived on Friday morning. It was a lovely day of brilliant sunshine, and the harbour made a perfect setting for the rather spectacular scene as the President's ship moved slowly past to its berth ahead of us, the Guards of Honour standing at attention and the music of the 'Star-spangled Banner' sounding across the water. The Colonel had long talks with the President over the meal and otherwise. The President has with him the usual crazy gang, who were discovered when Tommy went aboard sitting in a cabin in their under-shirts drinking vermouth. CRICKET was of course infested with G-men. After dinner the President went off to his plane and the Colonel followed after a conversation with Randolph, which however lasted so long that, after we had drunk all the whisky we thought proper, and then all the beer, and then all the cocoa, I was about to turn to Horlick's Malted Milk when the signal was at last given.

We had a very easy flight from CRICKET to ALBATROSS, passing over the A. Sea by early daylight, snowy mountain tops appearing above the quilt of clouds.

We were met on arrival by Molotov and co. and, after an inspection of a very smart Guard of Honour and the playing of the three National Anthems (it took me back to Sunday nights at home) and being cheered by the sight of Leslie and Miss Sturdee, who had preceded us by half an hour, set out on the long drive to Yalta. This took six and a half hours, including a longish interval for refreshments on the shores of the B. Sea (at a sort of Rest House where the table groaned with caviare and the pop of champagne bottles went on all the time like machine-gun fire). The road was long and often winding but it did not live up to the horrific description we had received.

Here we are installed in a large and magnificent palace of hybrid architecture, partly gothic and partly arabesque. The principal rooms, used for meals and offices, are of ample proportions, but the bedroom accommodation is more restricted and there is considerable competition for a cold tap. Although there seemed every sign of chaos when we first reached the house, this was surprisingly quickly reduced to order and, considering all the difficulties, we are now remarkably comfortably settled down. Today has been a day of brilliant sunshine in which it would have been churlish to bear any minor inconvenience in mind.

U.J. came to greet the Colonel in the afternoon and since then the first Plenary Session has taken place. I gather that it went well and the first results were satisfactory. (The subsequent dinner party did not go so well. U.J., as a republican, refused to drink the King's health and a jest by the President about 'Uncle Joe' did not go down.)

The crashed plane on the outward journey has of course thrown a shadow over the conference. Personally I have felt most the loss of Peter Loxley, who would have been a great prop in the Foreign Office in the years when a heavy load will fall on his generation. How cruelly hard for his wife at such a time.

7 *February*   In Black Sea area. There seem to have been various leakages in the Press and in any case our communiqué will be in tomorrow's, so I could spread myself a little more now were it not that the courier leaves in ten minutes.

We are in a large house overlooking the sea, with high rocky mountains rising behind. Today, with a sharp wind and brilliant sunshine, conditions could hardly be more pleasant and there is none of the arctic weather for which we came prepared. The house, built a century ago, is a remarkable mixture of Gothic and Arab [Muslim] styles. The public rooms are large and imposing, but bedroom and lavatory accommodation is more limited. Leslie and I share a small bedroom, completely lacking in pegs, shelves or wardrobes, and there is much competition for the single tap; but we are much better off than many of the delegates, for instance the sixteen American colonels who share a single bedroom. The food is excellent and provided lavishly, as are the wines with which we wash it down. I have caviare for breakfast as well as lunch and dinner, with lots of lovely butter. The only trouble is to avoid exhausting one's tummy with such unaccustomed work. As usual our hosts do everything in their power to help us and have even brought a large lemon tree by sea, complete with lemons, which was installed one afternoon in the conservatory.

9 February In the Black Sea area. The 'Big Three' are cutting steadily through their agenda. Agreement isn't always easy; but the atmosphere is excellent and it is already clear that there are going to be some good solid results. I haven't seen anything of the actual meetings, which are always held in the President's villa, and we haven't had nearly so much to do as on previous conferences, but there is a pretty steady flow of papers by daily 'Mosquito' and of course the usual late nights. A large part of the day seems to be taken up with the enormous Russian meals, as before all exactly the same and all excellent, with drinks ditto – vodka, white and red wine, champagne, liqueur (all local products) at both lunch and dinner every day. Caviare daily for breakfast, lunch and dinner. There is fortunately always a chance to walk some of this off in the afternoon.

The whole place is terribly knocked about, with scarcely a house anywhere intact. It must have been rather pleasant in happier days – the villages climbing up the slopes, with cypresses and vineyards, all very South European, the corniche road winding up and down between a rocky coast and a solid wall of cliff-like mountains, snow above and green below. The weather changes – sometimes dazzling sunshine, sometimes cloud and an occasional shower; but never the bitter cold and snow for which we came prepared.

We work in a room off the entrance hall, where there is a constant coming and going of young Foreign Office men, marines, Russian soldiers (very smart in white gloves), Chiefs of Staff and lesser fry, with an occasional bustle when the PM leaves for one of his meetings, dressed in a colonel's uniform, with high fur hat worn with points to back and front.

10 February In the Black Sea area. We came out here by Malta, spending two or three nights there on a cruiser. The first day was cold, but after that we had lovely sunny weather and the island looked most beautiful. One afternoon the ship's captain drove some of us up to St Paul's Bay in the north of the island, the traditional scene of the shipwreck. Beautiful soft colouring and the first spring flowers beginning to appear among the rocks.

There is a nip in the air, but it is often bright and sunny. We live in a palatial villa overlooking the sea, with a few large and imposing public rooms but with rather inadequate bedroom accommodation. I would not like to say how many of us share one bath. The Russians could not be more hospitable and have done everything possible for our comfort, though things have not been easy for them in a region almost completely devastated by the recent invaders. As before we are overwhelmed by the quantities of excellent food at every meal, course following course in an unvarying menu. The conference itself is going well in a friendly atmosphere and it is already clear that there are going to be really solid results. We are in close touch with home as a plane flies out every day with letters and newspapers.

11 February In Black Sea area. I enclose a menu to give you an idea of what a Russian meal looks like. Actually this was rather a special one in honour of Stalin and the President and our ordinary meals don't have more than about eight courses.

Fresh and pressed caviare
   Butter
   Pies
Fish 'Balyk'
Fish 'Shamaya'
   Herrings
Swiss Cheese
Game, hot and cold
Sausages, assorted
Fish – sturgeon
Sucking pig, horse-radish sauce
   Radishes
Cucumbers, pickled
Vol au vent of game.

Clear soup, game
Thick chicken soup

White fish and champagne sauce
   Fish 'Kefal'

Shashlyk of mutton
'Dzeiran' of mutton
Pilau of mutton

Roast turkey
  Sundry game

Peas à l'anglaise

Ice cream

Fruit

Cake and petits fours

Sweets

Chocolate

Almonds, roasted

Coffee

Vorontsov Villa, February 10th 1945

The conference is going very well indeed and some really important things have been tied up, as the final communiqué will show. No doubt it will be easy for the critics, who haven't been here and didn't have to overcome the many difficulties, to suggest improvements that might have been. [In the light of subsequent events it will be seen that this optimism was unjustified owing to the failure of Moscow to carry out the terms of the agreement reached at Yalta.]

Yesterday I went with Sarah and Tommy and a Russian woman guide to the President's villa, driving along the cornice road in a jeep (half-hour's drive) with lovely views of the very blue Black Sea. There we saw all the bustle and excitements of the arrivals for the afternoon session and then went on to visit Chekhov's house. He was a consumptive and came down here for a 'cure' in the last years of his life. Everything had been left just as it was at the time of his death and oddly enough the place seems to have come through the war unscathed, one of the very few houses in the town of which that could be said. This must have been a pleasant Riviera in its palmy days, but almost everything is now in ruins and I suppose many of the villas dating from pre-revolutionary times will never be rebuilt.

12 February Aboard SS – at – in the Black Sea area. The conference ended successfully yesterday. We had planned to leave today and I was sitting at the villa, snoozing off the effects of a lunch that had almost been too much for me, when suddenly the PM burst in like a whirlwind and said we must be off in half an hour. There was a mad rush to pack, very inadequate goodbyes to all the kind Russian staff who had looked after us so well and then off to the port where this ship had been anchored during the conference. It was a two-and-a-half-hour drive, fortunately daylight for an hour of it as the first half was over an extraordinary road climbing high along the coast and then over a mountain ridge with breath-taking twists and turns – huge towering rocks above and thousand-feet drops below.

It was a great joy to get aboard the ship and find everything clean and bright and welcoming, with familiar stewards from the *QM* and an excellent English dinner. It had originally been thought that we should live aboard during the conference and immense pains must have been taken to make the ship ready. I have the most beautiful cabin, complete with private bathroom and windows on two sides. Alas that we are only spending two nights.

The Russians have sent me a huge parcel, which I haven't dared to unpack, but no doubt it contains a supply of caviare and vodka as before. I hope to send it home in the ship. But, delicious as caviare may be, I must say that I was very glad to get back to bacon and egg for breakfast this morning.

13 February Sebastopol. You will have seen the Conference Report in this morning's paper. I'm sure you will agree that the PM's travels have been well worth while. Now Ulysses has begun his usual dilatory return and we are spending an idle day in our most comfortable ship – as somebody said, like Brown's Hotel compared with the Claridge's of the *Queen Mary*. We spent yesterday morning working quietly and in the afternoon went ashore and drove to Balaclava, where we saw the site of the charge of the Light Brigade – a long stretch of open grass as smooth as a polo ground and perfect for a gallop. Sebastopol itself is a pretty horrific sight. It must have been a large place, with good solid stone buildings, but it is almost completely wrecked – square miles of ruins with scarcely a house left. It is absurd to think of any little inconveniences the war has brought us compared with what these people must have gone through. Now they are coming back, thousands of them, with their children (nice friendly open faces), but how they make a living or find shelter in these heaps of ruins I cannot think. And this is only one of many Russian cities that have suffered such a fate. No wonder if they talk about Reparations.

The original intention had been to leave this morning for Athens, but that has been cancelled – rightly, for the situation there is not now one that calls for the presence of the PM.

Here at Sebastopol we have the morning London newspapers at 6 p.m. the same day.

16 February In a familiar villa. On Wednesday we flew to Athens. The journey began with a three-hour drive in the Crimea through bleak, snow-covered country and past many sights of war – the most spectacular of which was the remains of a wrecked train dangling from a high embankment down into the gap left by a blown up bridge. Once in the air we were soon in the bright sunshine of a more cheerful climate and the Aegean sparkled beneath us as we passed near or over one after another of the islands with such familiar names – Samothrace, Naxos, Imbros, Skyros (with the grave of Rupert Brooke pointed out as a speck of white on a hilltop) and Euboea. We were soon over Athens, circling round the Acropolis.

The PM's coming had been made known a few hours previously and there were excited little crowds all the way into town from the airfield. We drove straight to the Regent's house, where after a short conversation the Regent and the PM got into an open car, with two theatrically dressed Evzones standing on the running-boards, and were driven slowly past cheering crowds to the old Palace. There on a balcony they appeared before an immense crowd filling the principal square of the city (the scene of the firing that began the recent troubles). The Archbishop, a towering magnificent figure, and the PM made short speeches through amplifiers amid tremendous enthusiasm and repeated cheers from the crowd.

Later we drove down to the Embassy, where we spent the evening and dined. With some others in our party I drove in a jeep to the Acropolis and walked up to the Parthenon, floodlit in honour of the occasion.

We spent the night in our plane and at dawn set out for Alexandria (a three-hour flight), where we lunched in a cruiser. Lovely warm sunshine, a startling change from the Crimean snow of the day before.

20 February   We had an interesting short visit to Cairo, enjoying the sunshine at the familiar villa near the Pyramids, and flew back from there non-stop yesterday in just under fourteen hours, arriving at an airfield from which it took longer to drive to London (in a bus) than we had taken on the flight from Greece to Egypt.

The Emperor of Abyssinia called on the PM and the PM called on Ibn Saud, who had been invited to Egypt to meet President Roosevelt. The visit to Ibn Saud was made into quite a party. We drove for more than an hour across the desert to Fayoum, where he was staying as guest of the British Government in a recently opened hotel; with a remarkable troupe of relatives, ministers and retainers, including an astrologer and fortune teller, an official food-taster, a 'chief server of ceremonial coffee' and nine 'miscellaneous slaves, cooks, porters and scullions'. They had come from Jeddah in a destroyer, bringing sheep with them, which they killed and ate on the deck. The Royal Navy had constructed a special compass to indicate the direction of Mecca. At the end of the visit princely presents were produced. The PM received a wonderful sword and a trunk full of magnificent strings of pearls and a huge diamond (the latter said to be worth over £800 [according to *The Second World War*, VI, 349, the valuation of £1200 was attached]), bottles of scent etc. I received a little bundle containing a voluminous camel-hair robe with gold embroidery, a sort of kashmir head shawl with gold cord to wear round it and a jewelled gold dagger with belt.

23 February   A good deal of work was awaiting return here, but none of it at all exciting. In fact life seems a little humdrum after all the excitements of the last three weeks; but fortunately there is a sniff of spring in the air and the crocuses are out in the park.

28 February   I have just come back rather shattered from lunch with one of my Malayan friends, wife of X, whom I admired more than almost anyone in Malaya. He was taken prisoner at Singapore and only this morning she received confirmation of his death. She is incredibly brave about it and somehow we carried on an ordinary conversation, but poor thing she has lost terribly. He was the best sort of Colonial civil servant, who would certainly have gone to the top of the tree.

MARCH

The Germans were driven back across the Rhine in the north, centre and south. Cities taken included Cologne and Frankfurt. The PM visited the front.

The Russians captured Danzig. A Soviet-dominated administration was set up in Romania. There was deadlock in Moscow on giving effect to the Yalta agreement on Poland. Molotov refused to go to the San Francisco Conference. There were Soviet suspicions over contacts with General Wolff in Geneva, in relation to the possible surrender in Italy.

Mrs Churchill visited Russia on behalf of the Aid to Russia Fund. Mandalay was recaptured.

DIARY

March

1 Bridges took over as Secretary of the Treasury.

2 To Oxford in afternoon.

3 At Oxford.

4 At Oxford. There was an alert in the small hours, the first for months.

5 Returned to London. Lunch with Jock, just back from visit to Brussels with Mrs C.

6 News that the Americans have crossed the Rhine at Remagen.

7 To Chequers in afternoon.

10 Chequers. Duncan and Diana Sandys arrived for weekend. Film *The Fighting Lady*, US documentary on war in the Pacific.

11 At Chequers. Gen. Pile to lunch. Duncan suggested move of Colonial Office to Somerset House.

12 Returned to London.

14 Lunched with PM and Mrs C, the others being Lord and Lady Portal and Mr and Mrs Bevin.

15 Several days of sunshine now. I spent some time after lunch at Pelham Place gardening and basking in a deck-chair.

16 To Oxford.

17, 18 At Oxford.

19 Returned to London.

20 R was in town for a lunch party, after which she came with me to Pelham Place. Discovery of considerable ravages by moths.

23 Called at Dorchester on Dr Weizmann, who gave his impressions from his recent visit to Palestine. Lunch with Peter Brooke of Sarawak.

27 Dinner with Kathleen Walker, meeting Alec Adams and Tungku Maidin of Kelantan.

29 Lunch with Joy (on leave from Aden) with his wife and son and T.I.K. Lloyd [from Colonial Office]. To Oxford in evening with Prof.

30, 31 At Oxford.

LETTERS

11 March Mrs Churchill is full of the need for nurseries in which mothers can leave their babies when out shopping or working.

14 March Rather in need of a tonic after 3 a.m., 3 a.m. and 3.45 a.m. at Chequers. Ernie Bevin (at lunch here today) complained that a minute from the PM looked as if it had been written at 2 a.m., whereat Mrs C said, 'Yes. If only you would go to bed earlier, John Martin wouldn't look so pale and romantic.'

25 March No. 10. I am on duty here over the weekend. The PM, as you will have seen, has gone off to the Rhine battle. He spoke to me on the telephone last night, evidently delighted with our progress – many men across the river and few casualties.

I have been definitely offered Jock Macpherson's job in Washington, Colonial Office representative at the British Embassy (on his promotion to the West Indies) . . . My inclination is all against this uprooting at the present moment. All that Rosalind and I want is a little quiet domesticity at home. I think she would be rather heart-broken if we couldn't have our house at Pelham Place after all this longing and waiting for it. However the job is in many ways an attractive one and it is a difficult decision.

APRIL

The Seventh US Army drove east beyond Heidelberg. The French advanced across the Rhine on the right. Kassel was taken. The Ruhr was encircled. 'Germany's Western front had collapsed.' The advance to liberate Holland was halted, while arrangements were made for delivery of relief supplies to the rest of the country.

Roosevelt died.

The Russians took Vienna, from which they thrust forward up

the Danube. The Americans advanced on Magdeburg, Leipzig and Bayreuth and by the 19th had crossed into Czechoslovakia. The Ninth Army crossed the Elbe on the 12th and were about 60 miles from Berlin. American forces from Leipzig met the Russians on the Elbe. On the 16th Russian forces on the Oder started an attack on a 200-mile front and on the 25th surrounded Berlin.

A treaty was made between the Russians and the Lublin administration in Poland. There was failure to make progress with the Russians on giving effect to the Yalta agreement on the formation of a government of national unity. Sixteen leaders of the Polish Underground disappeared.

The Allied spring offensive opened in Italy. The Po and the Adige were crossed and there was a general rising of Italian partisans. On the 29th the Germans signed an instrument of unconditional surrender in Italy. Mussolini was killed.

Hitler died.

Himmler made proposals for surrender on the Western front through Count Bernadotte. The Allied reply demanded unconditional surrender on all fronts.

DIARY

April

1   Easter. At Oxford.
2   Returned to London after lunch.
4   At Houses of Parliament with King, PM and others examining arrangements for State Opening of Parliament.
5   Afternoon party for Dominion Conference representatives at Claridge's. Dinner party at No. 10 – speeches by PM, Fraser (New Zealand), Forde [Australia], Attlee and Sir R. Mudaliar [director, Imperial Bank of India, Madras].
7   A little gardening at Pelham Place.
8   A little gardening in afternoon. There have been no V-bombs for nine days. It looks as if we may have seen the last of them.
11 Memorial Service at St Margaret's for Peter Loxley and the others. At Mansion House for Lord Mayor's Easter Luncheon for Diplomatic Corps.
12 Death of President Roosevelt.
13 To Oxford in afternoon.
14, 15   At Oxford.

16 Returned to London.
17 P M's tribute to Roosevelt in House of Commons, preceded by attempt of Dr McIntyre [Scottish Nationalist Member for Motherwell] to present himself without sponsors.
18 Lunch with Dr Weizmann.
20 Left in P M's train after dinner.
21 Bristol visit. Conferment of Freedom on P M and honorary degrees on Bevin and Alexander. Visited Bristol Aircraft Factory – mock-up of Brabazon I. To Chequers.
22 At Chequers. Winant. Lord Camrose [Chairman of *Daily Telegraph*]. Dorothy Thompson and her husband Kopf to lunch.
23 Returned to London.
27 To Oxford in afternoon.
28 At Oxford.
29 Returned to London after lunch.

LETTERS

18 April I was in the House yesterday when the new Scottish Nationalist MP presented himself and tried to take his seat without sponsors – rather an absurd scene and an undignified prelude to the P M's tribute to President Roosevelt.

22 April We had a wonderful day at Bristol yesterday, a warm sunny Saturday morning – ideal for the crowds. The town was very much en fête, flags and decorations out and bells ringing, and thousands of cheering people in the streets. We had spent the night in our special train in a siding and arrived at Temple Meads after breakfast. The Lord Mayor was waiting with an open carriage and mounted escort and drove with the P M in state to the Mansion House, while the rest of us followed in cars. The air-raid damage is worse than anything I have seen except in the City of London, whole streets more or less destroyed. Little seemed to be left of Wine Street, which we passed, and half of those big shops opposite the Cathedral have gone.

At the Mansion House we had a glass of 'Bristol Milk' before the ceremony, at which the Lord Mayor and the P M made speeches. Then we drove on to the University Hall. It has been burnt out, but the walls stand and with a temporary roof and platform it is quite usable. The P M in his robes as Chancellor and with mortar board on squint looked like one of the later Roman emperors; but he made a good speech (impromptu) and it was altogether a very successful occasion. Afterwards we lunched with a select company in a smaller (undamaged) hall alongside.

After lunch we drove up to Clifton ... and then out to visit the aircraft factory before rejoining our train.

I thought Bristol and Clifton most attractive. The ancestors certainly chose a good town to live in. As you may have heard, the Colson Hall was recently burnt down – an ordinary accident and nothing to do with the war, which seems very bad luck on top of all the other destruction. St Mary Redcliffe has survived. The verger was on the roof fire-fighting and saw his own house burning a short distance away, but preferred to stay and save the church.

MAY

The Americans thrust down the Danube, reaching Linz on the 5th, and penetrated into Czechoslovakia as far as Pilsen and Karlsbad, but halted while the Russians occupied Prague. The Americans also reached Innsbruck, meeting with US forces from Italy. The British reached Lübeck and made contact with the Russians. Denmark was liberated.

On the 7th Jodl signed the instruments of surrender – all hostilities to cease at midnight on 8 May.

French troops landed at Beirut. Anti-French strikes followed and there was fierce fighting in Damascus. On the 31st the Commander in Chief Mediterranean was told to restore order and the French commander ordered a cease-fire.

The British advanced down the Irrawaddy. Rangoon was taken.

On the 23rd Churchill resigned, but accepted the King's invitation to form a caretaker government.

The San Francisco conference continued throughout the month.

DIARY

May

1 Rozie came to London for the day. We opened up 25 Pelham Place. Mrs Ingram re-installed. Dinner with Lord Provost of Edinburgh [Ian Falconer].

2 Lunched with Ben Gurion.

191

4 Montgomery reported surrender of German forces in Holland, North-west Germany, Frisian Islands and Denmark.

5 Eisenhower reported further surrender negotiations.

6 Awaiting outcome of negotiations at Eisenhower's HQ.

7 Jodl signed surrender of remaining German forces. Pug rang up in small hours, but we decided not to waken PM. Much confusion about official announcement, eventually postponed till tomorrow.

8 VE Day – a public holiday. PM broadcast at 3 p.m. from No. 10. Then to House, only just getting through the crowds in an open car. Crowds outside Palace. Balcony in Whitehall. Illuminations.

9 Another public holiday. Another warm day like yesterday and great crowds. Drove behind PM on round of visits to US, Soviet and French embassies. In evening he again appeared on balcony, made speech and led 'Rule Britannia'. Supper with Rowans. Cheered King and Queen outside Buckingham Palace.

10 Final committee on Honours List. Didn't get to bed till 4 a.m.

11 Lunch with PM, Sarah, Mary and James Stuart. PM had just seen Bevin and Morrison, who are willing to stay in Government until October or November and will agree to National Service.

12 To Oxford in morning.

13 At Oxford. Dinner with President at Corpus.

14 To Andover with R and David.

15–20 Idle days at Andover.

21 To Oxford. In evening left R and D at Oriel and returned to London.

23 PM tendered his resignation to HM at noon. At 4 he was asked to form a new government and kissed hands.

24 PM Cabinet-making all day. Evening argument with Brendan about Bretton Woods.

25 More Cabinet-making. List of Cabinet and other principal Ministers sent to MOI in evening for publication.

26 List of junior Ministers issued.
    To Oxford in afternoon.

27 At Oxford.

28 Returned to London. Bridges told me that PM had agreed to my return to Colonial Office (as an Assistant Under-Secretary).

Afternoon party at No. 10 for outgoing Ministers and new Cabinet.

29   At dentist for first time for three or four years. To bed at 3 a.m.

LETTERS

13 May   Monday was a day of order, counter-order and disorder. We heard early in the day that the Germans had signed the surrender, but there was much difficulty in arranging with Washington and Moscow the time to release the news. There were several transatlantic telephone calls and it was only the last of these, just before 6, when the PM was about to broadcast his statement, that decided him to postpone it. Meanwhile inevitably the news had got about and there were excited crowds waiting in the streets. After this fiasco I thought Tuesday might be rather an anticlimax; but it wasn't so at all and both Tuesday and Wednesday were days of real, unbounded, spontaneous happiness, enhanced by the generally bright, warm weather. I sat beside the PM in the Cabinet room while he made his broadcast. Then several of us crowded into the police car to follow his open car down to the House. There were comparatively few policemen in the streets and when we got round to Parliament Square we were soon surrounded by an immense, wildly excited crowd. At one moment I thought we should never get through. People clung on to our car on every side and several clambered on to the roof, so that in photographs it is completely invisible. Harvie-Watt, who had gone in the open car with the PM, had a finger broken in the mêlée. In the end we got through to the House. The chamber was crowded and there was of course great enthusiasm.

Later in the afternoon I strolled through the park and among the great crowd outside the Palace – a gay scene, with all the beds around the Victoria Memorial bright with tulips. (It was a sign of the good behaviour of the crowd that the tulips were still there the next day.) I was back in time to go on to one of the balconies in the Ministry of Health to see the PM with Cabinet ministers appear there and say a few words to the roaring mob that entirely blocked Whitehall from the Cenotaph to Parliament Square. After dinner with an old Corpus friend I wandered about admiring the illuminations.

On Wednesday the morning was uneventful, but in the afternoon one or two of us drove behind the PM on his visits to the American, Soviet and French Embassies. It was a triumphal progress through cheering crowds, particularly in Lower Regent Street and along Piccadilly, and only a mounted police escort got us through. I had supper with the Rowans, after which we came along to the office in time to see the PM's evening appearance on the Ministry of Health balcony, where he conducted the crowd in singing 'Rule Britannia'. Then again we paraded the streets and ended up at the floodlit Palace, where after a long interval we were rewarded by the King and Queen appearing and waving to us.

31 May The Colonial Office have asked for my return as an Assistant Under-Secretary. The PM, who said he didn't want service at No. 10 to stand in the way of people's promotion, has agreed. I am to have a month's holiday – in July – and start work in the CO on 1st August.

Naturally I shall have mixed feelings about leaving No. 10; but this is a very convenient juncture to do so and I had for some time felt that I had been a PS long enough and that I ought to get back to the CO soon . . . I have scarcely a moment in these unusually hectic days to think of all this. Bedtime was 2 a.m. on Monday, 3 a.m. on Tuesday and midnight on Wednesday. Just as well that R had not yet returned. Her sister gets back from the Fannies on Friday or Saturday, so that R will at last be free; but it is an awkward moment as her mother is not at all well. Meanwhile I have had one or two excellent lunches provided by a slightly rejuvenated Mrs Ingram at Pelham Place.

JUNE

The French garrison was withdrawn from Damascus; the British detachment moved in and peace was restored. Difficulties with the French over the administration of Italian territory in the Alpes Maritimes were settled.

Stalin agreed to a meeting of 'The Three' in Berlin in July. The PM invited Attlee (who accepted) to join the British delegation at the Berlin conference.

The British and American missions were ordered to leave Vienna. The US insisted on withdrawing their forces in Europe within the occupation zones previously designated.

Parliament was dissolved on the 15th. The General Election campaign began. The PM made tours in England and Scotland and broadcasts.

The San Francisco Conference concluded and the United Nations Charter was signed.

Okinawa was subdued. The Australians recaptured Brunei and Sarawak and Beaufort in North Borneo.

DIARY

June

1   At Academy Cinema – *Le Dernier Milliardaire* and *Horto-bagy*. Slept at Pelham Place for first time for months.

3   Read Inspector Thompson's book of reminiscences of service with PM.

4   Rozie and David arrived back from Oxford and returned to Pelham Place. PM's opening broadcast in Election campaign.

9, 10   At Pelham Place.

13   R and I lunched with the Churchills at the Annexe.

16   To Chequers.

17   At Chequers. Gen. Slim (of 14th Army) at lunch.

18   Chequers.

19   Returned to London. Bishop of Carlisle [who had married us] lunched at Pelham Place.

23   At Pelham Place, unpacking books etc.

24   At Pelham Place. We took David to the park to see the rabbits.

28   Rowans gave goodbye party for me at Cheyne Court. Afterwards festive dinner in the mess.

29   PM returned from his election tour. On late duty.

LETTERS

3 June   25 Pelham Place. At long last I write from this address . . . The garden is a sad wilderness with grass high like a crop of hay . . . The house is swept and garnished though much remains to be done. I anxiously await David's arrival – will he break this or that? Will he fall down the lift shaft? Will he dive from the garden into the area? I have just been at St Columba's for the first time in months and found it uncomfortably crowded in its small hall at the Imperial Institute . . . When it comes to the point it will be very sad to leave No. 10 and all it stands for. Now I must get on with a tiresome bit of work I have brought home with me – [security clearance of] a book of reminiscences by the PM's detective.

7 June   R and David are back at last. They arrived on Monday afternoon – the day of return of thousands of evacuee mothers and children . . . Last night I was on duty here (No. 10) and did not get to bed till 3.30 a.m. I need not tell you what a joy it is to have my family reunited again. I am thankful that this No. 10 life, which is only suitable for bachelors, is now coming to an end. Food seems to be more difficult in some ways than two years ago. R spent forty minutes in a fish queue. Potatoes were unobtainable the other day and we get rather a meagre ration of milk.

17 June   Here I am at Chequers for the last time as PS and fortunately it is a bright sunny weekend with the familiar countryside looking its best. I shall be very sorry when the time comes to say goodbye to a place where I have spent so many interesting and pleasant days . . . The Election is absorbing most interest here. On the way out to Chequers last night the PM's car was slowed down in a traffic jam just outside the White City where crowds were coming away from the greyhound races. Immediately he was surrounded by an extremely enthusiastic mob – smiling and waving and cheering – not a sign of un-friendliness or opposition. It was a remarkable demonstration and these were very much the 'common people'.

We had the Eastwoods to lunch one day, who rewarded us afterwards with a big parcel of potatoes from their garden – unobtainable in the greengrocers'.

DIARY

30 June   Took leave of PM and Mrs C at the Annexe. I ceased to be PPS to the PM at midnight.

As I observed in my contribution to *Action This Day* (edited by Sir John Wheeler-Bennett; 157), 'Although it was not easy to work for Churchill, it was, as all his staff agreed, tremendous fun and we would not have missed the opportunity for anything.'

INDEX

197

INDEX